T0325284

THE FINAL BATTLE

www.royalcollins.com

THE
FINAL
BATTLE

WINNING THE WAR AGAINST POVERTY

WANG JIAHUA

Books Beyond Boundaries

ROYAL COLLINS

The Final Battle: Winning the War Against Poverty

Wang Jiahua

First published in 2022 by Royal Collins Publishing Group Inc.
Groupe Publication Royal Collins Inc.
BKM Royalcollins Publishers Private Limited

Headquarters: 550-555 boul. René-Lévesque O Montréal (Québec) H2Z1B1 Canada
India office: 805 Hemkunt House, 8th Floor, Rajendra Place, New Delhi 110 008

Original Edition © China Democracy and Legal System Publishing House

ISBN: 978-1-4878-0959-1

To find out more about our publications, please visit www.royalcollins.com.

Preface

Humanity has long dreamed of eradicating poverty, improving people's livelihoods, and achieving common prosperity. As the largest developing country in the world, the People's Republic of China has successfully developed a Chinese-style pathway for poverty alleviation under several generations of leaders, and has made significant contributions to the cause of poverty reduction worldwide. Especially since the 18th CPC National Congress, General Secretary Xi Jinping has seen a new strategic opportunity for deepening reform. Taking the situation into account, he has proposed the strategic layout of building a moderately prosperous society, deepening reform, implementing the rule of law, and intensifying Party discipline. He has made a solemn commitment to eradicating poverty from the rural poor population by 2020, and has augured a new phase in accelerating China's economic development and achieving common prosperity.

In five years' time, 70.17 million rural residents living far below the current poverty line will be lifted out of poverty. This is the most rigid indicator for building a moderately prosperous society and achieving the "First Centennial Goal" of the great rejuvenation of the Chinese nation. The time limit is short, the cost of poverty reduction is high, and the difficulty of poverty alleviation is great. The battle against poverty will therefore not be an easy one. In fact, will be the most ambitious task that currently faces the Party, the government, and society. In the past few years, I have been fortunate enough to participate in a series of volunteer activities for poverty alleviation organized by the Poverty Alleviation Office of the State Council. Through participating in the design of some targeted poverty alleviation projects, I have been hugely inspired and educated. This book is based on my thoughts about poverty alleviation and development in China over the years.

The Final Battle: Winning the War Against Poverty is closely integrated with the national strategy of poverty alleviation, and tries to explain the strategic guidance from the perspective of combining national poverty alleviation policies and practices. Based on the realities of the government, society, and market, the book attempts to interpret the strategic guidance of poverty alleviation with a new vision, and explores the thinking and pathways of poverty alleviation in impoverished areas and for people living under the poverty line. It is hoped that this book will ultimately enlighten readers.

The book begins with an account of General Secretary Xi Jinping's devotion to and deep concern about poverty alleviation. Hopefully it will arouse the awareness and responsibility of the general public to care about poverty alleviation in China. Chapters 1 and 2 then elaborate on the strategic guidance and environmental conditions for the battle against poverty. On this basis, the following four chapters are devoted to explaining the strategic design, main directions, key links, and basic models of the battle. The book aims at rigorous logic, a reasonable structure, rich arguments, convenience of reading, and new exploration and understanding.

The year 2016 marks the start of the national battle against poverty alleviation. At the start of this year, I present *The Final Battle: Winning the War Against Poverty*. It is my sincere hope that this book will help raise awareness about the national poverty alleviation process, and lead enterprises, social organizations, and individual citizens to participate in the battle.

Wang Jiahua

Contents

Xi Jinping's Devotion to Poverty Alleviation

The High-level Forum on Poverty Reduction and Development was held on the morning of October 16, 2015 in the Great Hall of the People in Beijing, as scheduled. Xi Jinping's keynote speech, "Working Together to Eradicate Poverty and Promote Common Development" showed the effectiveness of the Chinese government's poverty alleviation and development policies to the world, and drew applause from participants both in China and abroad. Through his very personal and moving account, Xi shared his thoughts and feelings about poverty alleviation, gaining him a huge amount of respect from Chinese and foreign participants. Expressing his deep sympathy and empathy for impoverished people, he said:

For more than 40 years, I have worked in counties, cities, provinces, and the central government of China, and poverty alleviation has always been a significant part of my work. I have spent most of my energy on it. I have been to most of the poorest areas in China, including Shaanxi, Gansu, Ningxia, Guizhou, Yunnan, Guangxi, Tibet, and Xinjiang. In the past two years, I have visited more than a dozen poor areas, going to the homes of villagers and talking with them. Their lives are difficult. It breaks my heart. Whenever their situations improve a little, it makes me happy.

1. Strong feelings about poverty alleviation

Looking back through the life of General Secretary Xi Jinping, it is clear that he has always been deeply concerned about the public, particularly the poor. No matter where he has worked or what position he has held, he has always believed in helping the poor and the needy, and achieving common prosperity. He has worked tirelessly and persistently in this direction throughout his career.

(I) Liangjiahe

Liangjiahe – a rural village in northern Shaanxi Province – is now well known thanks to the fact that Xi Jinping worked there as a farmer and secretary of the Brigade Party branch. The story of his work with the villagers to fight poverty is still told among the older people of the area.

General Secretary Xi once recalled with great affection, "Looking back on the history of poverty reduction in China over the past decades, I have some deep and very personal experience. In the late 1960s, when I was barely 16 years old, I moved from Beijing to a small village in northern Shaanxi Province to work as a peasant for seven years. The poverty in rural China left a deep impression on me." The small village in northern Shaanxi that Xi was referring to is the now-famous Liangjiahe in Wenanyi Town, Yanchuan County. It was here that a young Xi first became aware of poverty in rural China, and thus began his struggle to lift the Chinese people out of poverty into prosperity.

In 1969, at the age of 16, Xi Jinping joined the "Go to Work in the Countryside and Mountainous Areas" movement. Leaving Beijing where he grew up, he took a series of trains and then buses, and finally walked nearly 10 kilometers to Liangjiahe, where he became a peasant. The young Xi Jinping gave people the initial impression that he was different from the rest of the group, with his sturdy build and calm determination. Another obvious difference was that he had the heaviest luggage among the 15 youths accompanying him, bringing a box full of books in addition to a change of clothes.

In the 1960s and 1970s, the level of mechanization in Chinese agriculture was very low, and farmers still followed very traditional farming methods. Xi worked hard in the fields, picking up dung, plowing, sowing, harvesting, and herding sheep with the villagers, day in and day out. People soon found out that this Beijing youth was not so delicate. He could bear hardships, and spared no effort. Working hard, he soon became a "real" peasant. After work, he would either study or tell the villagers stories about the outside world, winning unanimous praise. In January 1974, Xi Jinping joined the Communist Party of China, and was soon elected as secretary of the Liangjiahe Brigade Party Branch. This was a remarkable event. Anyone who lived through that era knows that the secretary of the Brigade Party Branch at that time was the head of a brigade. If he was not absolutely outstanding, a young man of 21 years old would not have been given this significant responsibility. Xi was aware of the weight of this responsibility on his shoulders. He led by example in all aspects of his work, wearing rubber shoes in the cold, windy winter, and leading the people to the ice dam. Usually, the villagers only dammed the branch ditch, but Xi was not afraid of hard work, and went to the main ditch where the villagers were afraid to go. Eventually, they all worked together to reclaim more good land and expand the area for food cultivation.

Xi Jinping worked very hard, and had some innovative ideas. In 1974, he read a newspaper report about the use of biogas for cooking and lighting in Mianyang, Sichuan Province, and went on a field trip to study it. When he returned, he led a group to create the first biogas tank in Liangjiahe, which allowed the villagers to improve their lives through burning firewood, illuminating the village, providing fertilizer for the team's production, and increasing the collective income. The advanced methods used in Liangjiahe attracted a lot attention thanks to the knowledge and ideas of Secretary Xi, and were followed by other villages.

(II) Zhengding

The famous historical and cultural city of Zhengding is also known as the town with three gates, the key to the sacred capital, and the intersection of eight directions. Zhao Yun – the ever-victorious general in *The Romance of the Three Kingdoms* – was a native of Zhengding. Thanks to the spread and longevity of the book, Zhengding also became well known. Chairman Mao once said, "Zhengding is a good place because of Zhao Yun." This historical and cultural city was destined to receive a good and pragmatic secretary who would leave its honor in modern China.

One day in early April 1982, Xi Jinping arrived in a green Jeep at the county Party committee compound in Zhengding County, Hebei Province, as Deputy Secretary of the county Party committee. He was 28 years old. A year later, he became Secretary of the county Party committee and left in May 1985, having worked in Zhengding County for three full years. He was down-to-earth, modest, and prudent, and devoted himself to doing practical things for the public, so that they could alleviate poverty and earn a living. Under his leadership, Zhengding County's economy of developed greatly, and the lack of food was solved. When he left Zhengding to take up his next post in Fujian, many people were reluctant to let him go.

When Xi Jinping took office, some people didn't think much of him. They said, "The son of a high cadre is just here for more power. He is only here for show. In less than six months, he will no longer be able to bear the hardships, and will end up leaving." Others said, "He's all talk, trying to control us." It was clear that people did not hold out much hope for the young county Party secretary. However, with his brains and tenacity, Xi had some surprises up his sleeve.

Xi Jinping found that Zhengding County was in a dead-end circle due to a long period of single operation in which high grain production was pursued at the expense of side industries like cotton, oil, melons, and fruit. After the annual payment of grain requisition projects, the remainder was not enough to provide for the people. Xi Jinping saw this, and felt for the county. He knew that the most urgent goal was for the villagers to rise out of poverty, produce enough food, and move away from the status of a high-yielding but poor county. Xi realized that high requisition had caused the disproportionate agricultural structure in Zhengding as well as the food shortages. So, together with Lv Yulan, then Deputy Secretary of the Zhengding County Committee, he reported the situation to the corresponding departments at the higher level, and requested that the base of requisition be lowered to lighten the burden. The Central Committee sent an investigation and verification team, and decided that Zhengding County's request was reasonable, so reduced the grain requisition from 76 million jin to 28 million jin. This greatly reduced Zhengding's economic burden and solved the problem of tight rations for farmers in the county.

With the food shortage solved, Xi Jinping focused on enriching the farmers. He read in the newspaper that some rural areas in the south had implemented a "household responsibility" scheme, with positive results. After an in-depth investigation and study, he found that the "household responsibility" scheme was simple to distribute, easy for farmers to accept, and very popular, so he proposed that the county committee promote it. With the committee's support, Xi Jinping decided to conduct a pilot project in the Lishuangdian Commune, which was economically backward and less productive. He established the idea of piloting first and gradually rolling out. After a year of practice, the agricultural output of Lishuangdian doubled, and the income of the peasants increased to more than 400 yuan, which caused a province-wide reaction. As a result, the "household responsibility" scheme was launched in Zhengding County, consolidating its the agricultural economic foundation and bringing living standards to a new level.

While the county's agricultural economy continued to develop, Xi Jinping began to explore comprehensive economic development for Zhengding. He and the county committee team took cadres to visit and study in the southern cities that were pioneers in Reform and Opening, in order to give them new ideas and allow them to think freely. Xi believed that Zhengding had major advantages in terms of its geographical location, being close to Shijiazhuang City, the 107 national highway, the Beijing-Guangzhou line, and the Shijiazhuang-Dezhou line railroad artery. For convenient transport, economic base, and high food production, economic development ideas had to be aimed at the city: what the city needed, they would plant or process. For this reason, he proposed that the agricultural development of Zhengding would deal with the relationship between food crops and cash crops, and asked the county to unify their thinking to develop a variety of business and planting specialties. In 1983, with Xi's direct leadership, the cotton cultivation area in the county increased to more than 170,000 acres, and the income from multiple operations reached 43 million yuan. The income of community members increased from just ahead 100 yuan to more than 200 yuan. In order to develop edible mushrooms, Xi also wrote to the director of Nanjing Huining County Fertilizer Factory, asking for advice on mushroom cultivation techniques. He sent people from the factory to collect tail sand – the raw material required for mushroom cultivation. At the same time, he also promoted the development of township enterprises. By 1985, the township-run enterprises and consortia in Zhengding, such as starch processing, meat processing and flour processing, had reached a certain scale, with an annual output value of 88.5 million yuan (an increase of 200% over 1980), placing the county's economic development in the forefront of Hebei Province.

(III) Fujian

Fujian is the province where General Secretary Xi Jinping served the longest. He was Vice Mayor of Xiamen from June 1985 to September 2002, when he was reassigned as Secretary of the Zhejiang Provincial Party Committee. He worked in Fujian for more than 17 years. Whether working in Xiamen, leading Ningde, or presiding over the whole province, he always cared about the public and their hardships. He made it a priority to lift them out of poverty. Under his leadership, Fujian underwent great changes, and many poor areas were successfully lifted out of poverty, especially the poor She minority areas. Xi formed a deep relationship with the people of Fujian, and his true devotion for the impoverished She ethnicity is widely praised today.

Fujian has a scattered and mixed ethnic minority population of nearly 800,000, of which the She is the largest, totaling 365,500 mainly in the Ningde area (more than half of the country's She population). In June 1988, Xi Jinping was appointed as Secretary of Ningde local Party committee, which was linked to helping the poor Banzhong She nationality township in Fu'an City. Within a month of his appointment, he came to do research in the She village, which has 60% of the population of Fu'an City. Three months later he visited villages and towns in nine counties in the Ningde area.

Xi Jinping was not afraid of hard work, and went tirelessly from villages and households. His personal devotion was touching. In order to gain a deeper understanding of the life of the minority people, he often spent days in a Jeep bumping along the rugged mountain roads and trudging through the muddy countryside, often too tired to even stand up straight. One day in the early summer of 1989, the sun was just climbing out of the mountain pass when Zhong Tongdi – the Secretary of the Party branch of Dalin Village, who was working in the rice fields – saw three people approaching the village on foot from afar. One of them pointed to a sweaty young man in the middle and said, "This is Xi, the Secretary of the local Party committee. He's coming to the village to get an idea of the situation." Zhong Tongdi knew that Dalin Village was accessible only by a steep, rugged, foot-wide mountain path from Fu'an City's Banzhong She nationality township government. It took more than an hour on foot to get there, even for those who could walk quickly. He said, "I was covered with mud, and my hands were all sweaty. However, Secretary Xi didn't mind at all, and shook my hand." Zhong Tongdi put down his seedlings and led Xi and the other three to the village, explaining the local situation as they walked.

During his work in Fujian, Xi Jinping took the lead in going to the "front line" four times. He went all over the poor areas of Fujian, performing careful research and investigation. He did not make empty statements or offer platitudes. He did his best to cure poverty and ignorance in Fujian, leaving valuable spiritual wealth behind in his wake.

Through his research, Xi Jinping found that the impoverished She area in eastern Fujian was very large, and the phenomenon of poverty and return to poverty was quite serious. The economy of the region was still in a natural or semi-natural state. Coupled with the fact that most She people lived in remote areas, inconvenient transport, inadequate information, and the lack of technology and personnel made it hard for east Fujian to develop. Faced with this situation, Xi Jinping formulated a series of policies to suit local conditions, such as: developing productivity according to local specifics; breaking away from the closed and single natural economy, developing into a commodity economy, and supporting and setting up economic entities; using the advantages of local natural resources to establish their own economic model;

changing the "blood transfusion" assistance model to the "blood generation" model of targeted poverty alleviation by internal and external linkage. Under Xi's leadership, Ningde was no longer a weak county, and the poverty alleviation rate reached over 96%.

Chixi Village is a She administrative village under the jurisdiction of Panxi County in Fuding City in the Ningde Region. In June 1988, when Xi Jinping was transferred to the post of Ningde Party Secretary, the villagers lived in thatched huts. They used wood chips and kerosene lamps for light, ate bitter vegetables and rice with salt water, and lived miserable lives. To remedy the situation, Xi Jinping launched an assault on poverty with the support of the state and Fujian Province's poverty alleviation policy. He proposed providing money and electricity first, and promoted the building of Fuding Mulberry Park Power Station. The latter was approved in 1991 and successfully completed in 1993. The people of Chixi were successfully connected to electricity and lighting, and also had the first dirt-knotted stone road to Panxi County in Fuding City as a result. In August 1994, Chixi Village started the relocation project of the She Village in Xiashanxi. By May 1995, all of the residents of this village had moved into their new homes. On December 4, 1996, the reservoir in Chixi Village was completed, with a total capacity of 73.5 million cubic meters and a total installed capacity of 3 × 12.5 mw hydroelectric generating sets. This is the largest poverty alleviation project in the history of Fuding City. The completion of the power station has enabled the residents of Chixi to increase their income by working, and the development of tourism has greatly increased their income. In 2014, the per capita income of Chixi Village increased from under 200 yuan in 1984 to 11,674 yuan in 2014, and the village financial income started from none to 250 thousand yuan in 2014. Since then, Chixi has earned the title of the "No. 1 Village in China for Poverty Alleviation."

At the end of the 1980s, Ningde implemented the "Welfare Project" for poor and remote places. It involved building roads where possible, and relocating people from places where the conditions were poor and roads could not be built, so that they could rise out of poverty faster. Xi Jinping promoted this project, and by 1993, 1,289 households and 6,235 people from 76 villages in the region had been relocated. A typical example was Dongling Village in Huotong Town, Jiaocheng District, Ningde. Dongling is located halfway up the mountain, and the living environment was very poor. It took more than two hours to go out and buy something. Village director Zhong Qingshuang recalls that once, when he woke up in the middle of the night, he found that a flash flood had reached his bedside. At Xi Jinping's request, they moved off the mountain, both to live safely and to completely escape poverty. Now, two- and three-story buildings can be seen everywhere in Dongling, and the village has developed planting industries such as bamboo, tea, and fruit according to local conditions.

In 1994, Fujian Province listed the "Welfare Project" as a practical people's project by the provincial Party committee and the provincial government. In May 1997, a research report from the provincial CPPCC was on Xi Jinping's desk, who was then Deputy Secretary of the provincial Party committee, and in charge of the province's agriculture and rural operations. The report reflected that although the province had made remarkable achievements in poverty alleviation in recent years, there were still some ethnic minority people living in houses with thatched roofs and mud floors in eastern Fujian. Xi Jinping devoted himself to finding a solution, and repeatedly summoned the appropriate departments for discussions. They performed in-depth research in eastern Fujian, in places such as Fuding and Xiapu, and formed a special research report, suggesting that further poverty alleviation in eastern Fujian minority areas was a priority. Xi asked for support in aspects such as policy and funding, and also went to Zhouning, Fu'an, and some old areas of the base village and minority villages. He found that the poorest regions were in the old areas and ethnic areas, and suggested that the ethnic areas be treated like the old base villages for support, down to the grassroots – especially the ones with the worst accessibility and lack of roads. Their aid would have to target the roots of poverty. Fujian Province was the first in the country to implement the "Welfare Project," with fruitful results. By the end of 2014, the province had implemented the relocation of 6,000 villages – a total of 1.01 million people.

These measures drew strong support from the public. People put up red couplets in their new houses to express their sincere thanks: "Creating a new world, with gratitude to the Party for their support."

(IV) Fuping

Xi Jinping visited the impoverished area of Fuping only a month after he became General Secretary. He said, "I have been to most of the poorest areas in China. In the past two years, I have visited more than a dozen such areas." On his second visit to the old areas, his purpose was to visit impoverished people in the old revolutionary base areas and do research, showing his genuine passion for poverty alleviation.

On December 29, 2012, General Secretary Xi Jinping braved the -10° cold to visit Fuping County in Hebei Province – a key county for poverty alleviation and development, located deep in the Taihang Mountains. There, he visited the needy and discussed strategies to alleviate poverty and become prosperous.

This visit was proposed by General Secretary Xi Jinping in order to understand the real situation of the poorest places and people in China. His goal was to think about the shortcomings of economic and social development, and to discuss plans to build a moderately prosperous society in all aspects. Xi stressed that no matter how long the road is and how difficult the conditions are, the trip must be completed. During the inspection, he gave instructions to his cadres:

> When you meet the public, you should listen to the truth and see it with your own eyes, allowing no falsification. Villagers should say what they have to say. It doesn't matter if they cannot say anything; the authorities should not engage in any training nor direct them to speak. Villagers should not be encouraged to decorate their homes before visits. They should maintain their actual lifestyles, and should leave things the way they are. They should not even add a new stool for the sake of this research.

The research project had a compact itinerary and pragmatic content. At 3pm on December 29, Xi left Beijing. In just over 20 hours, he traveled more than 700 kilometers, visited two poor villages, and held two seminars. He proposed that helping impoverished people to alleviate poverty should be put in a more prominent position. The various support policies should be tilted towards the old revolutionary bases and the poorer areas. They should change their plans according to local conditions, plan scientifically, guide with various classifications, and take advantage of the situation. They should help the old revolutionary areas and poor areas to alleviate poverty and become prosperous as soon as possible.

During the investigation, General Secretary Xi expressed his support for the people. His amiability left a deep impression on them. Tang Zongxiu, a 67-year-old villager, said, "The General Secretary knew that we are in difficulty here. He came to see if life was good. He didn't want us to suffer. He came into my house and sat down without wondering if it was clean or not. He said that my accent sounded like I was from Shanxi. He talked to me about life, which was very kind."

2. *Up and Out of Poverty*

During his tenure as Party Secretary in Ningde, General Secretary Xi Jinping took responsibility immediately, and pioneered the practice of poverty alleviation in the eastern part of Fujian. He also left behind various insightful opinions on alleviating poverty and becoming prosperous. In 1992, Fujian People's Publishing House published the book *Up and Out of Poverty*, which contains 29 articles that Xi wrote during his work in Ningde from 1988 to 1990. His scientific assertions about economic development and poverty alleviation are the ideological guidelines for winning the battle against poverty today.

(I) Weak birds can be the first to fly, and the poorest can become wealthy first

"How Can a Weak Hatchling Be the First to Fly? – Thoughts on Inspecting the Nine Counties of Ningde" is the first article in *Up and Out of Poverty*, and was Xi's first investigation report, written three months after he became the Party Secretary of Ningde. The dialectical idea put forward in this article is that the weak bird can be the first to fly, and the poor can become wealthy first.

For various historical and geographical reasons, in the 1980s, most of the Ningde area was still in a state of natural and semi-natural economic poverty, especially the remote She areas. Could a poor area in eastern Fujian become wealthy first? This was indeed a realistic question that needed to be answered. If this question was not answered correctly, it would be impossible to raise awareness about the need for poverty alleviation. After all, poverty of consciousness is bound together with economic poverty.

Xi Jinping took office in June. From early July to early August, he conducted an in-depth study of nine counties in eastern Fujian in collaboration with several leading comrades in the region. Through research, thinking, and studying, a positive and scientific answer was given. Xi said, "Is it worth discussing whether it is possible for weak hatchlings to fly first? In my opinion, is it possible, and there is an urgent need to talk about it." The answer is to step outside the box, depend less on superiors, eradicate laziness, think independently, liberalize the mind, and be open-minded. "Although an area might be poor, we cannot have a 'poor' mind. We should abandon the concepts of being content in poverty, waiting, depending, and asking others for help, and complaining about others. Cadres and members of the public should talk more about the dialectic of weak birds being the first to fly, and the poorest becoming wealthy quicker."

Xi went on to say, "It is necessary to understand the situation: it is its duty to solve the shortage of raw materials and funds. This attitude shift is the prerequisite for being the 'first to fly.' China cannot turn to others when facing difficulties, but must seek help from within." He believes that poor areas "are fully capable of extraordinary development when they are not constrained, and where they have unique advantages. Poor regions can rely on their own efforts, policies, strengths, and advantages to 'fly first' in specific areas to make up for the disadvantages brought about by poverty."

This idea is hugely innovative. The fact that poor areas such as eastern Fujian have been able to rise out of poverty and become prosperous proves the accuracy of this ideology.

(II) Recognizing that different regions have their own strengths

In order to alleviate poverty in eastern Fujian, the priority was to develop the economy, and finding the right direction and road was the key. Xi Jinping said, "To make the weak birds fly first, fly fast, and fly high, we must explore a way to develop the economy according to local conditions. On the mountain one lives on mountain products and sing folk songs; near the water one lives on the products of the sea and reads the literature of the sea."

Eastern Fujian was old, rural, impoverished, and full of islands; its advantage was the richness in agricultural resources. Therefore, Xi Jinping put the focus on the development and utilization of these special resources, developing township enterprises, agriculture, forestry, animal husbandry, sideline industries, and fisheries. Under Xi's leadership, special eastern Fujianese products such as forestry, tea, and fruit developed rapidly, and the progress of township enterprises accelerated, absorbing a large amount of surplus labor, expanding rural accumulation, and greatly increasing the income of farmers.

Different regions have their own strengths. Only through fostering these strengths and avoiding the shortcomings can it be possible to rise out of poverty. Regarding the actual situation of the Ningde area, Xi Jinping remarked, "We need to address problems according to local conditions, classify the situation, and guide things accordingly. We also need to know an area's abilities, and pay attention to the result." Based on local resources, Ningde's mountains and sea were leveraged in order to lift the area out of poverty into prosperity after the development of its agriculture and industry.

(III) Changing minds is the most important thing

An entrepreneur went to visit a poor peasant family in the west of China, to do research. Although he had seen a lot of disadvantaged households, he had never met such poor people, without even a pair of chopsticks to their names. The entrepreneur was shocked and upset, and wanted to help the family. He went around the back of the house and saw a bamboo forest. He thought to himself, "What's the point of helping people like this, when they are too lazy to even use the bamboo to make chopsticks?" The entrepreneur promptly left. This story tells a certain truth – that ideological poverty can have tragic consequences.

General Secretary Xi Jinping said, "Only through getting rid of the 'poverty' of the mind can China lift itself out of poverty and onto the road towards prosperity and wealth." In *Up and Out of Poverty*, he stated that the first step to poverty alleviation is to change the mindset restricted by poverty: "To help the poor, we must first change their mindset and eradicating the 'poverty' of the mind. Don't blame everything on poverty." Even if one is poor, one should not be shortsighted. Constant dripping wears away a stone. Poverty itself is not frightening; what should be feared is being short-sighted and having no ambition. When people have vitality within, poverty can be alleviated with determination. The people of east Fujian will never forget the General Secretary's wise advice. They played to their strengths, changed their mindsets, and repeatedly broadened their horizons. Keeping Xi Jinping's words in mind, the people of Guoyang Village broke into the market and explored new ways of becoming wealthy. In 1990, the village was awarded the title of "National-level Advanced Village for Minority Solidarity" by the National People's Committee. A young grape grower from the village, Zhong Juchun, was named "National Science and Technology Starfire Leader." In 1992, seeing that the benefits of cultivating tea seedlings were several times higher than those of grapes, the Guoyang villagers decided to follow the trend. Today, they cultivate tea seedlings that are exported to places like Guangdong, Guangxi, and Yunnan. Gantang Town has become a famous tea seedling breeding base in China. In 2014, the total industrial and agricultural output value of the village reached 8.6 million yuan.

Xi Jinping created a scientific roadmap for the development of the She region in eastern Fujian, consisting of market-led strategic thinking, and market-technology-resource development strategy, pursuing two-way opening and two-way development. Two-way opening means simultaneous opening to internal and external markets; two-way development refers to the simultaneous development of resources and markets. It is along this line of thought that Xi's blueprint for the development of ethnic areas in Fujian is gradually becoming a reality.

To break out of the vicious circle of poverty and ignorance in ethnic areas with weak economic and cultural bases, improving education is both an immediate and long-term solution. However, due to historical and natural conditions, for a long time the education level of the She people was generally low. The poorer a place is, the more difficult it is to educate people, and also the more necessary. The education of ethnic minorities became Xi Jinping's main concern. When he was in charge of Ningde, he insisted that the issue of education was absolutely not allowed to wait, and that "education must really be placed first, and efforts should be made to achieve a virtuous cycle in which education, science and technology, and the economy support and promote each other." To this end, from a strategic point of view, Xi made great efforts to cultivate cadres of ethnic minorities. Focusing on primary and secondary schools, he greatly improved the soft environment of building and developing the economy in previously disadvantaged area of eastern Fujian.

Guided by Xi Jinping's ideas, the cause of poverty alleviation among ethnic minorities in Fujian Province has been solidly promoted. The development of ethnic minority areas, including eastern Fujian, has been fruitful, and many poor villages (such as Chixi) have been transformed. Millions of ethnic minority people have risen out of poverty towards prosperity. In 2014, the per capita net income of farmers and ethnic minorities in Fujian province both exceeded the 10,000-yuan mark.

3. Profound reflections in *Zhejiang, China: A New Vision for Development*

Zhejiang, China: A New Vision for Development was written by General Secretary Xi Jinping during his tenure in Zhejiang. The book contains 232 articles from his column of the same name in Zhejiang Daily from February 2003 to March 2007. The short essays use Marxist positions, perspectives, and methods to explain the correct proposition of scientific, economic, and social development, and provide timely answers to some of the greatest issues of real-life public concern. The book also puts forward new and profound thoughts on the issue of poverty alleviation.

(I) Treating less developed regions as new economic growth points

On January 20, 2003, during the "two sessions" in Zhejiang Province, Xi Jinping – then Secretary of the provincial Party committee – attended a discussion held by the Wenzhou delegation of the Provincial People's Congress. He emphasized the need to treat the less developed regions as new economic growth points, pointing out that:

> Less developed areas are not burdens, and we should make policies and ideas
> to create more development opportunities and conditions for them. It is
> only when the less developed areas have also become moderately prosperous

that we can promote the province's overall prosperity and modernization. Undoubtedly, this is a new assertion. Zhejiang is an economically developed province; therefore, the less developed areas in the province have more room for development. Aiming at the less developed areas, the overall economic advancement of the province will accelerate. And it is only through overall advancement that a moderately prosperous society can be built.

He said that Zhejiang was made up of "70% mountains, 10% water, and 20% fields." Most of the poor people lived in these mountainous areas. There are also the difficult households in the islands and the general public of ethnic minorities. Zhejiang should continue to promote the overall development of less developed areas, and narrow the gap between developed areas. "In the less developed areas, we should advocate the concept of self-reliance and intensify the ability of self-development instead of waiting and relying on others" to achieve the overall coordinated and sustainable development of Zhejiang's economy.

(II) Helping those who are truly impoverished

Xi Jinping said, "In the poor areas, there are also households worth a million yuan. We alleviate poverty in the households that are truly poor, and grasp the dynamics within poverty. Our investments focus on things that could really benefit poor households." He also stressed the need to consider the actual situation in Zhejiang. It was necessary to grasp the specifics of impoverished areas in order to help villages and households directly. After Xi Jinping became General Secretary, this idea became a basic principle of poverty alleviation in China. To take targeted measures in poverty alleviation, we must identify who to support and how to support, so as to help those who are truly poor, alleviate poverty directly, get real results, and improve the effectiveness of poverty alleviation by taking targeted measures.

(III) By all means, benefit the public

In a nutshell, successful poverty alleviation lies in seeking truth and pragmatism from the very roots of the problem. Xi Jinping said, "At all times and under all circumstances, we must consider the fundamental interests of the public, testing our work and performance by comparing it to these interests. If what we do matters to the public, we need to try by all means possible. If what we do harms the public in any way, we must not do it."

In 2012, when investigating the development of poverty alleviation work in Fuping County, Hebei Province, Xi stressed, "Think constantly about whether the things we do are what the Party and the public need us to do. We have to work single-mindedly for the people, with their benefit in mind. We must help those in need. We must go into the poverty-stricken areas, sit in poor homes, and chat with impoverished people. This way, we will gain a greater understanding of the expectations of the disadvantaged people, solving their problems with devotion and enthusiasm."

4. Major ideas since the 18th National Congress

The 18th National Congress of the CPC elected Xi Jinping as the General Secretary of the CPC Central Committee, ushering in a new era of modern China's war on poverty. With the Millennium Development Goals (MDGs) achieved in China by 2015, General Secretary Xi Jinping's series of decisions and propositions on poverty alleviation have been deeply supported by the whole of the Party and nation.

(I) Following the example of the Foolish Old Man who moved mountains to win the battle against poverty

The story of the Foolish Old Man who moved mountains is a common Chinese fable. It tells the story of a man who was determined to move two mountains – Taihang and Wangwu – which were blocking his family's way.

This story is well known in China because it was told by Chairman Mao in 1945, referring to the two "mountains" of Japanese imperialism and feudalism, and the necessity of liberating China with the leadership of the Chinese Communist Party. Seventy years later, at the Central Conference on Poverty Alleviation and Development, General Secretary Xi Jinping invoked the Foolish Old Man once again, in the context of winning the battle against poverty. China has changed over the past 70 years. The two leaders used the example of the Foolish Old Man in different times and places, but they expressed the same truth: it is only through being determined like the Foolish Old Man that China can overcome all difficulties to achieve a final victory.

General Secretary Xi Jinping said that alleviating poverty, improving people's livelihoods, and gradually achieving common prosperity are the essential requirements of socialism, and the essential missions of the Party. He made a solemn promise to the nation to build a moderately prosperous society in all aspects. The battle against poverty has begun. We must move mountains, set goals, and work hard if we are to win it. By 2020, all poor areas and impoverished people must be moderately prosperous together.

China faces huge difficulties in building a moderately prosperous society. The size of its impoverished population is still large, the poverty rate is relatively deep, and the cost of poverty reduction is high; therefore, poverty alleviation will be difficult to achieve. The goal of releasing more than 70 million rural poor from poverty by 2020 is ambitious, as the timeline is very short and the workload is heavy. China must follow the example of the Foolish Old Man, taking the initiative, remaining realistic, and overcoming difficulties with perseverance in order to achieve the target of building a moderately prosperous society.

After Mao cited the example of the Foolish Old Man who moved mountains at the Seventh Congress of the CPC in 1945, it took nearly five years for the Party to liberate China. General Secretary Xi Jinping cited the same fable at Central Working Conference on Poverty Alleviation and Development, and proposed to build a moderately prosperous society by 2020 – also in five years. This may be a coincidence of history, but there is every reason to believe that under the wise leadership of the Party Central Committee with Xi Jinping as General Secretary, China will achieve its goal on schedule.

(II) Taking targeted measures to alleviate poverty

General Secretary Xi Jinping pointed out that we should insist on poverty alleviation through taking targeted measures. As for deciding who to support, we must identify the real poor population, the degree of poverty, and the causes. Then, it will be possible to apply policies to each household. Therefore, Xi asked for less acting, and more practical benefits to the poor. He ordered leading cadres at all levels in poor areas to go to the "front line" of poverty alleviation, be down-to-earth and realistic, and get things done properly with positive results.

Identifying those who are in real poverty involves taking targeted measures towards poverty alleviation. To do this, leaders at all levels should lead by example, taking staff deep into the grassroots, into people's homes and into the most remote areas to complete comprehensive surveys. These surveys should help to foster an in-depth understanding of who is really poor and how poor they are, rather than gathering surface-level information. It is only by going into people's homes, seeing how they live, listening to their stories, and seeing their circumstances that cadres can decide who needs poverty alleviation. In this way, there can be a clear goal and direction, and the policy can help the households that are truly poor.

The key to poverty alleviation through taking targeted measures is to help those who are genuinely in need. For a long time, the country's support for impoverished areas has been expanding year on year, but there are many problems, as the result has been unsatisfactory for some. Clearly, poverty alleviation efforts in the past were still developing. A phenomenon existed whereby some people remained poor despite receiving help year after year. There were even instances of helping the rich instead of the poor, assisting officials instead of the public, and helping the strong rather than the weak, which had to be stopped.

Targeted support should be implemented, with a policy for each household – a new method of helping people earn money, unlike the previous method of simply giving it to them. This way, poor households can be truly helped in accordance with local conditions, classified guidance, and targeted assistance.

Achieving real results is the core of targeted poverty alleviation. Empty talk is a burden, but practical work builds a nation. Leading cadres at all levels should undertake real work, and abandon the wrongful idea that making a little progress having a little wealth is enough. Following a realistic and pragmatic work concept, leading cadres should alleviate poverty step by step. They should educate the poor, free them from ideological poverty, and encourage them to stop complaining, relying on others, and being content with their impoverishment. Instead, they should leverage their own strengths and advantages. Promoting a mindset of self-improvement, self-reliance, and hard work, leading cadres should stimulate their internal motivation to change poor people's situations.

Since Xi Jinping took charge of the central government, he has visited the poorest areas and families many times, sympathizing with the people's hardships and solving their problems, setting an example for the rest of the Party. Early in the morning of January 19, 2015, he took a plane from Beijing to areas of exceptional and concentrated poverty in the Wumeng Mountains in Zhaotong City, Yunnan Province. As soon as he got off the plane, he transferred to a car and went to Ludian County to visit the poor people affected by disaster. Listening to a report about what had happened, he pointed out that poverty alleviation and development are the key aspects of its "First Centennial Goal," and is the most difficult task. Now, only five or six years from the realization of a moderately prosperous society, time is running out. It is necessary to enhance its sense of urgency and do real work, not just chant slogans. No one from disadvantaged areas and populations should fall behind. Through setting clearer goals with more powerful initiatives and more effective action, it is necessary to implement targeted measures in depth. Project arrangements and the use of funds should be more precise, digging down to the root and cutting to the chase, so that poor people really get benefits. When Xi Jinping went to visit the poor in a disaster-stricken area, the people were deeply moved and wrote a poem: "During the 'Great Cold,' he brings great love; the dragon sends a good year's snow. Thousands of magpies are chirping, and millions of people are smiling."

General Secretary Xi Jinping has repeatedly stressed that the implementation of targeted poverty alleviation relies on the "Six Precisions" – precise objects, precise project arrangements, precise use of funds, precise measures taken in households, a precise First Secretary of the county, and precise results. It is necessary to ensure that the benefits of the policies fall on the poor, so that impoverished households can become prosperous.

(III) Prescribing the right treatment, and taking targeted measures

A moderately prosperous society for China includes 7.27 million poor people. In such a society, no one is allowed to fall behind. In order to alleviate poverty successfully, General Secretary Xi Jinping has set a series of major targeted measures, including identifying and categorizing the root of poverty, prescribing the right treatment, and taking targeted measures.

In his speech at the 2015 High-level Forum on Poverty Reduction and Development, Xi said that in the implementation of targeted poverty alleviation, classification is the basic essence of the policy. It is necessary to apply policies depending on people and places, and depending on the causes and types of poverty. At the national level, it is necessary to delineate "five groups" according to the impoverished population: a group of people who develop production to alleviate poverty, a group of people who relocate to alleviate poverty, a group of people who use eco-compensation to alleviate poverty, a group of people who develop education to alleviate poverty, and a group of people who are covered by social security. In poor areas, Party committees and governments at all levels should develop self-reliance and self-improvement, pursue practicality, find the right development pathway for local conditions, find ways to solve real problems one by one, and use their own hard work to rise out of poverty and become wealthy.

In February 2013, Xi Jinping braved the cold to visit Bulengou Village in Gaoshan Township, Dongxiang Autonomous County, Gansu Province. The village is located in a steep ravine between two high mountains. The natural conditions are very harsh, and life is difficult. The village – with 68 households 341 people – had a per capita net income of only 1624.10 yuan. The poverty rate was as high as 96%. It was one of the poorest, the most arid mountain villages in the county. Ma Zhijian, Secretary of the Party Committee of Gaoshan Township, said that the General Secretary went into the village and gave them his assiduous and thoughtful attention. The village road was bumpy, with ankle-deep soil, but Xi walked all the way, his shoes and trouser legs covered with dust. Not caring about any of this, he sympathized with the people and their hardships, which was very admirable. He also repeatedly stressed during his visit that the villagers should adopt a mindset of self-reliance and self-improvement, find the right development pathway, work hard, improve the conditions for production and living, and rise out of poverty as quickly as possible.

The General Secretary's profound sentiments about poverty alleviation have set an example for China to follow, and have opened a door for exploration.

CHAPTER 1

Strategic Guidance in the Final Battle

The year 2020 is a significant historical node. By then, 70.17 million rural poor in China will have been lifted out of poverty, a moderately prosperous society will have been realized, and the "First Centennial Goal" of the great China dream will have been achieved.

Undoubtedly, the years 2015 to 2020 will see a tough and decisive battle to ensure that all poor areas and impoverished people will rise out of poverty, creating a moderately prosperous society. To win this battle, establishing scientific and strategic guidance becomes critical.

1. The strategic vision for poverty alleviation in the new era

Thought determines action. Winning the decisive battle against poverty contains strategically significant meaning to the well-being of the public, the ruling foundation of the Communist Party of China, and the long-term stability of the country. There is no choice but to win. Therefore, it is necessary to take charge of all poverty reduction activities by pursuing the strategic idea of poverty alleviation in the new era, to ensure that the final goal can be achieved on schedule.

(I) Using General Secretary Xi Jinping's statement about poverty alleviation as guidance

General Secretary Xi Jinping, who cares deeply about the poor, has deeply investigated and considered poverty-stricken areas and their residents, and has engaged in a series of meaningful discussions around poverty reduction. These discussions reveal the general rule of poverty alleviation, becoming the ideological guidance to ensure victory in the war against poverty. China must intensify its knowledge, accurately grasp the basic implication of General Secretary Xi's discussions about poverty alleviation, genuinely understand their essence, and unify its ideological understanding with General Secretary Xi's critical expositions, in order to form a consensus to alleviate poverty. China must insist on combining theory with practice, and guide its work practice with Xi's discussions about poverty alleviation. In order to win the battle against poverty, it is necessary to analyze the specific conditions of various regions, industries, and departments, and correctly apply a variety of strategies. As long as Xi's guidance on poverty alleviation is followed, it is possible to overcome all obstacles and maintain the correct direction, achieving the goal on schedule.

(II) Following the poverty alleviation policies of the Party Central Committee and the State Council of the PRC

In the new era, China still has a large impoverished population and a deep level of poverty, and faces high costs and great difficulty in reducing poverty. The tasks are strenuous and the timeline is pressing. China must adhere to the consistency of the Party Central Committee and the State Council on poverty alleviation policies. It must prioritize poverty alleviation as a major political project, enhance its sense of mission and responsibility, have the courage to take poverty alleviation as its obligation, and truly make a difference.

China must take the overall goal of poverty alleviation set by the Party Central Committee and the State Council as the basic standard, implementing it with no change or reduction. China must seize the day and work diligently to ensure that its various poverty alleviation projects can be completed according to certain standard and time. China must: take the basic principles of poverty alleviation established by the Party Central Committee and the State Council as the basis; intensify investigation and research; understand the root causes of poverty; take extraordinary measures; come up with exceptional methods and pragmatic solutions to problems; precisely target the poor and help them; and never leave an impoverished household or a poor population behind. In conclusion, it is necessary to implement the policies and regulations of poverty alleviation set by the Party Central Committee and the State Council, be consistent with their leadership, not seek pretexts with objective reasons or develop countermeasures, be realistic, and contribute all its strength to succeed in poverty alleviation.

(III) Comprehensively implementing the "Decision of the CPC Central Committee and the State Council on Winning the Fight Against Poverty"

In order to ensure that poverty can be alleviated among the rural poor, and that a moderately prosperous society can be built in all respects by 2020, the "Decision of the CPC Central Committee and the State Council on Winning the Battle Against Poverty" (hereinafter referred to as the "Decision"), which was issued on December 7, 2015, defines the political attitude, overall requirements, and six specific provisions that should be adopted to alleviate poverty. This decision is the basic proposition of the CPC Central Committee and the State Council on winning the battle against poverty, the basic standard for the national poverty alleviation work, and the macro blueprint for its final battle in 2020. China must insist on implementing all the provisions and requirements of the decision without any discount or shrinking, fully achieving all of the mission targets for poverty alleviation in both quantity and quality. In terms of the specific policy adoption in the battle against poverty, it is necessary to: focus closely on the strategic layout of the "Four Comprehensives"; establish and implement a development concept of innovation, coordination, ecology, openness, and exchange; and correctly handle the relationships among the following three aspects:

a) The relationship between fighting poverty and ecological protection

The ecological environment is the basis of human survival. Ecological protection cannot be suspended or weakened in the pursuit of poverty alleviation. Ignoring the natural and fundamental role of ecological protection because poverty appears to be the biggest challenge in building a moderately prosperous society is also not acceptable. Fighting poverty is not a case of blindly pursuing excessive economic development or unsustainable developments at the expense of the ecological environment.

To find a balance between fighting poverty and ecological protection, it is necessary to give equal importance to both. It should not unilaterally pursue pure economic development that disturbs the ecological balance and destroys the natural environment. Nor should it repeat the mistake of sacrificing the environment for economic growth and let future generations bear the sins it has committed. It is necessary to adopt the concept of green and sustainable development in poverty alleviation work. While developing its economy to alleviate poverty, it is necessary to also take ecological and environmental protection into account to promote the cohesive development of the economy and environment. It is only by pursuing the equal and coordinated development of poverty alleviation and ecological protection that China can fulfill the sustainable expansion of its economy and society, ensure the sustainability of poverty eradication, and reduce the proportion of ecological poverty.

b) The relationship between government leadership and the public

Fighting poverty through development is a complex systematic project. It is an important fundamental task for the coordinated promotion of the "Five in One" and "Four Comprehensives" strategies, which are related to the livelihood and well-being of all ethnic groups. Governments, as multiple resource holders, should play the role of instructors. They should play to their strengths in terms of organization and resources, activate the forces of the markets and society, and lead people out of poverty to become wealthy. As the object of poverty alleviation, people in poor areas are the beneficiaries of the fight against poverty through development. They cannot simply enjoy the results of poverty alleviation by not working hard and blindly waiting for government and social assistance. Relying only of the "blood transfusion" model of poverty alleviation will eventually lead to a return to poverty in poor areas. Following this model, the more help people in poor areas get, the poorer they become. The best form of poverty alleviation cuts poverty off at the root, stimulates people's sense of ownership in poor areas, and leverages their initiative. To alleviate poverty, it is necessary to follow the government's lead, gathering resources from all parties and enhancing social cohesion, and using the strength of the people to stimulate internal power. In this way, poverty alleviation and development will address both the symptoms and root causes, poverty will gradually decline, and a moderately prosperous society in all respects will be steadily and solidly established.

c) The relationship between targeted poverty alleviation and the development of concentrated and contiguous poor areas

Targeted poverty alleviation, which is a new measure for China to push it to a new stage and a realistic method of building a moderately prosperous society in all respects, emphasizes refinement and target-ability. It has clear targets, accurate methods, and great effects. However, the development of concentrated and contiguous poor areas is a regional method of targeted poverty alleviation, and the main focus of the fight against poverty through development. It is only by promoting regional economic development through regional development that China can solve the common problems faced by poverty alleviation in poor areas and build the foundation for intensifying targeted strategies.

A stream will be full if the river contains plenty of water. It is necessary to coordinate the relationship between the development of poor areas and targeted poverty alleviation; make overall plans based on regional realities; promote it step by step, by classification; organically combine targeted poverty alleviation with regional economic development; and fulfill the comprehensive, coordinated, and sustainable development of poverty alleviation.

2. Adopting the strategies of not falling behind and not leaving anyone behind

Not falling behind and not leaving anyone behind are the essential requirements and standards of building a moderately prosperous society, and the strategic positioning of poverty alleviation. A moderately prosperous society in all respects includes all Chinese people. The phenomena of falling behind and leaving people are not allowed to emerge. Poor rural areas are "the last kilometer" of building a moderately prosperous society in all respects. To reduce poverty for 70.17 million poor rural people by 2020, China must maintain strategies of not falling behind and not leaving anyone behind.

(I) Achieving global coverage of poverty alleviation indicators

This means that all poverty indicators for poor areas regarding education, medical treatment, housing, economic income, public services, transport, water conservation, and power infrastructure will meet the standards that have been set.

Global coverage of poverty alleviation indicators is a necessary condition for comprehensive poverty alleviation, and one of the objectives of a moderately prosperous society in all respects. Poverty is often a combination aspects, including impoverished lifestyles, backward education, lack of infrastructure, and lack of housing and medical security. These factors affect and interact with each other. If one indicator fails to meet the standard, it will lead to poverty. In such cases, poverty has not been alleviated, and a moderately prosperous society in all respects has not been achieved. Only when the global coverage of poverty alleviation indicators is achieved can China be a "Five in One" moderately prosperous society in all respects, with the comprehensive promotion and coordinated development of political, economic, cultural, and social systems, and ecological protection.

Realizing the full coverage of poverty alleviation indicators is the basic requirement for poverty alleviation and the basic measurement standard of a moderately prosperous society in all respects. This requires full consideration of the various factors that cause poverty in order to achieve all-round poverty alleviation; no index can be omitted. Achieving global coverage of poverty alleviation indicators requires that poor areas develop in leaps and bounds in the five aspects of political, economic, cultural, social, and ecological development. By 2020, all poverty alleviation targets must be achieved and sustained, and healthy economic development should be promoted in poor areas. People's democracy should be consistently expanded, cultural soft power should be significantly enhanced, and people's living standards should be improved in order to build a resource-saving and environmentally-friendly society. In short, by 2020, all of the 70.17 million rural poor under the existing standards will enjoy economic and cultural prosperity, political democracy, social equity, and good ecology.

(II) Strengthening poverty alleviation in the "three regions"

The "three regions" are the old revolutionary base regions, ethnic minority regions, and border areas. Most of these areas have a relatively poor natural environment, widespread and deep-level poverty, and large impoverished populations. They are the areas of the worst poverty in China. Due to location conditions, resource endowments, and historical factors, the "three regions" typify the current situation of accumulated poverty, and have long been the focus and challenge of poverty reduction in China. Enriching these regions has always been a particularly strenuous aspect of the task of building a moderately prosperous society in all respects by 2020.

Enhancing poverty alleviation in the "three regions" is necessary if China is to build a moderately prosperous society in all respects and common prosperity. A moderately prosperous society in all respects is moderately prosperous regardless of region, including all 56 nationalities. If a place is poor, it is not well-off, and if a nation is suffering, its wealth is not comprehensive. The goal of building a moderately prosperous society in all respects by 2020 and the particularity of the poverty in the "three regions" determine that poverty alleviation work must focus on the "three regions" in order to create a nationwide moderately prosperous society in all respects.

To enhance poverty alleviation in the "three regions," it is first necessary to direct resources to them, and offer prioritized and key support in terms of policies, funds, science, technology, personnel support, and publicity. Second, it is necessary to increase the transfer payment of the "three regions," accelerate the implementation of the "three regions" development scheme, and accelerate the building of major infrastructure projects and livelihood projects there. Third, it is necessary to enhance support for education. The government and society should concentrate on education in the "three regions," implementing the action plan of paired assistance for poverty alleviation through education, and fundamentally blocking the intergenerational transmission of poverty. Meanwhile, in these ecologically fragile areas, poverty alleviation work should also focus on ecological protection and development by integrating environmental and ecological protection, developing environmentally-friendly industries, and promoting the coordination of economic and social development with people, resources, and the environment.

(III) Standardizing public infrastructure

Public infrastructure refers to the basic facilities required for life and production in poor areas, including transport, water conservation, electricity, housing, the Internet, and the living environment. It is the basic condition and developmental foundation of economic society, and the basis for building a moderately prosperous society in poor areas.

Deficiencies or imperfections in public infrastructure seriously restrict the economic development of poor areas, and has become the biggest obstacle to poverty alleviation. Imperfections in public facilities have caused people in poor areas to suffer from adverse weather conditions, lack of food, clothes, and shelter, and limited transport. They have no way of developing production and improving their lives, and are no closer to achieving a moderately prosperous society. Adverse conditions of public infrastructure hinder economic development in poor areas, and also severely limit poor people's ideas about eradicating poverty. Therefore, to build a moderately prosperous society in all respects by 2020, China must raise the standard of public facilities in poor areas, remove obstacles to economic development in poor areas, and eliminate the stumbling blocks to the idea of prosperity.

To raise the standard of public infrastructure means that it is necessary to set the improvement of infrastructure in poor areas as the central project of poverty alleviation. Based on the natural geographical conditions of the poor areas, it is necessary to intensify scientific planning and make classified as well as time-bound implementation plans. It must coordinate the financial resources of the government and society, make efforts to accelerate implementation, and expedite the removal of development bottlenecks.

Firstly, construction should be carried out according to planning classification, so as to distinguish urgent demands in different regions according to the planning scheme. Urgent construction should be carried out first, and the most important elements should be completed in the initial stage. Urgent and smooth construction should be coordinated. The estates can be used and the income should be generated while the area is under construction.

Secondly, it is necessary to pay attention to the actual effect of investment. Special government support funds should be earmarked for specific purposes, which provides motivation to intensify supervision, ensure the amount of investment, and improve the use efficiency. In accordance with the principle of who invests gains, it is necessary to activate social funds and increase its participation in poverty alleviation and the development of public facilities in poor areas, in order to ensure the benefits to both supply and demand parties, improve the efficiency of construction, accelerate the building of external and internal transport channels in poor areas, provide safe drinking water for the poor, and improve the general service level of electric power in poor areas. Attention should also be paid to the actual effect of investment. Special government support funds should be earmarked for specific purposes, supervision should be strengthened, investment amounts should be ensured, and the use efficiency should be improved. It must expand broadband networks to cover poor villages; improve the level of rural Internet and financial services in poor areas; intensify the transformation of dilapidated rural houses in poor areas; ensure basic safe housing for poor households; continue to promote the linked improvement of the rural environment in poor areas; improve the living and production conditions in poor villages; and promote the building of attractive and livable villages.

3. Enhancing internal forces and the ability to benefit the poor

Building a moderately prosperous society in all respects is fundamentally a development issue. Development is the absolute principle. Poverty alleviation and prosperity in poor areas also depend on it. Development will not happen simply by waiting, asking, or relying on others. In order to alleviate poverty and gnaw down the hard bone of development, China must adopt the strategic method of enhancing internal forces and the ability to benefit the poor. To enhance internal forces is to encourage self-reliance in poor areas, supplemented by the help of external forces. To enhance the ability to benefit the poor means that all economic and social activities such as development should help people in impoverished areas to alleviate poverty and become wealthy. It is only by adhering to the strategic means of enhancing internal forces and the ability to benefit the poor that China can pool its efforts and move towards creating a moderately prosperous society.

(I) Relying on one's own efforts to reverse disadvantages

Relying on one's own efforts to reverse disadvantages means that people in poor areas should rise out of poverty through their own hard work instead of simply asking for money. Poverty alleviation will eventually depend on self-development. Practice has exemplified that the simple "blood transfusion" model of poverty alleviation has made it difficult to truly alleviate poverty and promote prosperity. Therefore, people in poor areas should be active instead of passive, relying on their own efforts to overcome their developmental disadvantages and fundamentally achieve stable poverty alleviation.

Relying on one's own efforts to reverse disadvantages is the summary of historical experience of poverty alleviation, the site of the battle against poverty in the new era, and the fundamental strategy of building a moderately prosperous society in all respects. Poverty alleviation projects in the past few decades have demonstrated that the previous pattern of simple material assistance will encourage being content with poverty, and will lead to worse ideological poverty. This pattern has no benefit for eliminating poverty, and can block development in poor areas, slowing poverty alleviation down. Therefore, poverty reduction work in the new era must instead stimulate people's sense of ownership in poor areas, improving self-development abilities, raising the sustainability of economic development, and completely blocking the root reasons for slipping back into poverty. People in poor areas are the main object of poverty alleviation work, as well as the biggest beneficiary of a moderately prosperous society in all respects. Only when all 70.17 million poor rural people are all self-reliant, can they pool into an irreplaceable main force for poverty alleviation. Relying on one's own effort to reverse disadvantages requires that:

a. In order to change their mindsets, ideas, and actions, people in poor areas should truly want to alleviate poverty, turn the pressure of poverty into the driving force for poverty reduction, and take practical actions to improve their living conditions and achieve prosperity;

b. People in poor areas should develop their strengths and avoid their weaknesses. Based on the enrichment of local ecological resources, they should leverage their individual advantages, and engage in extraordinary development in places with unique advantages in poor areas, so as to truly promote the sustainable economic development of the region.

As General Secretary Xi Jinping said, "poverty-stricken areas may rely on their own efforts, policies, strengths, and advantages in specific areas to make up for the disadvantages of poverty."

(II) Innovating specific self-restoration modes

To innovate self-restoration modes and make them more specific, the innovation of poverty alleviation mode used by industries should be used as a measure to realize the goal of poverty alleviation – that is, to promote innovation in the process of poverty alleviation by developing industries, and seek development through poverty alleviation by industries in the process of innovation. Industries are the focus of poverty alleviation and development, and this is a meaningful way to enhance the self-restoration ability of impoverished people.

The innovation of specific self-restoration modes is a must for targeted poverty alleviation and the fight against poverty in the new era. Poverty varies from region to region and from household to household. Therefore, it is necessary to identify the various causes of poverty in different impoverished areas, and adopt the appropriate self-restoration methods, rather than using the "one size fits all" method regardless of specific situations and simply copying the methods of poverty alleviation in other areas. A "blood generation" approach without local specifics will often fail to solve the specific problems of a particular poverty-stricken area, and may even hinder economic development and slow the pace of poverty alleviation. Poverty alleviation in the new era must be targeted, using the distinctive industrial model of the region. We can fundamentally eradicate the "root causes" of poverty and truly eradicate it only by adapting measures to local conditions, creating new ways of "blood generation" suited to the specifics of poverty-stricken areas, and enhancing the internal impetus of these areas.

In order to bring real benefits to people in impoverished areas, it is necessary to implement targeted poverty alleviation programs and use funds more accurately to find the root cause of poverty.

First, we should fully understand the importance of industry, clarify the role of industry, and intensify the basic understanding of relying on industry in poverty alleviation and elimination. Second, we should proceed from the actual situation, and promote industrial methods of poverty alleviation such as developing specific agriculture, resource-based industries, national and regional specific tourism, and service economies in different regions. Both the development of projects with low investment but quick results, and long-acting industry development is required. It is important that new models be explored for poverty alleviation in various industries, and new ways of self-restoration be created according to differences in natural conditions, factor endowments, economic levels, and specific market changes. Thus, it is possible to achieve notable results by improving the quality and adding benefits of poverty alleviation by development.

(III) Achieving sustainable development by combining internal and external factors

To achieve sustainable development by combining internal and external factors means that impoverished areas should rely on their own efforts to eradicate poverty and reach prosperity, and in the meantime combine it with the support of external forces. Self-effort is the internal factor, and external support is the condition. The internal factor is primary, and the external one is auxiliary. They combine and interact. If there is a lack of support from outside, people in these harsh-conditioned areas will find it difficult to build a moderately prosperous society in all respects by solely relying on their own efforts, and hence little progress will be achieved. Therefore, the goal of building a moderately prosperous society in all respects by 2020 may not be accomplished as planned. Similarly, if impoverished areas do not pursue their own development but rely only on external support, they will repeat their previous mistakes and be trapped in long-term poverty once the external support is withdrawn. Therefore, in order to win the battle against poverty, it is necessary to combine internal and external factors and form a joint force for poverty alleviation and elimination.

Most poor areas have a fragile ecological environment and harsh living conditions, making it difficult to eradicate poverty. In addition, in these areas, the level of economic development is low and educational resources are scarce. Most people lack scientific and cultural knowledge, meaning that there is insufficient intellectual support for poverty alleviation. Therefore, it is difficult for poor areas to alleviate poverty by themselves; they require external support. In this case, the government should play a leading role in supporting the development of poor areas in various forms, such as fiscal transfer payment, direct investment, system construction, policy support, and guidance, to provide the necessary economic conditions and favorable external environment for poverty alleviation. Then, those who become wealthy first should help the rest, for common prosperity, i.e. the regions that grow rich first should assist the poor areas to do the same through measures such as investment, technology transfer, and human resources assistance. Finally, it is necessary to encourage all sectors of society to offer charity to poor areas, including donations and educational support, to help people in poor areas eliminate poverty quickly.

4. Pursuing the strategy of "Prioritizing Determination and Education"

Poverty alleviation depends on determination, and achieving prosperity depends on wisdom. Therefore, to alleviate poverty, it is necessary to first be determined; to cure poverty, it needs to educate its people. In the fight against poverty, China must uphold the strategy of "Prioritizing Determination and Education." With a focus on improving the basic literacy and technical skills of the workforce in poor areas, education should be promoted in order to help them thrive, prosper, find employment, and settle down, thus laying a solid foundation for creating a moderately prosperous society in all respects.

(I) Alleviating poverty with determination and wisdom

Xi Jinping has said, "Poverty alleviation requires a rise in people's determination. We need to alleviate poverty from our minds." To eradicate poverty, "we must start from our ways of thinking and mindsets. It is only by eradicating poverty from our minds that we can alleviate it, first in the regions, and then across the whole country, embarking on the road to wealth and prosperity." This tells us that we cannot let poverty stifle our determination – we must first establish the ambition for poverty alleviation, which starts with mentioning and emphasizing the state of poverty less and doing more. It is possible to alleviate poverty with determination and wisdom. However, only by establishing the determination to alleviate poverty can we develop the wisdom for achieving prosperity. Poverty alleviation through education is an important aspect of the overall battle, as well as an important way to prevent the intergenerational transmission of poverty. The premise of improving internal power and enhancing self-restoration and independent innovation in poor areas is that people in these areas should completely change their thinking from relying on outside help to helping themselves. Through education, it is necessary to explore new ideas for poverty alleviation, find new ways of becoming rich, and stimulate the mental ability of people in poor areas to eliminate poverty and become prosperous.

(II) Emphasizing the benefit of education-based poverty alleviation for future generations

On September 9, 2015, General Secretary Xi wrote a reply to teachers who had participated in the Guizhou training class at Beijing Normal University during the 2014 National Training Program: "Poverty alleviation requires education. Providing children in poor areas with a good education is a significant element of poverty alleviation and development, and an important way of preventing the intergenerational transmission of poverty."

Knowledge changes destiny. Education is the ultimate solution to poverty, as it is a way of breaking the intergenerational cycle. It is only by relying on knowledge and skills that people in poor areas can improve their ability to fundamentally alleviate poverty and become well-off.

Education-based poverty alleviation is the focus of the new era. It requires a precise grasp of China's current development situation and an accurate judgment of the key points of national reform and development. Ignorance is the root of poverty. Poor rural areas are lagging in terms of the literacy rate and economic level, which indicates an urgent need for education to infuse the concepts of development, innovation, and hard work, to enhance the courage to fight aggressively, and to provide more knowledge and skills for people to change their fate. Education is the fundamental way of alleviating poverty in poor areas, and also an organic part of the national staff training strategy. Today, competition for personnel is a bargaining chip between countries. Education has become one of the most significant yardsticks to judge the strength and advancement of a country. It plays a leading, fundamental, and overarching role in economic and social development and national rejuvenation, and determines a nation's future.

Basic education must be given priority in education-based poverty alleviation.

As the Chinese saying goes, "When young people are strong, the country will be strong." Basic education is the foundation for rejuvenating the country through science and education. It plays an overall, fundamental, and guiding role in improving the quality of the Chinese nation, training personnel of all kinds and at all levels, and promoting socialist modernization. Ensuring that children in poor areas enjoy the same education as those in urban areas is a major challenge to poverty alleviation through basic education.

In April 2015, the 11th Meeting of the Central Leading Group for Deepening Reform deliberated and approved five reform plans, including the "Support Plan for Rural Teachers (2015–2020)." It proposed that by 2020, it is necessary to complete the building of a moderately prosperous society in all aspects and realize the modernization of education, for which the weak links are remote and poverty-stricken areas in the central and western regions such as the elderly population, minority areas, border areas, impoverished areas, and islands.

Therefore, the fundamental way to nurture wisdom and remove ignorance is to develop education. Compared with economy-based, policy-based, and project-based poverty alleviation, the education-based mode points directly to the root cause of poverty and backwardness, and cuts them off at the source.

(III) The Yulu Plan for poverty alleviation

The Yulu Plan is a poverty alleviation program for vocational education in poor areas. It aims to connect industrial transformation and upgrading with employment security based on basic education, and provides professional and skilled personnel for economic and social development in poor areas. The Plan aims for the alleviation of poverty in accordance with the "Decision of the CPC Central Committee and the State Council on Winning the Fight Against Poverty," and the goal of lifting 70.17 million people out of poverty by 2020 and building a moderately prosperous society in all respects.

It is necessary to be problem-oriented, focusing on improving the self-development capacity of those who have been lifted out of poverty, and promoting employment. It must make use of poverty alleviation funds from the government, and encourage the participation of all sectors of society. By providing financial support and guiding workers from poor rural families to receive vocational education and skills training, and thereby nurture industrial development leaders in poor villages, China will support and help the impoverished population to increase employment and development opportunities and raise income. It is fair to say that the Yulu Plan has achieved positive results since it was implemented during the 11th Five-Year Plan period. Since 2010, pilot reforms of the plan have been carried out to support and guide young people from poor families to receive secondary and higher vocational education and labor preparation training for at least one year. By the academic year 2013–2014, the number of pilot counties had increased to 203. The number of beneficiaries had reached more than 1.7 million. The next step should be based on the principle of targeted poverty alleviation, aiming at prominent existing problems and innovating a training pathway within the Yulu Plan, and hence transfer the policy mode from "broad irrigation" to a more precise "drip irrigation."

As a key step in improving the quality and efficiency of poverty alleviation, the "Decision of the CPC Central Committee and the State Council on Winning the Fight Against Poverty" states that by 2020, about 10 million registered poor will be lifted out of poverty through education. To eradicate poverty with the Yulu Plan, first, the two basic tasks of targeted poverty alleviation must be intensified, namely, identifying and filing poverty alleviation targets and locating officials in villages, and channeling poverty alleviation resources and measures to poor villages and households. Second, funding must be increased for vocational education, the standard of state grants for secondary vocational education must be raised, and children from poor families should be encouraged to participate voluntarily in vocational education and training. In addition to the state policy of subsidizing vocational education, children from poor families can also enjoy preferential policies such as student subsidies and loans from their original domicile. Third, secondary and higher vocational schools should be built, special education and distance education should be run well in poor areas, and special vocational education should be developed in line with the actual conditions of poor areas. To this end, an employment guarantee mechanism needs to be created, and employers must be guided and supported to establish labor service matching programs in poor areas, improve the effectiveness of vocational training, and avoid graduate unemployment.

5. Weighing up the long term and looking at the big picture

Pursuing the strategy of weighing up the long term and at the big picture means that in the battle against poverty, it is necessary to take a long-term view based on the overall situation and consider social and ecological benefits while focusing on economic development in poor areas. A moderately prosperous society in all respects is a society in which politics, the economy, culture, society, and ecology develop in harmony. Coveting immediate profits and overdrawing future assets is the last thing the building of a moderately prosperous society needs. Therefore, it is necessary to be visionary, pursuing the strategy of weighing up the long haul and into the big picture, leading the alleviation of poverty in parallel to social development, paying equal attention to industrial development and ecological protection, and developing universal measures and specific approaches simultaneously. This way, it will be possible to achieve coordinated, green, and sustainable development.

(I) Economic-based poverty alleviation and social development running in parallel

The parallel running of economic-based poverty alleviation and social development means boosting the economy of poverty-stricken areas, solving the poverty issue and achieving prosperity, and taking various social problems in poverty-stricken areas into consideration, promoting development there. Poverty is not a purely economic phenomenon; it is often closely and inseparably linked with social issues such as policy, culture, ecology, and education. Poverty alleviation in the new era must go hand in hand with social development.

The parallel running of economic-based poverty alleviation and social development is determined by the overall goal of poverty alleviation and is a necessity to build a moderately prosperous society in all respects. The overall goal of the poverty alleviation campaign is to ensure that the poor rural population has food, clothing, compulsory education, basic medical care, and safe housing by 2020. This creates a necessity for multi-tasking in poverty alleviation, involving ensuring the realization of economic goals and also addressing social and livelihood issues such as education, medical care, and housing. Economic-based poverty alleviation and social development are closely related and must go hand in hand. Without social development, economic-based poverty alleviation is not sustainable; similarly, social development without economic-based poverty alleviation is not progress, much less poverty alleviation. It is only by adhering to the principle of economic-based poverty alleviation and social development running in parallel, and economic building and social building being synchronized, that poor areas can become moderately prosperous in all respects.

The parallel running of economic-based poverty alleviation and social development call for developing the economy in poor areas while also consider improving education, medical care, and housing, as well as social and livelihood issues such as rural elderly care, left-behind children, and the disposal of women, the elderly, and the disabled. While developing industries to eliminate poverty, medical insurance and assistance should be carried out at the same time to ensure that the impoverished population has access to basic medical and health services. The introduction of the subsistence allowance system in rural areas is urgently needed to provide comprehensive policy support to those families who cannot rely on industrial support or employment assistance to escape poverty. Also, the care and service system for left-behind children, women, the elderly, and the disabled needs further development. For those living in areas with poor living conditions, fragile ecological environments, and frequent natural disasters, relocation projects should be in place. It is necessary to make unified arrangements for the export of labor services and promote stable employment and living of surplus rural labor in cities and towns in a planned way.

(II) *Attaching equal importance to industrial development and ecological protection*

To attach equal importance to industrial development and ecological protection means that industrial and ecological development should be performed simultaneously. Ecological development should be combined with industrial development, and the relationship between industrial development and environmental protection should be properly dealt with, so that people in poor areas can enjoy the benefits of economic development in a sound ecological environment. Protecting the ecological environment is the basis and prerequisite for sustainable development in poor areas, and it is a long-term plan concerning the future of poor areas and the well-being of people there. Ecological environmental protection and industrial development should be given equal importance.

Placing equal emphasis on industrial development and ecological protection is a realistic choice for targeted and sustainable poverty alleviation. The unsustainable cycle of natural ecology is one of the reasons for the slow pace of poverty alleviation in poor areas. Most of the poverty-stricken areas in China are impoverished due to ecological causes. Therefore, sustainable poverty alleviation in these areas starts with changing the ecological environment, intensifying infrastructure, and then improving the working and living environment of poverty-stricken areas, thereby achieving sustainable development and targeted poverty alleviation. Practice has proved that ecological poverty alleviation is a new and sustainable method of poverty alleviation in the new era.

Equal importance must be given to industrial development and ecological protection, taking industrialization of ecological development and innovation of industries as the direction. It is necessary to stick to sustainable utilization, treat the development and protection of resources equally, and pursue the protection of the environment and the development of industries in parallel. It is necessary to intensify ecological environment management and construction, step up ecological protection and restoration efforts, improve ecosystem service functions and poverty alleviation benefits, and truly achieve comprehensive, coordinated, and sustainable social development in poor areas. Ecological protection should be included in the evaluation system for poor areas' achievements in poverty alleviation, and ecological protection should be considered as a long-term performance evaluation indicator, thereby to ensure ecological improvement with rigid standards in poor areas.

(III) Placing equal emphasis on universal and special measures

The combination of universal and special measures means that in the battle against poverty, it is necessary to focus on solving both common and specific problems. Universal measures should be taken for common problems, while special measures should be taken for specific problems. Common problems are universal problems, so unified standards and policies should be adopted. Specific problems belong to individual cases, and should be distinguished and dealt with depending on the situation.

To alleviate poverty in the new era, it is necessary to adopt both universal and special measures. China's poor areas are large and widely distributed, and the poor are dispersed. Therefore, the cause of poverty varies – there are the common ones and the specific ones. For example, the lack of infrastructure is a common problem. Poor areas have incomplete transport, water conservation, electricity, education system, as well as backward medical and health conditions. To address these common problems, universal measures should be adopted, such as increasing capital input, and accelerating the improvement of basic public services such as transport, water conservation, electrification, education systems, and medical care in poor areas, so as to fundamentally change the phenomenon of poverty caused by lack of infrastructure. For another example, differences in the ecological environment is a specific problem. Although the poor ecological environment is a main factor leading to poverty, the conditions in the northwest and the southwest of China are very different. Therefore, it is necessary to adopt special measures according to the individual environmental conditions of different areas, formulate plans, and implement them according to scientific classification. It is only by taking both universal and special measures that China can eliminate all the factors that cause poverty in poor areas in the new era, and quickly lead poor areas out of poverty and towards a moderately prosperous life.

6. Viewing political achievement from the perspective of poverty alleviation

This involves using poverty alleviation achievements as an index to evaluate the political achievements of cadres, and identify and appoint cadres specifically to undertake poverty alleviation and elimination. Following this strategy is the political guarantee to alleviate poverty. It is necessary to take on-schedule poverty alleviation as the main index to evaluate the achievements of leading cadres, and assess, select, and appoint cadres based on the projects they have completed in this field. Through this strategy, it is possible to raise the effectiveness of poverty alleviation to a strategic height in order to ask Party committees and governments at all levels to focus on impoverished counties, villages, and to ensure the realization of the overall goal of poverty alleviation by the CPC Central Committee in 2020 as scheduled.

(I) *Viewing poverty alleviation as a political achievement*

Poverty alleviation and elimination are related to the building of a moderately prosperous society in all respects, and the consolidation of the Party's foundation of governance. Party committees and leading officials in poor areas should establish a view of their political achievements in poverty alleviation, regard poverty alleviation and elimination as the core and top priority of all their work, and enhance their sense of responsibility, mission, and urgency.

Making poverty alleviation a political achievement is the objective need of the sprint stage of poverty alleviation, and an assessment of the Party's governing ability. Poverty alleviation has reached this stage in cities and villages, and has launched a general offensive as the number one project before 2020. It is only by making poverty alleviation into a political achievement and intensifying the sense of responsibility and urgency of leading cadres at all levels that they can leverage their leading role in poverty alleviation, gather resources from all sectors of society, and work together to alleviate poverty. At the same time, poverty alleviation is a test of the abilities of leading officials at all levels in poor areas, as well as their political stance and attitude. They must answer to the Party and the nation, and make solid and effective efforts to alleviate poverty and live up to the trust placed in them.

To view poverty alleviation as a political achievement, it is necessary to strictly implement a chief responsibility system, with Party secretaries at the provincial, city, county, township, and village levels being responsible at the same time, and breaking down poverty alleviation projects year by year with strict goals and a high sense of responsibility and urgency. Leading officials at all levels must have the confidence and courage to assume responsibility and shoulder it without hesitation. They must never slack off or waver, and must fulfill their mission with full political awareness.

(II) Implementing transparent evaluation of poverty alleviation and elimination

This means that the indicators of poverty alleviation and elimination should be made transparent, so that the progress and results of poverty alleviation and elimination can be seen clearly and publicly. Evaluation affects the attitude, work mode, and performance of leading cadres, and thus reflects the work of poverty alleviation. Through the implementation of social evaluation and the publication of the results of poverty alleviation and elimination, the attention and enthusiasm of leading cadres at all levels for poverty alleviation can be aroused, and cheating can be avoided. Extensive public attention will also be attracted to the battle against poverty.

The implementation of transparent evaluation of poverty alleviation is a significant basis for the selection and appointment of cadres, and an effective supplement to the view of poverty alleviation as a political achievement. Poverty alleviation is the main basis for the performance evaluation, selection, and appointment of leading cadres at all levels. However, if there is no public supervision element, the evaluation will become a formality, which is not conducive to the establishment of the view of poverty alleviation as a political achievement. The implementation of transparent evaluation of poverty alleviation can encourage leading cadres at all levels to implement the Party's policy of poverty alleviation and elimination, change their work style to meet the realistic requirements of the battle against poverty, create an atmosphere of accountability, and nurture courage with shame-awareness. Only then can leading cadres at all levels be guided to establish an accurate view of their political achievements.

To carry out transparent public evaluation, it is necessary to establish and improve performance evaluation methods for poverty alleviation and elimination with the goal of significantly increasing the weight of poverty alleviation indicators in the evaluation of the economic and social development of poor counties, and ensuring that the evaluation process is transparent and open. Implementing transparent evaluation of poverty alleviation requires an accurate assessment index. Party committees and governments of all provinces, autonomous regions, and municipalities directly under the central government at all levels should quickly develop a set of indicators to form a system for the evaluation of poverty alleviation in specific counties according to their specific situations, especially for state-appointed key counties for poverty alleviation and development. These evaluation indicators should combine qualitative and quantitative methods, with the latter as the main indicators and the former as auxiliaries. And all quantifiable indicators should be quantified as much as possible, so as to enhance the objectivity of assessment and improve the rigor and authenticity of the evaluation.

(III) Implementing the feedback accountability mechanism

The feedback accountability mechanism is a mechanism to track the actual performance of poverty alleviation, and hold individual cadres accountable. It will follow up and claim responsibility of all aspects of poverty alleviation and elimination, and hold accountable those who cheat, conceal, or practice fraud whenever they are discovered.

The feedback mechanism is a significant supplement to the implementation of the transparent evaluation of poverty alleviation and elimination. The latter provides a reference standard for the implementation of the former. In turn, the former ensures the authority and authenticity of the latter, and enhances the credibility of the evaluation results. At the same time, the feedback accountability mechanism is a strong guarantee of the achievements of poverty alleviation. It can act as a deterrent, restraint, and supervision for leading poverty alleviation cadres, and can correct the performance deviations, thereby ensuring that work remains on the right track.

To implement the feedback accountability mechanism, it is necessary to formulate and improve mechanisms and measures for poverty alleviation elimination, divide responsibilities and develop limits of authority, and ensure that the decision-makers and the organizers are the ones who are responsible. In addition, making improvements to the feedback pathway and establishing a two-way communication mechanism is needed for the timely feedback of evaluation results. A poverty alleviation monitoring mechanism should be put in place to bolster the monitoring of rural statistics, improve monitoring capacity and data quality, and realize data sharing. A supervision system for major poverty-related funds and projects should be completed, to strictly prohibit extravagance and waste, practice strict economy, tightly control the expenses of the "Three Officials" (official overseas visits, vehicles, and hospitality), improve project management, and raise the effectiveness of the funds spent. It is necessary to deal openly with major poverty-related incidents, promote the sound development of poverty alleviation and elimination through handling these incidents, and consistently improving the level of poverty alleviation and elimination work.

The Strategic Environment of the Final Battle

The environment is the vehicle for action. To win the decisive battle of 2020, careful analysis of the corresponding environmental factors is required. Environmental factors are both domestic and international. In his keynote speech at the 2015 High-level Forum on Poverty Reduction and Development, Xi Jinping said that as the largest developing country in the world, China has always been an advocate and promoter of global poverty reduction and development. He added that the next 15 years will be a critical period for poverty reduction and development for both China and other developing countries. He called on the Chinese people to build consensus, work together to overcome difficulties, and commit themselves to win-win cooperation. This speech fully illustrates the interconnectedness of such environmental factors.

1. The development of poverty reduction from an international perspective

Poverty reduction is inseparable from economic growth and a secure and stable development environment. A stable and peaceful international environment is a prerequisite for poverty reduction in poor countries. With the development and change of the world political and economic pattern, the global poverty situation has taken on new features, and the pattern and practice of poverty reduction are also developing consistently.

(I) New changes in the global political and economic pattern

a) A shift in world politics from west to east

The global political pattern is formed by the main political forces in the world through a series of confrontations, differentiations, and combinations. This structure can take a relatively stable state in a certain period, but undergoes constant development and change. The current world political structure is comparable to that of China's Warring States Period (c. 475–221 BCE), in which countries abandoned old alliances and formed new ones. With the rise of emerging market economies, the dominating position of the United States, which was formed during World War II, is being weakened to some extent. Countries and communities such as China, Russia, Japan, and the European Union, and major developing nations such as India, Brazil, and South Africa have experienced a rapid rise in the process of economic globalization, and have formed a stable and balanced relation of cooperation.

However, after entering the 21st century, the overall strength of Western countries shows signs of weakening, while the national strength of Eastern countries increases, playing an increasing role in international affairs. First, the 2003 Iraq War caused great turbulence in the geopolitical and economic landscape of the Middle East and Europe, during which the United States damaged its international image and significantly weakened its soft power. Second, the international financial turmoil triggered by the subprime mortgage crisis in 2009 affected the whole world, and severely damaged the economies of the "hard powers" – major countries and communities such as the USA, the EU, and Japan. In contrast, many emerging countries, such as China, India, Russia, Brazil, and South Africa, have seized the development opportunities of globalization and have risen rapidly, playing a more active role on the global stage. This shows that the deification of Europe and the United States is wearing off, the Asia-Pacific region is becoming a key region in the world, and the global political center is shifting from the west to the east.

b) A shift in the center of the global economy from north to south

The wave of economic globalization that began in the 1980s has accelerated the evolution of the global economic structure, leading to a multi-polarization trend in the global economic pattern, with Europe and the United States occupying the dominant position and emerging economies in Asia rising rapidly.

Before 2008, the global economy maintained a growth trend, and the economic strength of developed economies, especially Europe and the United States, was still dominant, while emerging economies were still unable to truly dominate the world due to their own potential growth contradictions.

After 2008, global trade and investment suffered a heavy blow from the global financial crisis, and the global economic pattern changed dramatically. While the developed world is mired in slow growth, China and other emerging economies continue to rise. By comparing the "Three Economic Plates" – G7 (the USA, Japan, Germany, the UK, France, Italy, and Canada), the Asian Tigers (Hong Kong, Taiwan, South Korea, and Singapore) and the BRICS (China, India, Brazil, and Russia) within the core of the world economy, it is fair to claim that in Europe, the USA, and the G7 countries, the share of global GDP, global trade, and global investment has declined significantly, while the share of Asia and BRICS countries, especially China, has increased significantly.

This shows that the center of the world economy is shifting from north to south. The Southern Ring Economic Belt, dominated by emerging economies, is reshaping the global economic pattern. With its strong momentum of development, China has become a force to change this pattern.

(II) New specifics of the global poverty pattern

Changes in the world's political and economic structure have divided the global economic system into opposing groups, resulting in some new characteristics for international poverty patterns. Overall, the global poverty pattern shows the following new features:

a) A widening gap between rich and poor countries

The upsurge of economic globalization has promoted the growth of world trade and the economic growth of all countries in the world, but it has also aggravated the phenomenon of polarization between the rich and the poor among the nations of the world.

For one thing, the gap in ownership is bigger. Driven by economic globalization and the southward shifting of the center of the world economy, developing countries have leveraged their latecomer advantages to transform their economies, improving the quality of life for their people, reducing the number of people living in absolute poverty, and increasing their economic stock. On the surface, the economic gap between developing and developed countries is narrowing, but in fact, economic globalization has led to a more obvious imbalance in the economic development of every country in the world. The economic growth of developed countries with a high degree of globalization is much better than that of developing countries with a low degree of globalization. Economic globalization has, in fact, widened the gap between countries in terms of the possession of wealth, productivity, scientific and technological management ability, capital stock, and resource ownership.

Meanwhile, economic globalization has accelerated the imbalance of regional social and economic development. To a large extent, economic globalization is still reflecting the political and economic interests of developed Western countries, with little consideration of the interests of developing countries. Developed Western countries have exerted a major influence on the political and economic policies and cultural ideology of developing countries, thus affecting the national living standards of developing countries and leading to the widening gap between rich and poor nations. Although there are also poor people in developed countries, they account for a very small proportion of the overall population, while the number of poor people in developing countries accounts for a large proportion of the total population. Also, the regional social and economic development in developing countries is extremely unbalanced. Economic globalization makes this problem worse, resulting in the disastrous effect of rich countries becoming richer and poor ones growing poorer.

b) Increasing poverty in developed countries

The new changes in the global political and economic pattern have intensified the competition among countries. Due to weak competition in the capital and commodity markets, developing countries find it difficult to obtain the same labor income for the same work, and are unable to provide a higher level of social welfare for their poor population, leading to worsening poverty within their borders.

Within international market competition, developing countries often rely on cheap labor to exchange for international capital and commodities, which aggravates the income inequality of domestic residents. In order to obtain more scarce foreign exchange, developing countries have lowered wages and welfare for ordinary workers, bringing the living standard close to poverty and expanding the scope of their own poor population. In addition, compared with developed countries, the scope of social welfare policies in developing countries is smaller and the effect is weaker, which has made it difficult for governments to meet the increasing demand of low-income groups for social welfare and to eliminate poverty. Within international market competition, developed countries prioritize the competition for management and technical personnel, and can attract the world's scarcest human resources with high salaries and better welfare policies. Meanwhile, developing countries strive to lower labor costs in pursuit of capital in the international market by relying on intensive labor force, and find it difficult to improve social welfare. This perpetuates the existence of both absolute and relative poverty in developing countries.

c) *Substantial changes in the distribution of the world's poor*

The world's poor population has gradually developed from being mainly distributed in low-income countries to middle-income countries. There are now more people living in absolute poverty in middle-income countries than in low-income ones. With the rapid development of economic growth momentum in low-income countries, the amount of absolute poverty in middle-income countries is growing. Data shows that in 1990, about 90% of the world's poor lived in low-income countries, while today more than 70% live in middle-income countries. The reason is that as the GDP of low-income countries such as Nigeria, Pakistan, India, and Indonesia (the last two are more stable) grows, they join the ranks of middle-income countries.

There is no suitable, universal way to assess global poverty. However, whichever poverty scale is chosen, the majority of poor and vulnerable people are found to live in middle-income countries and regions in South Asia and sub-Saharan Africa. According to the World Bank's income breakdown, the vast majority of the poorest billion live in middle-income countries, among which 31–38% are in low-income countries, and 60–66% live in middle-income countries (see Tables 1 and 2). Measured by the Global Acute Poverty Indicator MPI (Multidimensional Poverty Index), South Asia is the region with the largest population size of multidimensional poor people and the largest number of poor people in the world, among which 40% live in India, followed by 33%–39% in Africa.

d) *The causes of extreme poverty are no longer resource-related*

Extreme poverty of any kind is becoming less about a lack of resources and more about national inequality and incomplete social security systems. It is widely believed that countries with higher per capita incomes have more domestic resources to spend on poverty reduction, and that the international aid system treats countries with higher per capita incomes differently, so extreme poverty is more likely to occur in countries that are starved of resources. Over time, however, poverty has become concentrated in middle-income countries rather than in those with more limited resources, which suggests that the main causes of extreme poverty have changed.

First is the national poverty gap. Economic globalization has brought about unprecedented global economic growth. However, at the same time, national inequality is growing in quite a few countries and regions, especially medium-

Table 1: Distribution of the billion poorest people in the poorest areas

Area	Number of Countries	Number of Regions	Total Population		The Billion Poorest (According to the MPI)		
			Population (Thousands)	Percentage of World's Population	Population (Thousands)	Percentage of the Billion Poorest	Average MPI
Europe and Central Asia	0	0	0	0%	0	0%	/
Arab Countries	2	2	33384	0.60%	20204	2.01%	0.348
Latin America and the Caribbean	4	13	7290	0.10%	4898	0.49%	0.363
East Asia and Pacific Region	3	18	5672	0.10%	3466	0.34%	0.335
South Asia	4	19	896722	16.70%	583715	57.95%	0.355
Sub-Saharan Africa	31	213	496471	9.30%	395009	39.21%	0.472
Total	44	265	1439539	26.80%	1007292	100%	0.375

Table 2: Income types of the billion poorest in their distributed regions

Income Types	Number of Countries	Number of Regions	Total Population		The Bottom Billion Poor (According to the MPI)		
			Population (Thousands)	Percentage of World's Population	Population (Thousands)	Percentage of the Billion Poorest	Average MPI
High Income	0	0	0	0%	0	0%	/
Medium and High Income	2	4	631	0.00%	400	0.04%	0.315
Medium and Low Income	15	79	924020	17.20%	620574	61.61%	0.375
Low Income	27	182	514888	9.60%	386318	38.35%	0.432
Total	44	265	1439539	26.80%	1007292	100%	0.375

high and medium-low income countries, in which rich social groups stymie the weak social groups' chance to make their fortune. This is bound to accelerate the polarization of social wealth and power, making the rich richer and the poor poorer, and exacerbating the polarization between the rich and the poor. According to data, poverty rates in middle- and high-income countries are as high as 40%, while poverty rates in low-income countries can be as low as five percent.

The second aspect is national social security systems, which aim to support the most vulnerable families and individuals, assist the poor and promote their employment, enhance social cohesion, and narrow the gap between rich and poor. The size and coverage of social security determines the actual impact on reducing poverty and narrowing the wealth gap. In sub-Saharan Africa, for example, the coverage of every social security system is less than a quarter of the population, while Romania, Mongolia, Chile, and Thailand cover most of the population and nearly 100% of the poorest. For many developing countries, enhanced social security systems can prevent famine, stop people returning to poverty, help reduce poverty, and alleviate extreme poverty.

(III) New changes in the methods and goals of world poverty reduction

Affected by the above factors, the methods and goals of poverty reduction around the world have also undergone new changes in donors, recipients, methods, and content of aid.

a) Changing implications of global partnerships

Global partnerships form one of the "Millennium Development Goals." The term refers to the aid relationships between the governments of developed and developing countries, with the former as donors and the latter as recipients. However, with the increasing prominence of global issues such as climate change, security, inequality, and the polarization of global economic powers, global partnerships are facing new challenges and experiencing changing implications. First, rising developing countries are critical of the existing rules and norms around global partnerships. They are unwilling to be mere recipients of the rules and make efforts with no return. The significant development of the emerging economies has brought economic growth, which in turn has incurred a rise in domestic tax and attracted overseas private capital inflows. Thereby, developing countries are becoming the main force of the global economy, accounting for an increasing share of the global economic pie. Hence, they are no longer willing to play the role of constant recipients, and want a place at the table in international affairs. Second, although developed countries acknowledge their responsibility as donors, their hope is to reduce this responsibility while not giving up their core influence in the formulation of international norms and the governance of international organizations.

b) Moving from financial aid to more diversified forms

In the new world political and economic structure, the international community puts more emphasis on cooperation, so the form of international aid has gradually diversified from being merely economic. In international aid, the relative scale and role of economic aid are getting smaller, with priority given to other types of aid such as technology. Recipients are more eager to gain experience from practice in order to develop self-reliance. The need for knowledge and experience is the main driving force behind the expectation that the recipients will continue to receive aid even if they are nowhere near being financially desperate. An evaluation of agricultural aid to Africa by the African Development Bank and the International Fund for Agricultural Development (IFAD) shows that middle-income countries are very keen to continue receiving IFAD loans, not because of the scale of the aid, but because of the international experience and best practices that come with it. At the same time, the reclassification of countries has led donors to become more aware of the importance of diversified forms of aid. When the scale of aid is reduced, donors are keen to carry out multi-field and multi-form cooperative aid with their recipients, especially with relatively wealthy and strategically significant countries, or post-conflict middle-income countries and former colonial countries. It is only by cooperating with such countries that donors can find more opportunities for economic cooperation and support from the international community, thereby achieving a win-win result.

c) The increasing importance of NGOs in poverty reduction

As service providers, non-governmental organizations are closer to the poor, and can offer more targeted aid and poverty reduction measures. With the transformation of the global political and economic pattern, NGOs have a louder voice in the world, and are playing an increasingly significant role in the process of international poverty reduction. NGOs provide social services to disadvantaged countries, especially those that do not have the resources to provide adequate goods, services, and supportive environments to help people achieve secure livelihoods. To meet the needs of the poor, NGOs provide a wide range of services in many areas, from livelihood interventions to health and education services, to more specific areas such as emergency response, promotion of democracy, human rights, finance, environmental governance, and policy analysis. At the same time, as civil and social organizations, NGOs emphasize participatory, people-centered, and power-based approaches to helping vulnerable groups express their needs. By representing disadvantaged groups and holding governments accountable for inefficient poverty alleviation, NGOs play a significant role in monitoring poverty reduction performance and pushing the progress of poverty reduction forward, which indicates that they will become a decisive force on the road to poverty elimination.

d) Social security projects as new and significant means of poverty reduction

Poverty reduction is the goal of social security, and social security programs are a significant means of international poverty reduction. Social security programs are operated by governments, non-governmental organizations, or other funders to provide security and assistance to disadvantaged groups with material support. The social security system contributes to poverty reduction through three channels: first, it directly transfers purchasing power to beneficiaries to reduce income poverty; second, indirect approaches are used, including providing insurance and protection against risks or shocks of livelihood to mitigate the impact on chronic poverty, helping beneficiaries recover from blows and reduce their possibility of lifelong exposure to poverty; third, "investment income," which means increased income through productive investment, or employment through social security programs. These three channels are indivisible from each other, and any social security project needs to go through them to achieve the goal of reducing poverty and narrowing the wealth gap. If social security programs generally work well, rapid poverty reduction can be achieved in the current context.

In the face of extreme poverty and a widening wealth gap, the role of the social security system will become increasingly prominent. It will be an important policy tool in the post-2015 development agenda, playing a central role in international poverty reduction practices.

(IV) Poverty reduction practices in major countries around the world

Poverty is a social phenomenon. Many countries around the world, both developed and developing, suffer varying degrees of poverty. Although these countries have different conditions, some have good practices and success in anti-poverty theory and practice, which can provide significant inspiration for China's successful implementation of poverty alleviation and the building of a moderately prosperous society in all respects during the 13th Five-Year Plan period.

a) Poverty reduction practices in developed countries

According to the international poverty standard (a per capita income of 1.25 USD per day), there is almost no extreme poverty in developed countries, and absolute poverty (a per capita income of less than 1 USD per day by the international standard) no longer exists. Poor people in developed countries are mainly the relatively poverty-stricken population, for whom developed countries have targeted social development policies and the implementation of various poverty alleviation and development plans for employment and income increase. Financial funds are mainly used to provide free public employment services, job-hunting assistance, vocational training, subsidies to enterprises that take in unemployed people and individuals seeking employment on their own, as well as to directly create jobs and support the unemployed in setting up small and medium-sized enterprises.

In the United States, the poverty line considers differences in family size. If the family income is below the poverty line, all the members of the family are defined as poor. In 1964, the Johnson administration declared a "war on poverty," and determined the absolute standard of poverty. The Council of Economic Advisers (CEA) set the poverty line at $3,000 a year (in 1962) for all types of families, and $1,500 a year for individuals without relatives. According to the Census Bureau's poverty line statistics, there were 4.62 million Americans living in poverty in 2010.

America's poverty reduction practices fall into two categories. The first is a series of measures specifically for the poor – public policies and welfare plans such as the rural loan programs of the Ministry of Agriculture, the work-study programs of the Ministry of Education, the neighborhood youth employment plan of the Ministry of Labor, and preferential policies to compensate for the disadvantages old people and women face in the economy. The second is the regional development policy for backward areas, which can be traced back to the Westward Movement, which lasted for more than a century after the founding of the USA. At that time, the US government issued a series of regionally directed regulations to develop backward areas, such as the "Development of the Tennessee River Basin and the Middle and Lower Mississippi River Act" of 1933, the "Regional Redevelopment Act" of 1961, the "Public Works and Economic Development Act and the Appalachian Regional Development Act" of 1965, and the "Federal Aided Areas and Aided Communities Act" of 1993.

The promulgation and implementation of these policies caused the impoverished population of the United States to drop rapidly and the incidence of poverty to reduce greatly, lifting the relatively poor out of poverty.

As for poverty reduction practices in the United Kingdom, the UK was the first country to establish an income poverty line. After the establishment of the modern welfare state, the phenomenon of absolute poverty in the UK was eliminated. In 1979, the problem began to shift to the relatively poor – a group that includes the unemployed, blue-collar workers, the elderly, and the disabled. The UK's backward areas are mainly concentrated in Northern Ireland.

The UK's anti-poverty measures include social welfare and regional development. Social welfare is enforced through legislation. Laws concerning social welfare in the history of the UK include the "Poor Law" of 1601, the "Old Age Support Law" of 1908, and the "National Relief Law" and "National Insurance Law" of 1948. Compared to the USA, welfare measures in the UK are sounder, more institutionalized, and more systematic. The UK is one of the countries with the best welfare laws in the world. Meanwhile, regional development policies are implemented with the unemployment rate as the main reference. Areas with an unemployment rate higher than the national average are identified as needing assistance. At first, unemployed workers were relocated to economically developed areas, and later, through the development of infrastructure, manufacturers were encouraged to create more job opportunities through measures such as investment, in order to accelerate the internal development of areas with high unemployment rates. The government has also adopted fiscal measures such as investment and employment subsidies to encourage the establishment of new businesses and small businesses in underdeveloped areas, creating more jobs. The establishment of free enterprise zones and duty-free ports will attract increasing numbers of enterprises to invest and set up factories in the areas in need, thus boosting the rapid development of the local economy.

As for poverty reduction practices in Japan, the nation's comprehensive national strength is relatively strong. It developed rapidly in a very short time after World War II, and became the richest country in Asia, with many anti-poverty examples that are worth emulating.

After the war, Japan's economy was severely damaged, especially in the rural areas, where it lagged severely behind. In order to remedy this situation quickly, the Japanese government adopted and implemented several laws and decrees, such as the "Law on the Revitalization of Mountain Villages" and "Law on the Revitalization of Underdeveloped Areas," and the special development of Hokkaido.

Generally speaking, the Japanese government implemented its anti-poverty development strategy in two stages. The first stage ran from 1955 to 1962, with the main goal of intensifying the building of rural infrastructure and public facilities and promoting cooperation and organization among farmers. In this stage, the Japanese government took three main measures. Firstly, it formulated a plan to promote the development of the countryside, and launched the building of 4,585 municipalities with a scale of 900–1000 households. Secondly, it established a new rural development system by means of a rural revitalization association. Thirdly, it raised building funds through collective fund-raising among farmers, loans from financial institutions, and financial government subsidies. The second phase was from 1967 to 1979 – 13 years in which Japan promoted the development of its countryside. In this stage, the government's work was focused on three aspects: firstly, intensifying the building of infrastructure and public facilities for agricultural production and rural residents; secondly, attracting industries to rural areas (the "Law on Promoting Attracting Industries in Rural Areas" was promulgated in 1971); and thirdly, proposing and implementing the goal of making the countryside into an attractive and comfortable place to live.

b) Poverty reduction practices in developing countries

At present, the poor population of the world concentrated in low-income countries in developing countries, and South Asia and sub-Saharan Africa are still the key regions for global poverty reduction. Among the multidimensional poor population, 51% live in South Asia and 28% in sub-Saharan Africa. Based on international assistance, these countries are exploring long-term poverty alleviation policies and measures suited to their national conditions.

India has the largest number of poor people in the world. The scale of the poor population is huge, and the differences in its regional distribution are obvious. The impoverished population in the eastern and middle regions accounts for more than half of the total poor population, and mainly consists of small farmers, marginal farmers (with cultivated land of less than half a hectare), landless farmers, and low castes. The causes of India's persistent poverty are deeply rooted and complex: informal, insecure employment with low pay, discrimination against ethnic minorities and poor castes, gender inequality, and high fertility rates in poor states and poor social groups.

Starting from its Fifth Five-Year Plan, the Indian government set poverty alleviation as one of its main goals, and has helped and promoted the development of poverty-stricken areas through the implementation of various programs. India advocates a strategy of meeting basic human needs, mainly by directly providing daily necessities such as food, housing, medical care, and education services to the poor to eradicate poverty. The 1960s saw a spectacular "Green Revolution" aimed at increasing agricultural productivity and food supplies to address poverty in rural areas. Later, the gap between rich and poor widened, which made it difficult for the poor to reap any substantial benefits. Thus, in the early 1970s, India adjusted its strategy and implemented the "Rural Poverty Alleviation Plan" to stabilize growth, eliminate poverty, and meet people's minimum needs. The plan has a long timespan and is arranged in chronological order, including the "Small and Marginal Farmers Development Plan" of 1970, the "Arid Areas Development Plan" of 1972, the "Integrated Rural Development Plan" of 1978, and the "National Rural Employment Plan" of 1980.

While implementing the strategy of meeting basic needs with the reduction of rural poverty, India has also instigated a regional preference policy and increased the development of the poor areas in the northeast frontier. Specifically, the government has integrated the forces and resources of all sides, and has mobilized the functional departments of society to invest in the movement of regional development in the northeast frontier area. For example, the government has expedited the building of infrastructure such as roads, railroads, and energy facilities, and has implemented new industrial policies such as horticulture, agriculture, and forestry, thereby speeding up the flow of capital. In 1996, the government issued the "Focus on the Northeast" policy, requiring 10% of the annual budget funds to be invested in the northeast region every year.

As for poverty reduction practices in Bangladesh, it is a traditional agricultural country, with nearly 900,000 people living in the countryside. However, more than 80% of the rural population are sharecroppers, as the land is mainly in the hands of a few landlords. These sharecroppers earn their keep by selling their labor, and thus lead extremely difficult lives. Therefore, extreme poverty is relatively common. In this case, relying solely on increasing local agricultural productivity is not the root solution to poverty. In its long-term anti-poverty explorations, Bangladesh has created a unique method of alleviating poverty – microfinance.

Microfinance originated from Gralmeen Bank (GB), which was founded in 1974 by Muhammad Yunus – a professor at the economics department of Chittagong University in Bangladesh, and winner of the 2006 Nobel Peace Prize. GB pioneered many new ideas, such as extending the services of banks to the poor, eliminating exploitation by borrowers, and creating self-employment opportunities for the vast unused human resources pool. The long-term vicious circle of "low income – low savings – low investment – low income" will be transformed into a virtuous circle of "low income – loan – investment – more income – more savings – more investment – more income." Microfinance is an institutionalized and organized financial service that is provided to the poor without mortgage guarantee in accordance with the principle of commercialization. Through careful organization, it ensures that the poor can benefit from microfinance. GB states that it only provides loan services for landless or assetless people, and adopts the method of whole loan and installment repayment to disperse loan risks. In addition to focusing on loan services for women, non-financial services such as education, nutrition assessment, and health care are also provided.

GB has made impressive achievements in the practice of poverty alleviation. Microfinance solves the problem of capital shortage and directs funds precisely to the poorest, thus compensating for the targeting bias caused by regional targeting measures and inefficiency in the exercising of poverty alleviation funds.

South Africa is a middle-income developing country with the most developed economy in Africa. However, the development of various sectors and regions of its economy is unbalanced, and the dual urban-rural and black-and-white economic specifics are obvious. In the early 1980s through to the early 1990s, the South African economy suffered a recession due to international sanctions. The new government formulated the "Rebuilding and Development Plan," which emphasized enhancing the social and economic status of black people. The "Growth, Employment, and Redistribution Plan" was launched in 1996 to promote economic growth, mainly by promoting privatization, reducing fiscal deficits, increasing labor market flexibility, promoting exports, loosening foreign exchange controls, encouraging the development of small and medium-sized enterprises, and increasing employment, and thereby gradually lessening unequal distribution. The Accelerated and Shared Growth South Africa Initiative was launched in 2006 to increase government intervention in the economy and promote employment and poverty reduction through intensifying infrastructure, implementing a sector-first development strategy, and intensifying education and human resources training. In 2009, South Africa's GDP per capita reached $5,824.

From 1994 to 1999, the South African government raised and invested 12.5 billion rand in the building of low-cost housing to alleviate the housing problems of black urban residents.

In terms of education, the educational opportunities of black people are far lower than those of white people due to the long-standing Apartheid education system. In January 1995, South Africa officially implemented free and compulsory education for children aged 7–16 and withdrew the Apartheid-era textbooks. The government has consistently been increasing investment in education and emphasizing on the reform of the teaching curriculum, the education funding system, and the higher education system. At the same time, the influx of immigrants from Taipei and Hong Kong in the early 19th century, as well as the investment and entrepreneurship of a large number of people from Mainland China since the 1990s, have left a deep imprint on education in South Africa, which is characterized by diversification.

2. Poverty reduction practices in China

In the modern era, China is fighting a new war against poverty. Since the announcement of the Reform and Opening policy, it has intensively developed poverty alleviation projects and mobilized society to eliminate poverty. Over the past 30-plus years, China has significantly reduced its own poor population, and has promoted radical poverty reduction. It has played a powerful role in reducing global poverty, setting an example for other developing countries. However, the road has not been smooth. The phenomenon of falling back into poverty, the dispersal of the poor population, and the increase of poverty reduction costs have compromised progress. The task of poverty reduction remains strenuous, and there is no room for any slacking in the fight against poverty.

(I) Chinese-style poverty alleviation

Since the launch of the Reform and Opening policy, China has made significant efforts to reduce poverty, blazing a trail that is uniquely Chinese. The government has taken the lead, incorporating poverty alleviation and development into the country's overall development strategy, taking a development-oriented approach to poverty alleviation, and encouraging public participation. Hence, a large-scale pattern of poverty alleviation has been established through the coordinated efforts of the government, society, and the market, and a multi-subject social poverty alleviation system with public participation has been formed. The results have proved that this Chinese style of poverty reduction is correct and successful.

a) Significant reduction of rural poverty

As the largest developing country in the world, China's impoverished population used to account for 20% of the world's total. However, after more than 30 years of reform, opening, and development, the impoverished population has been greatly diminished and the poverty rate has been consistently reduced, thus making fundamental changes the situation of poverty in China. In 1978, 770 million people still lived in poverty in China's rural areas; in 1985, the number dropped to 760 million. Based on the 2000 poverty standard (the per capita net income of rural residents was 865 yuan), the number of people living in poverty dropped from 94.22 million in 2000 to 26.88 million in 2010, and the incidence of poverty fell from 10.2% in 2000 to 2.8% in 2010. During the implementation phase of the new poverty alleviation program, the number of people living below the 2,300-yuan poverty line decreased from 122 million in 2011 to 80 million in 2014. Thanks to the joint efforts of the central government and local governments at all levels, the poverty reduction target for 2014 was overfulfilled, with poverty eradicated for 12.32 million rural people, accounting for 14.9% of the total impoverished rural population. By 2015, the impoverished population in China's rural areas had been cut down to 70.17 million.

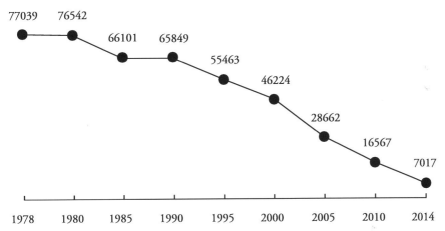

Changes per year in the size of the rural impoverished population after launching the Reform and Opening policy (unit: ten thousand)

b) Improvement in infrastructure and public services in poor areas

With the implementation of poverty alleviation policies, infrastructure and public services in poor areas have been improved, which is mainly reflected in education, healthcare, housing, and transport.

The education level of farmers in poor areas has been improved. Monitoring statistics on poverty alleviation show that in 2012, 81.4% of the rural labor force in contiguous poverty-stricken areas had junior high school degrees or below, 12.6% had senior high school degrees, and 6% had junior college degrees or above. Compared with 2011, the number of junior high school graduates has increased by 8.4%, the number of high school graduates has increased by 4.3%, and the number of college graduates and above has increased by 3.3%. Of the rural labor force in key counties, 82.5% had junior high school degrees or below, 10.5% had senior high school degrees, 1.7% had technical secondary school degrees, and 5.3% had junior college degrees or above. Compared with 2011, the number of students that received junior high school education or below has increased by 13.5%, the number of high school graduates has increased by 3.5%, and the number of secondary school graduates has increased by 0.7%.

Medical conditions and healthcare systems have been improved. Among impoverished administrative villages, 94.6% had health clinics in 2012, an increase of 13.6% over 2011; there was one doctor for every 1,111 people and one certificated rural doctor for every 1429 people; the average government subsidy for village clinics was 3,938.10 yuan – an increase of 801.30 yuan over the previous year; the participation rate of the new rural cooperative health care system reached 91% – an increase of 1.9% over 2011. As for the administrative villages in key counties stuck in extreme poverty, 85.7% had clinics in 2012; the number of hospital beds for per 1,000 people was 5.9 – a 168.2% raise compared to that of 2011; there was one doctor for every 1,111 people, and 77% of the rural doctors had certificates – an increase of 4% over 2011; the government provided an average subsidy of 4,786 yuan to health clinics; the participation rate of the new rural cooperative medical system reached 92% – an increase of 1.6% over 2011.

Housing standards for rural residents were improved. In impoverished counties and villages, the standard of building materials for rural residents has been improved. The proportion of brick and concrete buildings has increased slightly, while that of buildings made of mud and wood has decreased. In 2012, the per capita housing area of rural residents in 13 autonomous regions (excluding Tibet) was 30.5 square meters. In terms of the materials, buildings made of mud and wood accounted for 42.2% of the total in 2012 – a decrease of 2.8% from 2011; buildings made of brick and wood accounted for 27.4% – a decrease of 0.9% compared to that of 2011; brick and concrete buildings accounted for 27.2% – an increase of 3.1% over 2011. In addition, only 0.8% of rural families are still living in thatched houses.

Great achievements have been made in transport. Over the past five years, 550 billion yuan of vehicle purchase tax funds were invested, 92% of county seats in contiguous impoverished areas now have roads of grade-ii or higher level, 86.5% of administrative villages have smooth roads, and 309 ropeways have been replaced by bridges. During the 12th Five-Year Plan period, China's highway network continued to expand, with the total length of open highways reaching 4.57 million km and the length of expressways exceeding 120,000 km. The "7918" national expressways network was completed, and the length of rural roads exceeded 3.97 million km. In

81% of the villages in the western region, roads were unobstructed. The technical level of national and provincial trunk roads was gradually upgraded, 96% of the counties had roads of grade-ii or higher level, and road maintenance and management levels continued to improve. The density of postal outlets increased significantly, with 8,840 post offices in townships and towns being rebuilt. The total number of postal outlets in China reached 53,000, including 145,000 express delivery outlets. The coverage of key express delivery enterprises in townships and towns reached 70%.

c) Accelerating economic development in impoverished areas

With the implementation of various poverty alleviation measures, the economy of poverty-stricken areas has developed, the income of farmers has increased year by year, and the living expenses of poverty-stricken farmers have seen an increase.

The income level of the poor has increased year by year. In 2010, the per capita net income of poor rural households accounted for 33.8% of the national per capita net income, which was 2.3% lower than in 2000. Calculated at constant prices in 2010, the income of poor rural households was only equivalent to the national average around 1990, which means that the per capita income of poor rural households in 2010 was about 20 years behind the national average. The income of poor peasant households mainly comes from household business operation and agriculture. It is worth noting that the transfer income of poor households increased from 39 yuan in 2005 to 188 yuan in 2010 – a nearly fourfold increase, which is inseparable from the national policy support for poverty alleviation and the increase of transfer payments. In 2012, the per capita income of farmers in the 14 most impoverished counties was 4,849.6 yuan, up 472.20 yuan year-on-year (a 10.8% increase), and the per capita income of the residents in these districts was 61.2% of the national average. The per capita net income of farmers in the 592 key counties was 4,623.50 yuan, increasing by 715.50 yuan or 18.3% year on year, and the per capita net income of residents in these counties was 58.4% of the national average. Household business operating income continued to increase, with wage income growing the fastest. Data showed that the household business operation income of the 14 most impoverished counties was 1,781 yuan, accounting for 37.4% of the total income; and the per capita wage income was 2,917.10 yuan – a year-on-year increase of 574.60 yuan, or 24.5%; the business operating income of these households was 1,822.90 yuan, accounting for 37.6% of their total income. The per capita wage income in key counties was 2,750 yuan – a year-on-year increase of 882 yuan, or 46.9%. The transfer income grew rapidly, and went above the national average of rural areas. With the continuous intensifying of national policies to benefit, strengthen, and enrich farmers, the per capita transfer income of rural residents in the 14 most impoverished counties was 98 yuan in 2012 – a year-on-year increase of 63.20 yuan, or 181.6%, contributing 13.5% to the increase in farmers' income. The transfer income of key counties reached 107 yuan, with a year-on-year increase of 20 yuan, which is 22.9% – 1% higher than the national average of rural areas.

The living expenditure of rural poor households has increased, and the Engel coefficient (the proportion of total food expenditure in total personal expenditure) has fallen. With the rapid growth of rural residents' income, the living expenditure of poor rural households has also continued to increase, and their living standards have improved significantly. In 2010, the per capita living expenditure of poor rural residents was 1,490 yuan – an increase of 14.1% over 2000, and the average annual growth rate reached 7.9%. In the same year, the per capita living expenditure of rural residents in China was 4,382 yuan – an increase of 162.4% over 2000, with an average annual growth rate of 10.1%. Although the living expenditure of the poor has achieved steady growth, the per capita expenditure is still less than one-third of the national level. In 2010, 52.6% of the poor households had expenditure higher than their net income, which means that more than half of poor households did not make ends meet. In 2010, the Engel coefficient of poor rural households declined, and the per capita expenditure on food, clothing, and housing was 1,193 yuan – an increase of 1.1 times over 2000. The expenditure on food, clothing, and housing accounted for 80% of the total living expenditure – a decrease of 0.3% from 2000. In 2010, food expenditure of poor farmer households accounted for 64.4% of living consumption expenditure – a decrease of 0.9% from 2000. Except for the consumption of clothing, food, and housing, which meets basic survival needs, poor farmer households spend very little to improve their quality of life. In 2010, the per capita expenditure on household equipment and services of the poor was 60 yuan – equivalent to 25.6% of the national level; the per capita expenditure on transport and communication was 94 yuan – equivalent to 20.4% of the national level; the per capita expenditure on culture, education, and entertainment was 48 yuan – equivalent to 13.1% of the national level; the per capita expenditure on health care was 72 yuan – equivalent to 2.1% of the national level.

d) New breakthroughs in the innovation of poverty alleviation development mechanisms
Since the Reform and Opening period, especially after the 18th National Congress of the Communist Party of China, China has made remarkable achievements in poverty alleviation and development. One of the main reasons for these achievements is continuous innovation of poverty alleviation and development mechanisms.

After more than 30 years of work, poverty alleviation and development have a clear mission target, overall plans, specific scope and focus of support, and corresponding organization. Poverty alleviation and development mechanisms have seen a series of significant changes and innovations.

The first is to promote the operation of targeted poverty alleviation and elimination, targeting individuals and suiting the remedy to the case. On the premise of accurately identifying poor villages and households, the tasks are to: improve the precise management mechanism of poor households and population; achieve the "Six Precisions" – precise objects, precise project arrangements, precise use of funds, precise measures taken in households, a precise First Secretary of the county, and precise results); ensure dynamic management; and gather human, material, and financial resources to ensure the feasibility, effectiveness, and accuracy of targeted poverty alleviation.

The second is to innovate the management system for poverty alleviation and development, and the formation of a new pattern of the "five-level linkage" joint efforts to tackle tough problems. The tasks are to: promote the responsibility system for poverty alleviation and elimination, putting leaders of the Party and the government at all levels in full charge of implementing the "four counties": responsibilities, powers, funds, and tasks; intensify the main responsibility of the county-level Party committees and governments for poverty alleviation and elimination; improve the performance evaluation mechanism of poor counties; increase the weight of poverty alleviation evaluation indicators such as poverty alleviation achievements and farmers' income; and guide the Party and government leaders of poor counties to shift their work focus to poverty alleviation and development.

The third is to encourage public participation, forming strong synergy and improving the effectiveness of poverty alleviation. Based on government-led reform and innovation, it is necessary to leverage the leading role of the market and the joint role of helping and promoting self-improvement to form a large-scale poverty alleviation work pattern that is coordinated by the government, the market, and society, and truly meets the public's need. The poor must develop greater awareness of self-development and stronger abilities to increase income and wealth. Poverty alleviation must reach those who truly need it.

e) Significant contributions to international poverty reduction

China is the world's largest developing country and has always been an active advocate and a powerful promoter of poverty reduction in the world. It has embarked on a pathway of peace, harmony, tolerance, prosperity, and sharing. It has achieved its own economic and social development, and has also promoted the progress of other developing countries within its capacity, and has made significant contributions to the cause of global poverty reduction.

As the first developing country in the world to achieve the poverty reduction goal of the "Millennium Development Goals," China has accumulated and formed its own distinctive experience in the process of poverty reduction, including: regarding accelerated development as a fundamental measure to promote poverty reduction; improving the production and living conditions of the public in poverty-stricken areas and improving the living standards of the poor as the central tasks of poverty alleviation and elimination; strong government leadership as a significant guarantee for poverty reduction; intensifying the self-development ability of poor areas and poor people as the main way to alleviate poverty; the extensive mobilization of social forces to participate in poverty alleviation as an effective model for promoting poverty alleviation and development; stimulating the public's self-reliance, hard work, initiative, and creativity as the inherent vitality of poverty alleviation and development; and carrying out international exchanges and cooperation as a significant supplement to poverty alleviation and development. These valuable experiences have great significance for the poverty reduction and development of other developing countries, and have become an important aspect of China's major contribution to global poverty reduction.

At the same time, China has played an irreplaceable role in global poverty reduction. Over the past 60 years, it has provided nearly 400 billion RMB in aid to 166 countries and international organizations, and has dispatched more than 600,000 aid workers. It has announced the unconditional exemption of government interest-free loan debts by heavily indebted poor countries and the least developed countries seven times. It has provided medical assistance to 69 countries and regions in Asia, Africa, Latin America, the Caribbean, and Oceania. It has also provided assistance to more than 120 developing countries to implement the "Millennium Development Goals." China proposes to build the Silk Road Economic Belt and the 21st Century Maritime Silk Road, to establish the Asian Infrastructure Investment Bank and the Silk Road Fund to support developing countries in the building of infrastructure interconnection, and to help them enhance their own development capabilities in order to integrate more seamlessly into the global supply chain, industrial chain, and value chain, and inject new vitality into the international poverty reduction cause. The 2015 High-level Forum on Poverty Reduction and Development, and Rural Development held in Beijing on October 16, 2015, is a significant testimony to

China's sharing of development concepts with the world and fulfilling the promises of major powers after achieving tremendous economic development.

(II) Poverty alleviation in China

Since the period of Reform and Opening, China has persisted in driving poverty alleviation through development, and has implemented large-scale projects. Great changes have taken place in the appearance of poverty-stricken areas. More than 600 million people in China have successfully lifted themselves out of poverty, made world-renowned achievements, and given great contributions to global poverty reduction. However, at the same time, poverty is still the most prominent shortcoming of building a moderately prosperous society in all respects. Currently, poverty alleviation work has entered the critical stage of tackling tough issues.

a) The impoverished population is still large

After more than 30 years of poverty alleviation and development, the number of rural poor and the incidence of poverty in China have changed greatly. However, due to the large rural population base in the country, the number of absolute impoverished rural populations and the low-income rural population are still relatively large. According to the current poverty standard, there are still 70.17 million people in absolute poverty in the country. In terms of trends, the decline in the size of the rural poor and the incidence of poverty in the country has become increasingly gradual. This indicates that the effectiveness of the country's rural anti-poverty policies has shown a diminishing marginal effect, and the situation facing rural poverty alleviation and development is becoming increasingly severe.

After the implementation of the "National Eight-Seven Poverty Alleviation Plan (1994–2000)" and the "China Rural Poverty Alleviation and Development Program (2011–2020)," the number of poor in the country's rural areas has gradually decreased, and the distribution of the poor population has become increasingly concentrated. From the perspective of geographical distribution, the poor population is mainly concentrated in the central and western regions, and shows a trend of further concentration in the central and western regions. From the perspective of terrain distribution, the poor population is concentrated in the alpine mountainous area. Due to its harsh natural environment, weak public service facilities, and the difficulty facing poverty alleviation, the poor population shows a trend of further concentration in this area. From the perspective of ethnic distribution, the poor are gradually becoming concentrated in ethnic minority areas. Because poverty reduction in ethnic minority areas is slower than other areas, the country's rural poor are showing signs of concentration in these areas.

b) The cost of poverty alleviation is increasing

Significant results have been achieved in poverty alleviation and poverty alleviation across the country since the period of Reform and Opening, especially in recent years, under the appropriate leadership of the Party Central Committee, the State Council, and the Party committees and governments at all levels, with support from corresponding departments and all echelons of society, and economic and social development in poverty-stricken areas has seen huge changes. However, from a long-term and overall perspective, problems such as large impoverished areas, large impoverished populations, deep poverty, and uneven development still exist in China. The gap is gradually widening between the rich and the poor, between urban and rural areas, between the east and the west, and between regional industries. As a result, it is becoming increasingly difficult to alleviate and eradicate poverty.

First, the relative poverty of farmers has become increasingly prominent. China has eliminated the sort of extreme poverty in which the most basic needs for food and clothing cannot be met. At present, poverty is mainly reflected in the growing urban-rural gap in income and consumption. It is also reflected in the inequality of development rights and opportunities for farmers caused by the dual urban-rural structure. Farmers are lacking inability, are extremely vulnerable, are socially excluded, and are generally in the relative poverty of a weak position.

Second, the existing impoverished population poses the greatest challenge for poverty alleviation and elimination. From the perspective of this population, after decades of poverty reduction practices, China's current 70.17 million poor are mostly distributed across a few poor and old areas. The reason is that it is difficult to get a piece of the pie from the ever-developing market economy. In short, it is more difficult for these groups to alleviate poverty. From the perspective of the economic driving force for poverty reduction, in the next five years, China's economic development will remain at a medium to high-speed level. To use economic growth to lift the poor out of poverty and into moderate prosperity, it is necessary to change the development mode while maintaining a stable economic growth rate. Poverty alleviation has higher requirements for economic development, making it harder for the remaining poor people to rise out of poverty.

Third, poverty spreading from rural to urban areas. There are more people in China's rural areas, and less land. With the acceleration of industrialization and urbanization, many surplus rural laborers have moved to cities, and a large population of migrant workers has appeared. Due to system restrictions such as household registration, migrant workers find it difficult to access welfare benefits such as urban education, medical care, and insurance. They live in the lower echelons of the city, and are in danger of falling into poverty. In 2009, the World Bank estimated that 150 million rural migrants (living outside their registered permanent residence for more than six months) had migrated to cities. In 2003, migrant workers who had gone elsewhere to work for more than six months accounted for 9.2% of the total impoverished population. The consumption-poor population accounts for 11.7% of the poor population. This shows that the impoverished population of migrant workers is not small, and should not be ignored.

c) The fight against poverty needs to be intensified urgently
As far as China is concerned, the tasks of solving poor people's problems in terms of production and living, and realizing common prosperity are still highly urgent and very difficult. It is necessary to enhance the consciousness and determination to do a good job in poverty alleviation and elimination, with greater determination, greater intensity, and more effective measures. Solid poverty alleviation and elimination should be performed to ensure that all poor people across the country will be lifted out of poverty by 2020, achieving the goal of building a moderately prosperous society in all aspects.

First of all, the pace of making relevant legislation should be accelerated in order to lay a solid legal foundation for poverty alleviation work, so that the work has laws to follow and is implemented in accordance with current legalities. Second, the coordination of poverty alleviation funds should be reinforced, and efforts should be made to improve the allocation and standards of special funds to bring true and tangible benefits to poor areas and impoverished people. Third, loan policies must be formulated to promote the self-employment of poor people. In addition, the issue of poverty must also be solved in areas of rich resources. For example, northern Shaanxi has abundant coal, oil, and natural gas resources. However, due to the current policies and system, the profits and taxes of established projects have been largely transferred, and the original products are shipped out. An industrial chain cannot be formed locally. As a result, poverty in resource-rich areas is still a problem. In short, many of the issues in the fight against poverty must be resolved quickly to ensure smooth progress.

(III) The basic task of China's poverty alleviation

2020 is the deadline for China to build a moderately prosperous society in all respects. The Fifth Plenary Session of the 18ᵗʰ Central Committee of the CPC pointed out that lifting the rural poor out of poverty is the most difficult part of this task, and it is also a landmark indicator for it. The "Decision of the CPC Central Committee and the State Council on Winning the Fight Against Poverty" issued on December 7, 2015, made clear arrangements for poverty alleviation after 2015, stating that "winning the fight against poverty is the bottom-line goal of building a moderately prosperous society in all respects." By 2020, to achieve "Two Worry-frees," "Three Ensures," and "Two Guarantees," the core is the latter. "Two Worry-frees" means to ensure that the rural poor do not have to worry about food and clothing, that the per capita disposable income of farmers in poverty-stricken areas has increased above the national average, and that the main indicators of basic public services are close to the national average. The "Three Ensures" are to ensure compulsory education, basic medical care, and safe housing. The "Two Guarantees" are to guarantee that all impoverished counties and all poor rural people are lifted out of poverty under China's current standards.

In general, it is necessary to lock down the current 70.17 million rural poor population and complete five poverty alleviation tasks:

a) Develop specific industries

The development of specific industries for poverty alleviation (also known as poverty alleviation through industry) refers to the resources of poverty-stricken areas, cultivating specific and advantageous industries, and using industries to drive the economy, increase farmers' income, and achieve local poverty alleviation. Using industry is the first choice and the main means to alleviate poverty. If there is no industry support to alleviate poverty and raise incomes, it is an empty endeavor. In poverty-stricken areas, to alleviate poverty and raise incomes, China must intensify its "blood making" ability, develop industries to obtain a stable income, and truly achieve the goal of eradicating the roots of poverty.

At the third meeting of the Leading Group for Poverty Alleviation and Development, Xinjiang and Tibet Aid, held by the Ministry of Agriculture in 2015, Vice Minister of Agriculture Yu Xinrong pointed out the specific targets for poverty alleviation through industry: 30 million out of China's 70 million rural poor need to alleviate poverty through the development of industries, that is, to achieve the goal of building a moderately prosperous society in all respects by 2020, the task of poverty alleviation through industry is to lift 30 million poor people out of poverty.

To alleviate poverty through industry, one must select the right industry. The key to alleviating poverty and becoming prosperous is driven by industry. The choice of industry should be based on the grasp of subjective and objective conditions such as local resource endowments and the wishes of the people. Through professional market surveys on the status quo of various resources in poverty-stricken areas, combined with the overall consideration of the production supply-side and the market consumption side, it is possible to find industries suitable for local poverty alleviation and development and press the fast-forward button for poverty alleviation. In addition, for the poverty alleviation projects that are introduced, it is necessary to assess whether they align with the actual development of the local area. They must not be divorced from reality, nor should they blindly pursue overly ambitious poverty alleviation projects.

The second step is to build a relatively complete industrial chain as the core of poverty alleviation through industry. The industry must become bigger and stronger to truly become a way of achieving prosperity from poverty. It cannot stop at simple agricultural product planting and the development of a single product. Industrial development and construction must be realized in a way that can link various production factors, expand production scale and product types, and extend production and product chains. Industrialization in poor areas cannot simply follow the traditional production methods, and cannot stop at the initial processing of products and the development of primary products. Instead, it should expand the capacity of industrial linkages, increase the level of industrial value, and derive the comprehensive development effects of industries. This is extremely important for improving the ability of industries in poverty-stricken areas to alleviate poverty more broadly, developing the economy of poor areas, and creating a lasting mechanism for poverty alleviation and prosperity.

b) Develop education

Poverty alleviation through education refers to the development of basic and vocational education in poverty-stricken areas to enhance the employability of the poor, promote employment, and lift a proportion of the population out of poverty. The implementation of education for poverty alleviation and elimination is a significant strategic component of promoting human resource development and national development in the new era. It is also one of the 10 key tasks of poverty alleviation, and an aspect of development identified by the central government.

To cure poverty, China must first cure ignorance; to help the poor, China must first support wisdom. The only way to prevent the intergenerational spread of poverty is through education. Implementing educational development for poverty alleviation and elimination, and accelerating the development of education and human resources in poverty-stricken areas will help improve the basic cultural knowledge of the public in poverty-stricken areas and the ability of laborers to rise out of poverty and earn a living. It is also conducive to improving the economic development of poverty-stricken areas and undertaking industrial transfer from developed areas, raising the capacity and improving the accuracy of public services.

Poverty alleviation through education requires the state's education funding to continue to tilt toward poverty-stricken areas, focusing on basic and vocational education, helping poor areas improve school conditions, and providing special care for children from poor rural families, especially left-behind children. By 2020, the Educational Poverty Alleviation Project should benefit every poor family, so that disadvantaged children can receive a fair and quality education, and that laborers in poor areas can acquire more practical skills and break the intergenerational transmission of poverty.

c) Relocation and resettlement

Relocation for poverty alleviation refers to the relocation and resettlement of poor rural people from areas with harsh living conditions, in order to fundamentally improve their living and development environment, and alleviate poverty successfully. In 2015, during the 13th Five-Year Plan period, the "Relocation of Poverty Alleviation and Relocation Work Plan" stated that it would take five years to implement relocation for poverty alleviation and resettlement of the registered poor people from impoverished areas. During this period, the task of relocating 10 million people will be completed, helping them to move into a moderately prosperous society in all respects at the same time as the rest of the country, that is, completing the task of lifting 10 million people out of poverty through relocation.

Relocation and resettlement for poverty alleviation is a systematic project. It is necessary to carefully investigate and study, formulate specific methods, and organize and implement them according to the plans, to ensure that the relocation is possible, stable, and beneficial. First, the relocation and implementation plans should be incorporated into the overall plan for local economic and social development. The implementation should be organized on an annual basis, with the resettlement area as the basic planning unit, and overall arrangements for village layout, infrastructure, and public services. Second, priority must be given to poor villages and people located in seismically active zones and threatened by geological disasters such as mudslides and landslides. It must be ensured that the per capita housing construction area of the central subsidy does not exceed 25 square meters, and the public must not be indebted to or affected by relocation for poverty alleviation. Third, more effective resettlement methods must be explored, which can be centralized resettlement, decentralized resettlement, and resettlement by moving to the city for work, relatives, and friends, so that the relocated people have the right to choose and are not forced or ordered. Fourth, funds should be earmarked for the building of housing and supporting facilities for relocation in the resettlement area. Overall plans should be put in place to use the increase- and decrease-linked surplus indicators for urban and rural building land in poverty-stricken counties within the province to ensure that by 2020, the production and living conditions of the relocated people will reach the level of a moderately prosperous society.

d) Combining ecological protection and governance

Poverty alleviation through ecological protection refers to transforming the economic development mode of poverty-stricken areas by protecting and restoring the ecological environment, ending the vicious circle of poverty and ecological destruction, and taking into account the strategic goals of ecological improvement and poverty alleviation. Specifically, poverty alleviation is combined with ecological protection, and the poor people who have established files and registered become ecological protection personnel and forest rangers. In this way, those who cannot move from ecologically fragile areas can be converted into paid workers on the spot, allowing some of the poor population to be lifted out of poverty.

Ecological protection is a positive and tangible way for China to break through the bottleneck of poverty alleviation. The bottleneck of economic and social development in ecologically fragile areas lies in the low carrying capacity of resources and the environment. Rational use of resources and improvement of the ecological environment are the only ways to alleviate poverty and achieve sustainable regional development. Until the resources and environmental carrying capacity of the ecologically fragile areas are significantly improved, the means to promote economic growth and regional development for the purpose of reducing poverty will lack a stable foundation.

The most important way for ecological protection to alleviate poverty is to base itself on regional resources (including natural and human), and fully activate all positive factors, strive to improve the ecological environment, and build the foundation for poverty alleviation and development in ecologically fragile areas.

One aspect of this is to make full use of special products and landscape resources in these areas, relying on them to develop an ecological economy, promote regional employment, and have a competitive advantage that can attract foreign investment. Another aspect is to make full use of human resources in impoverished areas. The poor are the direct victims of ecological deterioration, and they can expand their own development space and enhance their development capabilities through continuous ecological improvement. To alleviate poverty through ecological protection, local poor people must be encouraged to improve the ecological environment and be responsible for ecological protection.

e) Implement poverty relief policies

To solve the total or partial loss of working capacity among the poor, the social security policy will help them to coordinate rural poverty alleviation standards and the rural subsistence allowance standards, and increase other forms of social assistance to help them rise out of poverty. It is impossible to alleviate poverty and raise incomes in a "one size fits all" manner. For the poor who are indeed incapacitated, a comprehensive social security policy must be used. A Politburo meeting on November 23, 2015 clarified the scale of poverty alleviation through social security policies for the first time. By 2020, all of the 20 million+ people who have completely or partially lost the ability to work must be included in the coverage of the rural minimum living standard guarantee system to achieve the poverty alleviation through social security policies.

Poverty alleviation is a "blood transfusion" for those who are unable to rise out of poverty themselves. Through the implementation of various bottom-line policies, a public livelihood security network is imbued with measures such as a subsistence allowance policy, medical assistance, special hardship support, and temporary assistance. The minimum living guarantee is the last barrier to poverty alleviation. Efforts must be focused on protecting the basics, and ensuring low-income support to help the poor in good time. It is necessary to provide assistance to poor people in the medical assistance category, either to afford current treatment, or to pay debts accrued by illness. Through reducing medical expenses and solving the issue of lowered family income due to illness, work must be done to eradicate poverty caused by illness. Meanwhile, it is necessary to target the poor people who are unable to work under the minimum living standard system, and follow the requirements of the "two-line integration" of poverty alleviation and the minimum living standard.

(IV) Basic requirements for China's poverty alleviation

Eliminating poverty, improving people's livelihoods, and achieving common prosperity are the essential requirements of socialism and a significant mission of the Party. Since the period of Reform and Opening, through planned large-scale nationwide developmental poverty alleviation, the country's poor population has decreased significantly, and the appearance of poverty-stricken areas has changed significantly. However, there are still very strenuous tasks ahead for poverty alleviation and elimination as it enters a sprint period of tackling tough issues. The situation is pressing, and time is of the essence. Party committees and governments at all levels must increase their sense of urgency and initiative, clarify their thinking, intensify responsibilities in the fight against poverty, and adopt more powerful, more targeted, more direct, and more sustainable measures.

a) Leveraging political and institutional advantages

Winning the battle against poverty is a difficult and decisive battle that marks China's leap through historical stages. It must be based on national conditions and leverage the country's political and institutional advantages. This is the basic guarantee for us to alleviate poverty.

The leadership of the Communist Party of China is the greatest political advantage in the fight against poverty. It is the fundamental guarantee for poverty alleviation, and the fundamental political principle that the nation must adhere to. The central government decided that the leaders of the Party and governments of provinces, districts, and cities with the most significant element of poverty alleviation should sign a letter of responsibility and commitment. According to the requirements of the central government, responsibilities should be implemented at all levels, and the five-level secretaries of the province, city, county, township, and village should work together. It is stipulated that the First Secretary and the work team stationed in a poor village should build the two-committee model of leadership, and implement the task of poverty alleviation to the last mile. The leadership of the Party is its unique political advantage and the core of its leadership in poverty alleviation. Party committees and governments at all levels must obey orders, heed commands, and implement the poverty alleviation and prosperity indicators on time and according to the nodes without compromising.

Government-led leadership is a specifically Chinese element of poverty alleviation, and a major institutional advantage. Economic growth cannot automatically achieve poverty reduction. It is necessary to adhere to the government-led poverty alleviation system and leverage the government's leading role in the endeavor. The government must formulate economic and social development strategies and poverty alleviation plans that are suitable for poverty-stricken areas, and organize the mobilization of resources from all regions, departments, and industries to support poverty alleviation, so as to ensure that projects are prioritized, funds are guaranteed, and measures are emphasized.

Social participation is a fine tradition of the Chinese nation and a significant factor in winning this battle against poverty. China has always embraced the traditional virtues of helping the poor and treating people with kindness. It must pursue east-west cooperation in poverty alleviation. The provinces and cities that are the first to develop in the east must help the western provinces, districts, and cities to alleviate poverty. The Party, government and military agencies, and state-owned enterprises and institutions must participate in targeted poverty alleviation. Private enterprises, social organizations, and individual citizens must participate in the building of a Chinese-style social poverty alleviation system, which will continue to develop and improve, and form a strong joint force for poverty alleviation.

b) Expanding the coverage of infrastructure in impoverished areas

This is a major requirement for China's economic and social development during the 13th Five-Year Plan period. In the decisive stage of poverty alleviation and the building of a moderately prosperous society in all respects, expanding new development space and shaping a new pattern of regional development requires the effective use of the guiding role of infrastructure development. From the perspective of scientific development, it is necessary to genuinely understand the great significance and far-reaching impact of expanding the coverage of infrastructure in impoverished areas.

This involves expanding the coverage of infrastructure in poverty-stricken areas, including infrastructure consisting of information, energy, telecommunications, water conservation. A comprehensive transport infrastructure network should be created consisting of railroads, highways, water transport, civil aviation, pipelines, postal services, urban water supply, power supply, gas supply, and an underground pipe network. Flood control and waterlogging prevention facilities should expand the space for infrastructure building, considered with the main tasks of cultivating new development momentum, deepening the implementation of innovation-driven development strategies, building a new industrial system, and forming a new development system. It should also involve coordinating with the expansion of land development space and industrial development space, and uniting with the expansion of opening up, intensifying cooperation, and mutual benefit and co-building and sharing, and exploring ways, methods, and measures to expand and develop new spaces.

To expand the coverage of infrastructure in poverty-stricken areas, it is necessary to improve the living standards and life quality of impoverished people, improve their well-being, and promote their overall development in accordance with the new situation and new specifics of the decisive stage of poverty alleviation and the building of a moderately prosperous society in all respects. First, China must: insist that development is the first priority; adhere to the principle of first guiding and moderately leading; maintain a certain development speed; promote infrastructure building in a systematic manner; strive to achieve a moderately advanced allocation of infrastructure capabilities; and provide a solid foundation and strong guarantee for maintaining medium- and high-speed economic growth. Then, it must: highlight key areas, intensify weak links, optimize the layout structure, improve security capabilities, support the implementation of major economic and social development strategies in poverty-stricken areas, and optimize the development structure of poverty-stricken areas and urban and rural areas.

c) Promoting the equalization of public services in poverty-stricken areas

Equalization of basic public services is an institutional arrangement for expanding the coverage of public finances so that all poor people can share the fruits of reform and development. In terms of basicity, extensiveness, urgency, and feasibility, compulsory education, public health, basic medical care, basic social security, and public employment services are necessary to establish a social safety net and guarantee the basic survival and development of all poor people. Basic public services are the main thrust of the current equalization of basic public services in China.

The first step is to establish a unified urban and rural public service system. This, along with improving the level of basic public services for urban-rural integration, is a long-term development project. It is also a basic requirement for current poverty alleviation and the building of a moderately prosperous society in all respects. The design of the system should be accelerated to make it clear that urban and rural areas will be established. A unified public service system is the main aspect of poverty alleviation in the new stage.

The reform of the compulsory education system in poor rural areas must be promoted, focusing on the implementation of the education funding guarantee mechanism. On the basis of exempting tuition and miscellaneous fees, it is necessary to clarify the expenditure responsibilities of governments at all levels for compulsory education in poor rural areas. It is necessary to convert the original tuition and miscellaneous fees into central, provincial, city, and county government input; raise additional funds through the provincial government; exempt all expenses including tuition and miscellaneous fees for compulsory education in poor counties; and gradually narrow the gap between urban and rural compulsory education in poor areas and the quality of education.

A new rural cooperative medical system must be fully implemented. Central and provincial governments should gradually increase the proportion of input to stabilize farmers' expectations on them for the long-term development of new rural cooperative medical care in poor areas. It is necessary to improve the protection methods against serious diseases, taking into account the prevention and treatment of common and frequently-occurring diseases; intensify the building of the three-level health service network in poor rural areas; gradually expand designated medical institutions, so that impoverished farmers have more choices, and promote medical institutions to improve service quality and reduce prices; ensure that farmers in poverty-stricken areas who leave to work elsewhere are allowed to seek medical treatment in qualified hospitals in other places, and then reimburse them at participating places with corresponding certificates; intensify the management and supervision of medical funds, establish and improve the tripartite restriction mechanism of new-type rural cooperative medical management organizations, insured people, and medical units; regulate the operation of insurance funds, and improve the efficiency of the use of funds.

The minimum living guarantee should be fully implementing for poor rural areas. The central and provincial governments should formulate corresponding laws and regulations on the minimum living guarantee for poor rural areas as soon as possible. All regions must calculate the annual per capita consumption level and per capita basic living expenses of the poor according to the most basic living needs of impoverished farmers and the level of local economic development, and determine the minimum living security standards for poor rural areas. The source of guarantee funds should follow the principle of government input as the mainstay and include the funds for the minimum living guarantee in poor rural areas in the fiscal budget. According to the level of economic development in different regions, it is necessary to rationally divide the proportion of funds burdened by governments at all levels, taking into account the financial difficulties of poor counties and townships, and reducing the proportion of burdens as much as possible. It is necessary to increase financial transfer payments at the central and provincial levels to ensure that the funds for the minimum living guarantee in poor rural areas are fully in place. It is necessary to intensify the communication and collaboration among the departments of finance, civil affairs, education, labor security, and health; integrate various beneficial agricultural policies; and realize the transformation from single assistance to comprehensive assistance.

Pilot projects for a new type of poor rural social endowment insurance should be carried out. It is necessary to: incorporate the building of the rural social endowment insurance system into the economic and social development plan; clarify the responsibilities of central and local finances, and increase public financial investment in the building of the social endowment insurance system in poor rural areas; explore the establishment of a multi-Party financing mechanism for the poor population's individual contributions, collective subsidies, and government subsidies, and a new type of poor rural social endowment insurance system based on personal accounts, supplemented by overall planning adjustments; straighten out and improve the management system of poor rural social endowment insurance, and improve the fund operation and supervision system. In the design of the system, full consideration should be given to the connection between urban and rural areas in poverty-stricken areas in the future.

The second step is to reform and adjust the relationship between the central and local governments, and establish a regional coordinated development mechanism. The focus is to establish a system for the reasonable division of labor between the central and local governments, so that the responsibilities of basic public services in poverty-stricken areas are commensurate with their financial resources.

Labor must be divided reasonably between the central and local governments for compulsory education in poverty-stricken areas. The central and provincial governments have to take on more compulsory education responsibilities in poverty-stricken areas. The central government should undertake two major coordination projects: (1) Increase the expenditure on compulsory education in the poor rural areas of the central and western regions, bearing all of the tuition and miscellaneous fees exempted in the rural areas (including counties) in the poverty-stricken areas of the central and western regions; (2) Balance the gap in financial education funding between regions through the central fiscal budget. For example, it can be determined that provinces where per capita financial education expenditure is lower than 80% of the national average will be supplemented by the central government to the level of 80%. The provincial government has increased expenses for compulsory education in poverty-stricken areas through the provincial budget. Governments at the city and county levels in poverty-stricken areas are mainly responsible for managing the quality of education and some of the funding obligations, such as building schools.

The division of labor between the central and local governments in public health and basic medical services in poverty-stricken areas should be reasonable. The general principle is that the responsibility for public health lies with the central government, and the financial resources are shared between the central government and provincial governments, with the central government as the mainstay. It is necessary to gradually reduce the financial burden of the municipal and county governments in poverty-stricken areas and the share of residents (partially resolved through basic medical insurance). It is recommended to increase the proportion of fiscal medical expenses in the GDP to 3%, and the increase will be shared by the central and provincial finances. The central government uses transfer payments to balance the inequality of medical and health expenditure among poor areas.

The division of labor between the central and local governments in basic social security in poverty-stricken areas should be reasonable. The central government must issue corresponding policies as soon as possible to unify the arrangements for the basic social security system in impoverished areas, and improve the overall level of social security in impoverished areas. It is necessary to increase the transfer payment from the central government to provincial finance, improve the provincial budget and distribution system, and guarantee social security funds in poverty-stricken areas. While improving the social security system for urban residents in poverty-stricken areas, it is also necessary to formulate effective measures to make overall plans and solve social security issues in poor rural areas, especially for poor migrant workers. It is necessary to divide labor reasonably between the central and local governments in public employment services in poverty-stricken areas. Public employment services are within the scope of the local government's responsibilities. Urban employment services are mainly implemented by the city government. For poverty-stricken areas, the provincial government and the central government should provide certain special subsidies for employment training. The government of the outflow area is responsible for the employment training of impoverished farmers, including vocational education and training before employment of rural middle school students in poor areas. This is because it is reasonable to subsidize the vocational training of poor migrant workers displaced by the government, but this is very difficult in practice. Therefore, the central and provincial governments need to provide special subsidies based on the number of poor migrant workers in the outflow areas and the scale of training, and establish an employment assistance system specifically for poverty-stricken areas and disadvantaged groups.

The third step is to coordinate the supply of basic public services for migrant workers in poverty-stricken areas. Solving the problems facing migrant workers in poverty-stricken areas involve regional coordination as well as the connection between urban and rural areas. It requires a unified policy by the central government to properly resolve the territorial management of basic public services for migrant workers in poverty-stricken areas. These workers are creating wealth and becoming taxpayers of governments. Therefore, the government should assume greater responsibility in the provision of basic public services for migrant workers in poverty-stricken areas.

As for providing compulsory education for children of migrant workers in poverty-stricken areas, in response to the difficulty of linking up compulsory education funds in places that suffer an outflow of people, a nationwide education voucher system for compulsory education will be implemented. Children of migrant workers in poverty-stricken areas can go to school in any region of the country with these education vouchers, and the state will provide financial support in accordance with the education vouchers provided by schools; or, according to the actual number of local compulsory education students in recent years, special financial transfer payments for the compulsory education of children of migrant workers in poverty-stricken areas will be made. In the case of insufficient public education resources for migrant workers in poverty-stricken areas, the threshold for calibrators of private schools should be lowered, and the government should purchase services from such schools. Local governments should increase their assistance to schools for children of migrant workers in poverty-stricken areas, and provide necessary financial subsidies in terms of school venues, teaching equipment, and office expenses to reduce their school costs.

A basic social security system should be established for migrant workers in poverty-stricken areas. For migrant workers in poverty-stricken areas who are willing to receive the new type of rural cooperative medical care in the place where their household registration is located, effective measures should be taken so that the cost of seeing a doctor in the inflow location hospital can be reimbursed in the outflow location. For migrant workers in poverty-stricken areas who wish to receive basic urban medical care in migrant areas, the governments of these areas must lower the minimum payment base so that most migrant workers in poor areas can afford the personal payment for urban basic medical care. In areas where conditions permit, it is necessary to gradually explore effective ways for migrant workers to use the new rural cooperative medical system and the basic urban medical system. In terms of basic medical care, a unified nationwide network will be implemented as soon as possible so that the personal accounts of the floating population in poverty-stricken areas can be transferred. At present, the proportion of migrant workers in poverty-stricken areas who have work injury insurance is still low. Legislation needs to be passed to make this sort of insurance compulsory for hazardous industries and to regulate related tariff issues. It is necessary to establish a transitional endowment insurance system that suits the specifics of migrant workers in unstable and poor areas. A system model that combines social pooling and personal accounts can be adopted to first establish individual pension insurance accounts for migrant workers in poverty-stricken areas that can be transferred across regions, and then to include them in the social pooling of pension insurance when the time is right.

Public employment services must be improved for migrant workers in poverty-stricken areas. It is necessary to implement an employment information card system for migrant workers' in poverty-stricken areas as soon as possible, and integrate the management and services into the overall information network. It is necessary to accelerate the building of a comprehensive information exchange platform that reflects the changes in the labor force in poor areas. On this basis, China will realize the connection of public employment services across urban and rural areas and across regions in poverty-stricken areas, so that migrant workers in poor areas can enjoy the same treatment as urban residents in terms of introduction to jobs, vocational training, employment, unemployment registration, and labor contract management.

d) Implementing the responsibility system for poverty alleviation work
This requires starting from the leadership team and the implementation of the chief responsibility system; intensifying the responsibility assessment of poverty alleviation work; implementing the one-vote veto system for poverty alleviation work; and insisting that leading cadres lead by example when putting poverty alleviation work in place.

First, it is necessary to think carefully, clarify tasks, keep responsibilities in mind, and fully implement various poverty alleviation targets to ensure that the poor will rise out of poverty and earn a living as quickly as possible. Secondly, it is necessary to increase the management of poverty alleviation funds. Illegal misappropriation of poverty alleviation funds must be severely punished. It is necessary to integrate all kinds of poverty alleviation resources, open and develop new channels for poverty alleviation funds, and ensure that they are used well. Thirdly, it is necessary to refine the identification mechanism of the targets of poverty alleviation and elimination, strictly control the check to ensure their authenticity, and firmly implement the accountability system. Violations of discipline such as the abuse of power, back door dealings, pseudo-poverty, and ignorance of policies and regulations should be dealt with seriously and pursued to the end. In short, it is necessary to implement poverty alleviation projects with a responsibility system. Anyone who fails to complete a specified poverty alleviation project to the specified deadline should implement the one-vote veto system, take accountability based on the situation, and deal with it seriously.

2016 is the first year of the 13th Five-Year Plan, and the first year in China's battle to alleviate poverty. Under the solid leadership of the Party Central Committee and the State Council, China must analyze and understand the domestic and international environment of the fight against poverty, and work hard to make a good start. It must win the battle, ensuring that all poor people and areas are lifted out of poverty on schedule, and working with the people to build a moderately prosperous society in all respects.

CHAPTER 3

Strategic Design of the Final Battle

On October 29, 2015, the "Proposal of the Central Committee of the Communist Party of China on Formulating the 13th Five-Year Plan for National Economic and Social Development" was formally adopted.

In China, there are more than 20 million poor people who are completely or partly incapacitated and unable to work. All of them can be included in the coverage of the basic living allowance to achieve social security policies and alleviate poverty. Based on this initial plan, this chapter proposes a strategic design for the decisive battle of 2020. The author believes that combining some successful practices in modern countries, and considering China's long-term development, the key to the development of its rural areas (including impoverished villages) is to build a social ecosystem that integrates elements such as industry, projects, policy funds, staff training, and market development. Therefore, the decisive battle of 2020 should focus on the implementation of the "Million Farms in Thousands of Counties and Ten Thousand of Townships" plan, the "Well-off College Incubating Talent" plan, the "Trillion Policy Financial Support" plan, and the "Consumer Poverty Alleviation Social Action" plan.

1. The "Million Farms in Thousands of Counties and Ten Thousand Townships" plan

A farm is a new type of village that gathers several planting and breeding farms, integrating agricultural production, agricultural product processing, sightseeing, leisure and tourism, and residence into one – i.e. primary, secondary, and tertiary industries. It is both the basic organizational unit in rural areas and the basic industrial format. It is characterized by sound organizational structures; complete systems for education, medical care, and services; operation of planting, breeding, work, and sub-categories; and social cohesion. The "Million Farms in Thousands of Counties and Ten Thousand Townships" plan refers to the integration of industrial layout and living environment design in accordance with the development needs of farms in the poverty-stricken villages in the process of promoting poverty alleviation and reaching prosperity.

(I) International reference points for the "Million Farms in Thousands of Counties and Ten Thousand Townships" plan

International examples have shown that the evolution of the rural mode to the farming mode has formed an inevitable and irreversible trend along with a regularity of its own, which is accompanied by the development of national food security and urban-rural integration. General Secretary Xi Jinping has repeatedly emphasized that projects related to agriculture, rural areas, and rural people are the top priority. Old revolutionary base areas, ethnic regions, border areas, and poor areas should set poverty alleviation and development as the top priority in projects related to agriculture, rural areas, and rural people, so that there is a focus. Since poverty alleviation and development is a significant part of the work related to agriculture, rural areas, and rural people, it is necessary to examine the global historical evolution of agriculture and rural development for poverty alleviation in poverty-stricken villages, and learn from the example of foreign farm development to provide a reference for the "Million Farms in Thousands of Counties and Ten Thousand Townships" plan.

a) The development of urban-rural relations in global society, and the historical evolution of farm building

The author has been abroad, and personally believes that the development of countries and regions in East Asia that are close to China (such as South Korea and Japan) is worthy of note. The histories of these countries and regions have many similarities with China's national conditions. They also have a tradition of small-scale peasant economies as the foundation of agricultural cultural life, but their industrialization is now relatively advanced. The level of urbanization is relatively high, as is the rate of farm building. However, at the same time, farm development has also encountered many practical problems, which China can heed for the purpose of research and discussion.

(1) In the initial stage of national development, the "scissor gap" between urban and rural development is large, and building farms is impossible. In the early stages of national development, South Korea and Japan had very low economic levels, with an urbanization level of only 10%–15%, and they were poor and backward traditional agricultural societies. The urbanization level in China in the early stage of Reform and Opening was about 18%. In order to break this state of poverty and weakness, China must first develop industry, because there is no capital to engage in modern agriculture; it is only possible to engage in industry first. However, industrial development needs cities and towns as carriers, and the level of urbanization will increase accordingly. At this stage, the "scissor gap" between urban and rural development cruelly exploited the countryside, and farm building was more or less neglected. This is the initial stage of industrialization, when the urbanization level has risen to 15%–30%. At this point, the rural areas are poor and weak, and the urban-rural development gap is rapidly widening.

(2) With the development of industry, cities and towns become prosperous, while the rural environment deteriorates on a daily basis. From the perspective of world history, the development of industry causes tertiary industries to develop rapidly, and cities and towns become prosperous. The development of urban tertiary industries is supported by a large amount of cheap labor, resulting in a significant outflow of rural population, the gradual decline of traditional rural villages, and a deteriorating rural environment. Since the start of the 21st century, the model by which industry feeds agriculture and cities in supporting the countryside has become a serious political proposition. The level of urbanization at this stage is 30%–50%.

(3) The further development of the secondary and tertiary industries and the improvement of the social and cultural level will inevitably lead to a continued substantial reduction of the rural population. At the same time, with the increase of public financial resources, the gap between urban and rural social security and public services will gradually narrow, the building of new rural areas will be put on the agenda again, and the demand for building farms will increase. At this point, the level of urbanization will have reached 50%–70%.

(4) When the level of urbanization reaches 70%, the national economy is considered to be highly developed. At this time, the proportion of the agricultural population will become extremely small, the proportion of the urban population will be very large, and the social security, public services, and production factor markets

between urban and rural areas will usually be consistent. The country's subsidies for projects related to agriculture, rural areas, and rural people will become even greater, the support for the building of farms in poverty-stricken areas will be unprecedented, and the role of farm owner will become a respected identity. However, the proportion of the total national expenditure is not necessarily high. After all, the proportion of the rural population is very low, but this is very significant for farmers' income.

A recent survey report pointed out that the income ratio of agricultural and non-agricultural income in Japan remains at 86%–97%, and 140% in Taiwan. In Japan, this proportion reached 86% in 2005, either due to the combination of agricultural development and the processing industry, or the combination of agriculture, the processing industry, and rural tourism; the proportion in Taiwan was also very high, reaching 77% in 2004. In terms of the proportion of professional and part-time households, Japan had less than 11% of professional farmers, and part-time farmers accounted for 84%; in Taiwan, professional farmers accounted for less than 10%, and part-time farmers accounted for more than 90%. That is to say, after rural development reaches a certain stage, it is actually part-time. As well as planting and breeding, it will be combined with industries such as processing, tourism, and e-commerce to increase economic benefits by raising the added value of agricultural products. In addition, national policy support occupies a significant position in rural development. Direct or indirect financial policy support can increase the transfer income of farmers and help narrow the income gap between urban and rural residents. The proportion of policy funding to the income of agricultural workers is 58% in Japan and 63% in South Korea.

From this point of view, the building and development of farms does not mean that the countryside will completely disappear, nor does it shake the fundamental status of agriculture. Food security occupies an important position in the national strategy. A country cannot completely rely on foreign imports for its food, even if the imported food may be cheaper. At the same time, striving to narrow the gap between urban and rural development, consistently improving the living environment of farmers, and improving their quality of life are also the strategic focus of a country's integrated urban-rural development. Therefore, the development of farms has an irreplaceable positive effect.

b) Overview of foreign farm building
As mentioned above, the farm-building models and developments in East Asian countries such as South Korea and Japan are worthy of study and discussion. The following is a brief explanation.

• South Korean farms

South Korea's urbanization rate is very high, reaching 41% in the 1970s, reaching 77% in 1994 at the end of the 20th century, and now standing at around 90%. They paid close attention to farm building in the early stage of urban development during a period of low urbanization, and encouraged farmers to build farms in order to improve the living environment of rural people.

In the initial stage, when the urbanization rate was low, the proportion of agricultural production on farms was large, and the government's investment burden was heavy. With increasing urbanization, South Korea has begun to transform its farm development mode from government-led to farmer-led and government-supported. According to data, after 2005, the "New Village/Farm Movement" in South Korea implemented a model in which rural villages submit applications, which are screened and evaluated by government departments, and then given support. South Korea's "New Village/Farm Movement" has a great reputation, and has been copied in some African countries. However, from the perspective of the rural areas alone, even though the government has spent a lot of money on the new village/farm movement, the rural areas are still in severe decline, especially since the rural population has dropped sharply, and is aging fast.

The South Korean government's support for farms continues to increase every year. The Comprehensive Development Support Association for Korean Agriculture and Fishery Village Areas is a permanent institution at the government level, and is subordinate to the Ministry of Agriculture, Forestry, Fisheries, and Food of the Central Government. It was formed by the merger of the Water Conservancy Association, the Land Development Association, and the Farmland Development Association, which were originally under different government departments, in the year 2000. The Association is responsible for the promotion of farm development outside of metropolitan areas, and its purpose is to encourage better and more efficient use of rural resources, giving rural areas more value and economic capacity. Meanwhile, there are some new positive developments in South Korea. For example, the trend for returning to farms and villages has begun to gather steam. Returning to agriculture refers to the return of migrants, or the migration of urban populations to farms to engage in agricultural work. According to South Korean law, urban people can go and work on farms, productive people can buy farmland, and white-collar workers can work in agriculture. Returning to the villages means that urban people go to live in the countryside, or return to provide for the elderly. Mindsets are changing. In the past, farms were seen only as food production bases. Now, people understand that they are spaces for life, production, employment, and leisure. However, overall, this situation is still rare.

South Korea's "New Village/Farm Movement" started early. However, the urban economy is highly developed, and rural problems have become increasingly prominent. The main reason for this is the shocking degree of rural decline. The government and all sectors of society recognize that the countryside has irreplaceable value. Therefore, over the years, the South Korean government and related institutions have devoted a lot of manpower and material resources to farming issues, trying to boost farms and maintain the healthy development of the countryside. Statistics show that farm building in South Korea has evolved from the early "New Village/Farm Movement" to today's situation of farm support, that is, using top-down economic assistance and technical support to achieve the goal of comprehensive stimulation.

Gangwon Province has carried out the "New Village/Farm Movement" throughout its territory since 1998, including the exceptional Meihuli unit. There are 72 households, 244 people, 144 hectares of arable land, 320 hectares of mountain forest, a clean and attractive environment, sound and suitable houses, developing green

Rice fields and 100 mu of Korean ginseng planting fields at Meihuli Farm

industries, and agricultural products. The industries there are very distinctive. The rebuilding of village roads, water conservation facilities, and farm houses at Meihuli Farm is supported by the government. After being rated as an outstanding unit of the "New Village/Farm Movement," the farm was awarded 500 million won by the government. It was also rated as a "Green Rural Experience Village," and was awarded 100 million won the Ministry of Agriculture, Forestry, Fisheries, and Food of South Korea and Gangwon Province respectively. The South Korean government strongly encourages farms to engage in planting to avoid abandoning farmland. According to a local farm owner, about 80% of the input cost of production materials such as seeds, fertilizers, and pesticides is government subsidies, making farms are more profitable. In addition to rice, the farm also grows crops such as high value-added ginseng and tobacco. The average income of farmers is more than 50 million won per household per year (the average number of people in each local household is 3.3), and the per capita income is equivalent to about 134,000 yuan.

Sillim-myeon in Wonju City is a farm that forms part of South Korea's informatization pilot. The farm consists of 401 households and 1,667 people in a total of four wards (actually natural villages) in Hwangdun 1 & 2, and Songgyeon 1 & 2.

The penetration rate of phones in Sillim-myeon is 100%, and it has 200 computers and an electronic trading market. These facilities and equipment are the result of investments by governments at all levels. Their farm operations are mainly high-tech greenhouses that grow large peppers and tomatoes, as well as clean vegetable processing and packaging, open fish farms, computer rooms for student internships, logistics centers for agricultural products, and gyms for residents.

From the point of view of data, since South Korea has few resources, so it has had to build a tradition of conservation and efficient use. In building farms, they focus on revitalization, guiding farmers to apply for construction support, which is screened and provided by government agencies, along with training and support for model projects. If a project is successful and additional funds are added, the work will continue to be tracked and maintained, rather than being implemented by high-level executives.

Despite the success of building and renovating South Korean farms, it is difficult to reverse the possibility of population loss and decline even in the more successful farms. This phenomenon is likely to be maintained in South Korea, and it may be difficult to rejuvenate and return to the former prosperity of the rural population and sound social structure.

Growing large peppers in the greenhouse on Sillim-myeon Farm

Mechanized graded packaging of agricultural products on Sillim-myeon Farm

- JAPANESE FARMS

Japanese villages/farms are administrative organizations, and villages, towns, and cities are all first-level administrative organizations. A village covers a large area. Japan now emphasizes six industries, including primary, secondary, and tertiary. The modernization of agriculture and large-scale land use have largely concentrated on large farmers through leasing.

The trend of diversification and leisure in the building of farms in Japan is relatively obvious. Farming people live in small houses, and their homesteads are often linked with their farms. The aging of the rural population in Japan is a serious issue, but the countryside has not been abandoned. The cultivated land is still intensively maintained, some by families, and some by large households. Some even regard agriculture as a form of heritage, almost like a museum. In fact, it is being developed and utilized as a cultural resource. The degree of urbanization in Japan is very high. In the early 1960s it was 63%, in 2001 it was 86%, and it is now more than 90%. From 1945 to 1970, the number of villages decreased to 8% of the original in 24 years, including large-scale mergers. After 2010, it was reduced to 2%. However, the

A Japanese farm

Recreational area on a Japanese farm

countryside has not been abandoned, and the maintenance and restoration of the rural landscape is still a priority.

A report stated that in 2013, the average age in rural Japan was 65. A typical case is a widowed peasant man whose son left to work in the city, and whose two daughters work as a civil servant and doctor in nearby cities. He is 76 years old, he is still farming, running a family farmstead of 12 hectares along with professional services. He believes that his son will come back from the city when he is old. The phenomenon of the empty-nest elderly population in rural areas is very serious.

One small village in Japan is producing pottery. Even though it does positive work in protecting traditional handicrafts, the economic benefits are negligible, and there are few visitors. The pavements of the village is properly hardened, and obviously the hope is to restore the history and preserve the original culture through restoration.

Hokkaido's farms are landscaped with lavender and flowers to attract tourists, and a lot of thought has been put into offering activities such as tractor rides and go-kart rental. In the suburbs of cities, farm bases are often used as urban farms to perform educational functions. For example, there is a kindergarten that has invested in a sweet potato farm so that the children can visit and participate in the planting, growing, and harvesting. There is also a cherry farm in Hokkaido, which dates back several generations. The cherries used to be exported, but now they are mainly sold to big cities. The farm also receives tourists to visit and pick fruit. Business is booming.

Japan's modern culture and public administration are not very different. All residents of the country are treated fairly as citizens, but there is a big difference between economic density and population density. Hokkaido, for example, has been developed for many years, but still has a small population of only five million people, most of whom are concentrated in the capital. Considering the small size of the country, the high population density, and the high economic development in Japan, there is no big difference in public services between urban and rural areas, and the government and the private sector have invested a lot of financial resources and efforts for the balanced development between urban and rural areas. However, even in this case, farms in the northern region are still in decline.

c) Insights and revelations from the construction of foreign farms
(1) With the rural population continuing to decline, the decline of the countryside as a whole is inevitable. Modern urban life and work are very attractive to young people in rural areas, so most leave their villages and go to cities, even in a society like Japan, where the difference between urban and rural areas is very small. As a result, the rural population continues to decline and grow older, with an inevitable consequent decline of the countryside as a whole. To a certain extent, what is happening in rural Japan today will be the future of rural China. Therefore, it is necessary to examine the development of Japanese farms and the strategies to cope with them, and have a clear understanding of the reality and future development of China's rural areas. The pace of farm building should be accelerated, but this does not mean that the decline and aging of the rural population can be reversed.

(2) Urban and rural factors should flow in both directions, and new ideas should be developed for rural development strategies and planning. With the rapid advancement of agricultural modernization and new urbanization, traditional rural villages are evolving into communities and farms, which is manifested by the drastic reduction of the farming population, the continuing decline of villages, the accelerated construction of farms with different themes, and the continuous streamlining and shrinking of rural living space. The development of poor villages is no exception. This trend also raises a demand for the integration and optimization of public services and facilities in rural communities to avoid waste. Therefore, in order to have a two-way flow of urban and rural elements, rural development strategies and plans must have new ideas. According to the example of South Korea and Japan, in a situation of high

urbanization and modernization, urban and rural resources should be able to flow in both directions, so that farmers can move to cities and urbanites can return to farms and villages.

(3) It is necessary to reduce production risks and improve production efficiency. China's rural areas are very different, especially poor villages, and the reasons for poverty vary widely. In the future building and development of farms, it is necessary to adapt measures to village conditions. Many areas can also maintain agricultural production methods, but it is necessary to promote large-scale production and management according to the situation. Japan used to have a farmer's association, i.e. a large rural network that organizes supply and marketing and all aspects of operation. In China, the best way to develop is to use leading "big money" agricultural industrialization enterprises, which can reduce state input, lower risks, and improve production efficiency. Of course, it is also possible to join together in corporatization, marketing local specialties, reshaping local customs and folklore, and developing integrated cultural resources.

(II) Developing the "Million Farms in Thousands of Counties and Ten Thousand Villages" plan

a) The general significance of building farms

It is easy to see from international cases that farm is an organizational unit and a production space for modern agriculture. Farmsteads rely on mechanization and modern organization to upgrade agricultural production and improve its efficiency, gradually developing from backward traditional agriculture to a global-level industry. At the same time, the living space and infrastructure of farmsteads have improved enormously, along with the living standard of villagers, which is conducive to narrowing the gap with urban residents. This implies that the construction and development of farms in China is a universal trend. The benefits of farm construction are:

(1) It leverages the advantages of rural resources, especially building farms with independent decision-making processes and diversified forms of management, which focus mainly on planting, breeding, and eco-tourism, supplemented by the processing and marketing of agricultural products, and which implement intensive management of production factors like land, technology, and capital.

Firstly, it optimizes the allocation and integration of rural resources. The development of farms attracts a lot of superior resources such as personnel, capital, and technologies. Plus, it can also optimize the allocation of land-based agricultural resources. Many idle resources such as barren mountains, wasteland, and wastewater can be revived and utilized. At the same time, farm management is not merely a simple expansion of land scale, but also a new type of development under the premise of optimizing structure and pursuing high quality and efficiency. By utilizing modern agricultural technologies, increasing capital investment, improving the quality of the operators, and ameliorating production equipment, it is possible to consistently reduce production costs, maximize the output of land and the productivity of labor forces, and switch agriculture up from extensive to intensive growth.

Secondly, it enables rural areas to leverage their potential advantages on natural resources. Through the building of farms, most operators gain advantages in information, technology, capital, and management, and can respond quickly to market demands. Oriented by the market, based on science and technology, and through specialized production and intensive management, products that meet the market's demand should be developed, which will leverage the potential advantage of rural natural resources. This will promote the adjustment of the structure of agricultural production, accelerate the formation of leading regional industries, and lay a foundation for industrialized agriculture.

Thirdly, farm building makes rural areas more competitive. The managing mechanism and the corporate governance structure of the modern enterprise system have been introduced to farm management, which defines the relationships of interest among investors, operators, and laborers. The clear definition of property rights and the clear division of responsibilities motivate and galvanize the producers and operators.

(2) The construction of farms provides an opportunity for deeper agricultural reform. Chinese farmers are not the first to create farmsteads – the new micro-organizational unit in rural areas – but they can be brought to life through the practice of the vast majority of rural Chinese areas, providing an opportunity for deeper agricultural reform and development.

Firstly, farms fit into the mainstream of rural development. Agricultural developments in developed countries have all started from family peasant households and developed into farm management. In European and East-Asian countries and territories including Taiwan, the farming industry is flourishing. From the strategic consideration of agricultural development, rural labor transfer and new urbanization are closely related to farms. Farm construction is an inevitable choice to enhance the competitiveness of China's international agricultural market. It is a necessary stage in realizing agricultural modernization, and an inevitable choice and mainstream direction for the cultivation and development of rural market subjects.

Secondly, farms can adapt to the mainstream rural population division. In China, even though the current land circulation system still has certain constraints regarding the development of farms, the shift of the agricultural population from the primary industry to the secondary and the tertiary industries will be accelerated, and the proportion of the agricultural population in the labor force will fall sharply with the deepening reform of the rural land management system. The management pattern of farms meets the needs of this population differentiation precisely.

Thirdly, the development environment for farms is constantly improving. National and local governments at all levels see the importance of issues concerning agriculture, rural areas, and farmers. Especially during this period of poverty alleviation, under the guidance of the strategic planning of poverty alleviation by the CPC Central Committee and the State Council, the environment for building and developing farms will undergo unprecedented improvement including financing policies for farm operation in poor villages, the policies for enriching, strengthening, and benefiting farmers, the security protection policies, and the investment policies for infrastructure building.

Fourthly, the organization and management of farms must be standardized further. Thus far, China has not paid adequate attention to farm building, and management is carried out in a loose manner. With the continuous development and expansion of farms, organization and management will be normalized, the form of organization and its financial system will be refined, and corresponding associations will be established.

Fifthly, the production and operation of farms is more specialized and market-oriented. Farms must transform from extensive management to intensive management, and the internal structure must be refined. Advanced equipment and technologies could be put to best use, making the production process more professional and market oriented. At the same time, the division and cooperation between farms must be more socialized, making it easier to leverage the advantages of local capital and manpower, forming competitive edges and specifics of different products, so as to promote the development of China's rural economy to a higher and deeper level.

(3) The building of farms guarantees that farmers' quality of life will improve. At present, the state-driven integration strategy of urban and rural areas and the new-type urbanization strategy provide an opportunity to narrow the gap in living standards between urban and rural residents. During the evolution from villages to farms, the community function of the farm is made prominent; farmers' living space is relatively separate from the production space, which is conducive to the

rapid improvement of the infrastructure related to living and production functions. Intensive and efficient use of service agencies for community education, elderly care, and medical care has significantly improved the quality of life of rural residents.

b) Policy advantages of building farms in poor villages

The author believes that the building of farms in poor villages is the only way for those villages to alleviate poverty, become wealthy, and develop in the long run. During the critical period of poverty alleviation, the policy has provided inborn advantages for the building of farms in poor villages.

(1) It offers ways to cultivate personnel. In view of the problems of the low quality of rural personnel and low level of operation and management, the state has designed and implemented the special "Rain and Dew Program" and the "Training Project for Entrepreneurial Leaders in Poverty-stricken Villages" to provide targeted training for students who leave education after graduating from junior high school. The purpose is to enable people from poor families with the ability to work to gain the skills, enthusiasm, and motivation required to start a business.

(2) It provides financing channels for farm construction. In response to the problem of limited financing channels, the Party Central Committee and the State Council attach great importance to the issue. In 2015, the Poverty Alleviation Office of the State Council signed a financial support agreement of nearly four trillion yuan with the China Development Bank and the Agricultural Development Bank. In December 2014, the State Poverty Alleviation Office, the Ministry of Finance, the People's Bank of China, the China Banking Regulatory Commission, and the China Insurance Regulatory Commission issued the "Guidance on the Innovative Development of Small Credit for Poverty Alleviation," which provides poor households eligible for loans with no collateral, no guarantee, benchmark interest rates, and financial subsidies for small credit products and services for poverty alleviation of less than RMB 50,000 for a period of three years, and has formed a basic financing channel for the construction of farms in poor villages.

(3) There are improvements to the social environment. Since 2014, China has designated October 17 each year as "Poverty Alleviation Day," with the purpose of calling on and encouraging society and the Party to participate in the country's poverty alleviation work and forming a strong synergy for further development, as laid out by General Secretary Xi Jinping on the first "Poverty Alleviation Day" in 2014. At the High-level Forum on Poverty Reduction and Development in 2015, Xi delivered a keynote speech titled "Working Together to Eradicate Poverty and

Promote Common Development," expressing his concern for the poor with his personal experience of poverty reduction in China. The environment for private enterprises and for society to participate in poverty alleviation has been improved.

(4) Living space is guaranteed. Surrounding the main goal of poverty alleviation, ministries and commissions under the State Council and local governments at all levels have formulated corresponding planning ideas in nine areas, namely clear roads at village level, safe drinking water, electric power supply, renovation of dilapidated buildings, cultural development, informatization of poor villages, and poverty alleviation in terms of rural tourism, education, and public health. The building of related infrastructure is advancing and improving in all respects.

c) Building farms lays the foundation for poor villages to eliminate poverty and become prosperous

For a long time, China's agriculture has been small-scale due to a large population and less land available for farming. The "small" element of the term "part-time small-scale" has long been the main characteristic of Chinese farmers, especially in poor villages. After more than 30 years of the household contract responsibility system, population growth and institutional factors such as problems relating to land property rights and social security have meant that the agricultural industry has become fragmented, with farmers leaving the profession and the countryside emptying out. Due to the fragmentation of smallholders, coupled with the turmoil of speculative capital and the dramatic fluctuations in the prices of some agricultural products, the healthy development of the agricultural industry has suffered major negative effects, as have the steady growth of farmers' income, the development of rural society, and the stable operation of the national economy. However, poor villages can change this fragmented small-scale production model by building farms as the new basic organizational unit, and greatly improve their living environment.

In comparison, farms have a larger operation scale, more concentrated land, and mass production, which are all to the benefit of performing scale efficiency and reducing production costs. To improve the competitiveness of products in the market, farms can choose to pursue specialized, professionalized, and standardized development. Therefore, the farm development model will promote the continuous updating of technology and equipment for agricultural production, as well as aspects such as transport, storage, sales, and processing. Mechanization will be enhanced and the utilization rate of new varieties along with new technologies will be raised, so that agricultural productivity is improved, accelerating the speed of poverty alleviation of poor villages.

At the same time, farming is also conducive to extending the agricultural industry from pure agricultural production to secondary and tertiary industries such as processing and services, expanding agricultural value-added space and the agricultural industry chain, increasing employment opportunities, and providing employment opportunities for poor people with working ability. Farm management also helps to promote the transformation of impoverished farmers from part-time smallholders to vocational farmers and then to professionals. Moreover, the building of large-scale farms will promote the creation of public facilities in poor rural areas where it was previously difficult to make a difference. The living function of communities will also gradually improve.

In conclusion, the building of farms in poor villages is conducive for those areas to lay a solid foundation for poverty alleviation and prosperity.

(III) The conception and pathway selection for the building of farms

a) The concept of building farms

The farm proposed by the author is an organizational unit integrating functions such as producing products, processing products, sightseeing, leisure, elderly care, and living space. It is a new type of rural form. In the building of farms, it is necessary to plan and design a pathway combining agricultural production, agricultural processing, farming culture, regional natural features, and folk customs of the area, pursuing specific themes, so as to maintain its original flavor and avoid a loss of perspective.

The farm is divided into a production area and residential area. The residential area is located in the middle of the farm, and is classified into administrative (including the Party organization), food, shopping, medical care, education, elderly care, leisure, and recreational zones, reaching the living standard of urban communities. specific building modes should be designed in consideration of the local environment and cultural conditions. It is necessary to return the land to nature, establish agriculture based on ecology or sightseeing, or build creative agricultural parks, so as to restore agriculture to its original form.

In short, the farmstead we envision should have both community and productive functions. The development and construction of the farm should maintain the originality of its landscape, the ecological balance of the local area, and the virtuous cycle of the ecosystem.

The "Million Farms in Thousands of Counties and Ten Thousand Villages" plan is based on this idea. The building of farms is a shortcut for poor villages to rise out of poverty as quickly as possible, and also a direction for the future development of China's rural areas. According to the National Bureau of Statistics, by the end of 2014, there were still 14 contiguous special hardship areas and 832 poor counties in the country, which should be remedied by 2020. According to the planning principle of the scientific and reasonable layout of each natural village and village group with the existing administrative village as the center, it is not only correct but also feasible to implement the construction of a million farms.

b) The farm-building pathway

As for the selection of a pathway, the author believes that under the premise of succeeding in cultivating the poverty alleviation leaders in poor villages, the following two pathways should be adopted according to the specific situation: the cooperation between a farm and its assisting enterprises; and independent business development.

• COOPERATION BETWEEN A FARM AND ITS ASSISTING ENTERPRISES

This means that an enterprise and a farm operate together, with joint investment and joint management. This has many advantages: first, it greatly reduces the risk of farm operation, which need not be described in detail; second, it guarantees the safety of the micro-credit funds for poverty alleviation, because the investment funds of the farm mainly come from the micro-credit for poverty alleviation, and the enterprise is responsible for the normal withdrawal of the equity capital when the loan period expires; third, it lifts more poor people out of poverty and into prosperity, as the farm fully aggregates and plays the "hat" value of poor groups. By helping enterprises, poor farmers can become shareholders, poor groups can change their status and receive regular dividends, asset income, and wages, thus lifting more poor groups out of poverty and into wealth.

At the same time, the farm is also the rear production base of its cooperative enterprise – a fact that can greatly reduce the enterprise's alternative cost and time spent choosing raw materials. The enterprises will also benefit. The "Decision of the CPC Central Committee and the State Council on Winning the Fight Against Poverty" states that it is necessary to "improve the identification system for leading enterprises in poverty alleviation and enhance the ability of enterprises to stimulate poor households to gain more income." In this way, the assisting enterprises will be developed and expanded, and will go on to cooperate with more farms in a wider scope, lifting more poor farmers out of poverty towards prosperity, and achieving positive interactions. In the author's view, this path can be summarized in one sentence, that is, boosting enterprises, stimulating farmers, balancing justice and benefit, and mutual assistance between the rich and the poor.

• INDEPENDENT BUSINESS DEVELOPMENT

This means that the farm develops and operates independently in terms of project funds, technology, venues, and marketing. What should be noted is that China's existing farms are small in scale, usually covering only a few to a dozen hectares of land, with low labor productivity and products of low output value and poor quality. The quantity and quality of agricultural products impose restriction on their own development. At the same time, there is a lack of long-term planning and insufficient development energy. Although some projects have achieved initial results in the short term, the problems of lacking development momentum, having difficulty expanding, and having low rates of return on capital still exist due to the lack of medium- and long-term development projects and the incapability of forming industrial pillars. Therefore, in order to develop well on its own, a farm should make subtle plans, and reinforce the management of quality control, cost accounting, and cost control, so that the sustainability of building farms and development should be enhanced.

(IV) Examples of farm building and supplementary reading

a) Ecological farms in Taiwan

Ecological farms in Taiwan are well planned and designed, rationally distributed, resource-based, and differentially developed. They advance with time, innovate constantly, combine production with research, and provide considerate service. They are supported by the government and promoted by the public. They perform marketing through networks, conduct publicity, play a leading role, support farmers, enrich people, pay society back, and achieve win-win cooperation. The building of farms in Taiwan is positive and unique in many aspects.

(1) It considers ecology and takes a long-term view. The original purpose of the building of ecological farms in Taiwan was to create peaceful harbors in the countryside close to nature and fields, far away from worldly troubles and modern urban life. Therefore, in the process of farm construction, they do not give priority to economic benefits, but to the protection and improvement of the environment and the restoration of ecological functions. They often do years of work and invest a lot of money in improving the environment. In the process of planting or breeding, they basically do not apply chemical fertilizers and pesticides, and some even do

not use agricultural fertilizers at all. The main measure to improve production is to restore, improve, and fertilize the ground year by year, to ensure that the ecological environment is not polluted by foreign chemicals, and to ensure that their products are original, nutritious, safe and healthy. This farm management model is very different from the mentality of many Mainland investors who are eager for quick success and profit, and who do not understand the management philosophy of Taiwanese farmers. However, in the long run, these ecological farms are very viable, because with the development of the economy, humanity's influence on nature has touched almost every corner of the earth, even some remote mountainous areas. When more and more environments are polluted and ecologically destroyed, and when it is difficult to find ecological living environments that are not damaged in this way, such painstakingly managed ecological farms will become precious. People will want very much to go there for leisure, sightseeing, relaxation, and new experiences. Many ecological farms in Taiwan were originally built for the purpose of "pleasing oneself," not for making money, but after years of operation, many of them have eventually become places that please people, and have gained rich returns in the process.

(2) Taiwanese farmers have built farms with their own specific and distinctive features. Since the original intention of building is to create an ideal environment for life, many ecological farms in Taiwan have obviously integrated the thoughts, ideas, and pursuits of their founders. Farms in Taiwan have distinct features, and make a deep impression on the people who visit. For example, the Ageless Tribe farm in Datong Village, Yilan, was founded by seven indigenous Tayan families who returned to their native land. The main concept of the farm is to return to nature and learn from it. The houses are made of natural materials such as wood and thatch, which blend cohesively with the local environment. The people who live on the farm follow the ancient laws of man and nature, being self-sufficient through farming, weaving, hunting, planting crops, and caring for animals. The food and ingredients provided by the farm are all organic, free from chemical fertilizers and pesticides. Many of them can be picked and eaten without washing. Each dish made from these fresh and authentic ingredients is unique and original, presented in a stylish and distinctive way. After years of operation, the Ageless Tribe farm has become one of the most acclaimed projects in the development of foreign tourism by native Taiwan residents, attracting global attention. However, in order to protect the ecological environment of the farm, Ageless Tribe strictly controls the number of visitors per day. Although visitors can only stay on the farm for a few hours, they can still enjoy everything it

has to offer – sampling rice wine and delicious food, singing and laughing, enjoying nature, and forgetting their worldly troubles.

Another example is the Lavender Forest Farm, which was built with love by two Taiwanese women who wanted to escape city life. They selected a location with an exceptionally beautiful environment, far from the hustle and bustle of the city. They built the farm themselves, and planted fragrant lavender from which they extract essence and make their own essential oil soap. Its distinctive characteristics attract many visitors who are interested in the environment, as well as customers who like lavender products. Thanks to its flourishing business, several more branches of the farm have been established in the Taiwanese countryside.

Qinglin Farm in Guanyin Township, Taoyuan, has dozens of kinds of sunflowers from all over the world. In addition to viewing the blooms, visitors can also try special sunflower products created specially by the farm including tea, steamed rice, chicken with sunflower oil, and braised hock.

Another example is Bo's Farm, which is home to more than 20,000 insectivorous plants like pitcher plants, flytraps, sundews, and sarracenias. Visitors can learn the secrets of insect-eating plants under the guidance of farm commentators. Similarly, at the Binlang Phalaenopsis Farm, visitors can see various types of phalaenopsis collected from all over the world, witnessing the entire growing process from tissue culture cultivation of seedlings to beautiful blossoms. Along the same lines, the popular Flower Blossom Leisure Farm specializes in planting rare trees and exotic flowers and plants in a fresh, attractive environment.

(3) Ecological farms in Taiwan adjust measures to local conditions and innovate constantly, following the ideas of the philosopher Laozi in paying special attention to local characteristics and historical and cultural resources. They see great value in development measures that align with local conditions, and espouse the theory of letting nature take its course, imitating it, and conforming to its rule, rather than sticking to convention or copying the old farming model, certainly not relying on human or mechanical power to remake nature. In the building of ecological farms in Taiwan, people try their best to use local materials and turn them into "gold," so as to explore and manifest local specifics at minimum cost. Imagination, creativity, and innovation are also major features.

(4) Ecological farms in Taiwan feature refined construction and high quality. Most are "small but perfectly formed." They do not deliberately pursue area and scale, nor count how many crops they plant, nor how much yield they achieve, nor how large the batches of products are. Instead, they concentrate on fine management,

deep processing, the integration of creativity, and an improvement in quality. Some products are in limited supply, with small quantities but fine quality. Taiwanese farms pursue success through guaranteeing high quality and unique features. For example, some tea farms only pick one type of spring tea, and then process, prepare, and package it to make it the best of its kind. When not producing fine tea, the operators devote the rest of their time to management, allowing the tea trees to grow healthily, and preparing for the production of more high-quality spring varieties. Other farms use streams to breed ornamental fish like rainbow trout and diamond tetra. Visitors can buy food to feed the fish, and can enjoy them in their natural habitat, but they are not for sale. However, they are a huge draw for tourists. In this way, the farm maintains the lasting and significant vitality of the product, and also minimizes the consumption of resources and ensures good benefits. Its practice is very much in line with the fact that Taiwan is relatively small, mountainous, and not suitable for large-scale, mechanized farming. In contrast, the agricultural industry on the Mainland, in both mountainous areas and plains, is preoccupied with the area of coverage, amount of production, and output value as significant assessment indicators. The aim is always to grow bigger and stronger, favoring only large-scale farms and ignoring the practical benefits. In always trying to produce higher yields per unit area, they neglect the need for the soil to recuperate. In wanting to sell more products, they ignore the excessive consumption of resources and the possible pressure on the environment. In fact, these practices lack competitive advantage in mountainous areas, and are not conducive to sustainable development. Ecological farms in Taiwan can avoid competition by digging into their own specifics, exploiting their strengths, and avoiding their weaknesses. China will achieve resource-conservative and sustainable development by refining the building of farms and improving the quality and efficiency of production. This pathway is worthy of being considered and referenced by mountainous areas in similar situations.

(5) Ecological farms in Taiwan devote attention to word of mouth and local sales. Due to their small scale, they place great emphasis on word of mouth rather than the brand of their products, believing it to be more important. They therefore make more of an effort to ensure product quality and customer satisfaction. To guarantee that their products are safe and nutritious, they strictly control the use of chemical fertilizers, pesticides, and herbicides. They would rather increase input and sacrifice output to ensure the quality of their products. In order to offer products with the best flavor, many ecological farms in Taiwan open free of charge to tourists, to attract them to buy the freshest and ripest agricultural products. Ecological farms in Taiwan

are mostly located in remote suburbs, so they have to encourage tourists to make the trip. If they can sell their produce locally, the quality will be higher, and sales costs will be lower. For example, if tourists buy local eggs produced on the farm itself, the authenticity and freshness of the eggs can be ensured, and the transport, damage, and marketing costs accrued by the farm in bringing the eggs to the market can be saved. If eggs are labeled for export sales, they could go bad if stored improperly or for too long. If a product is passed several times from one hand to another, undergoing several steps in transport, the end consumer will blame any quality problems on the farm. If a brand is not well maintained and operated, years of accumulated public recognition will be destroyed. However, many enterprises on the Mainland now spend a great deal of money on advertising, creating a false reputation, building brands, and establishing images rather than concentrating on the quality of their products. They prefer to sell their products far away, preferably abroad, yet ignore the local market and neglect what lies close at hand.

(6) Ecological farms in Taiwan put emphasis on participation, and intertwine education with entertainment. They try to attract tourists to spend time, buy products, and enjoy services, and also participate and interact. Many farms are equipped with areas for fruit picking, barbecues, games, fishing, farming experiences, and crafts. With guidance from service staff, tourists can enjoy farming, operating, picking, feeding, and processing ingredients. They can bake their own sweet potato and roast chicken, or use the ingredients provided by the farm to process and make specific products. Some farms hold frequent lectures and competitions related to agriculture, and many schools regard them as outdoor teaching facilities. Families also go to farms for weekends away, keen to escape busy city life, relax, and enjoy being close to nature, learning things that cannot be taught in the city or classroom. That's why these farms are so popular.

b) Additional material

China's agricultural competitiveness is lagging by world standards: one jin (500 g) of every seven jin of grain is imported. On the one side are full granaries of domestic grain thanks to twelve consecutive years of increasing harvests; on the other side are more than 100 million tons of grain imported at low prices. The price inversion between China and abroad give prominence to the backward situation of China's agricultural competitiveness, and creates a strong impetus to adjust food policies. Statistics show that in the first 11 months of 2015, grain imports amounted to 113 million tons – an increase of 27.3% compared with the same period in 2014. For the second time in history, the number exceeded 100 million tons. In addition, China's total grain output in 2015 was 621 million tons, up 2.4% compared to the year 2014.

According to Chen Xiwen, the Deputy Leader and Office Director of the Central Rural Work Group, "The 13th Five-Year Plan has proposed new policies, such as experiments with crop rotation and the fallow system, as well as the implementation of grain storage on the land. When there is an oversupply of food, some land is left fallow to reduce the amount produced, and when there is a shortage of food, the land is quickly put back into use. Grain storage is governed by technology and strategy (i.e. the scientific use of arable land resources), which sends a signal to adjusting the current grain output."

Ma Wenfeng, an agricultural analyst at Eiger Agriculture, says, "It is fine to cut output, but not to reduce the area of arable land. It is up to the farmers themselves to choose whether to withdraw or not from grain cultivation." He adds, "Farmers will naturally plant less grain if they earn less, but we should not push forward grain reduction at the expense of farmers' interests."

According to the proportion of imported grain, one jin in every seven jin of grain in China comes from abroad. Soybeans make up more than 70%, and the rest mainly corn substitutes such as barley, sorghum, DDGS (dried distillers' grain and its solubles), and cassava. Aggressive imports impact domestic corn production and sales.

Treasury sales have been directly impacted by cheap import substitutions. The current state reserves of corn have an enterprise sales price of 1,400 yuan per ton, which is 0.7 yuan per jin, while the original purchasing price was about one yuan. Apart from the loss of storage charges, each ton of corn will have a loss of at least another 500 yuan.

What is inside the national treasury cannot get out, and what is outside the national treasury cannot get in. High grain stocks have exacerbated the difficulty of collecting grain in China. How tight is the storage capacity? The State Grain Administration reports an extraordinary situation: "China's grain stocks are currently at a new high. The amount of grain stored by various grain and oil storage enterprises is unprecedented, as is the amount of the state's policy-related grain stored in the open air and in simple storage facilities."

Chen Xiwen points out that the imports of corn substitutes such as barley, sorghum, DDGS, and cassava have severely impacted domestic sales of corn, causing overstocked commodities. This is the main problem that China's grain market is facing at present. Therefore, the question for the Chinese government and farmers is what measures can be taken to regulate domestic food prices in order to control the arbitrary increase of imported corn substitutes.

In the context of the twelve consecutive years of increasing harvests for the national grain output, some believe that a moderate reduction in grain output should be considered. What's more urgent is the necessity of adjusting the structure of grain production. The focus of grain production and reform should shift from the demand side to the supply side. When the supply side has excess yield, it is necessary to focus on the transition to a state of balance between grain supply and demand when adjusting the planting structure. Any adjustments and decelerations should not be excessive. At the same time, it is necessary to maintain intense effort and pace to tap into the new potential of grain production. The key point is to shift grain production from merely a growth in quantity to an overall growth in quantity, quality, and efficiency, moving away from relying on resources and material input to relying on scientific and technological progress and the improvement of the quality of the labor force.

Food shortage is a very serious issue because of the huge fluctuations experienced in the first two declines in food production. The first major fluctuation occurred in the 1980s, when grain production declined for four consecutive years until 1989, when it returned to pre-1984 levels. The second time, starting in 1999, food production fell until 2003, when it reached 430 million tons, and then, stimulated by a series of policies, it rebounded from 2004 until 2008, when it surpassed the 1998 level.

Chen Xiwen remarks, "It was like taking one step forward and two steps back. It took 10 years for grain production to recover. Based on the lesson of history, the Chinese government should be particularly cautious in adjusting its grain policy. The price-setting mechanism for grain, the subsidy policy for farmers, and the reform of grain storage policy should fully consider the interests of farmers to avoid another significant drop in grain output."

A third grain reduction reform has been revealed. "In fact, we have been considering grain production capacity for a long time – as far back as 2014, when the No. 1 document of 2015 was discussed," says an official from the Ministry of Agriculture. "Planting areas can be reduced, but production capacity still needs to be guaranteed through technological upgrades and land restoration."

(This additional material is from *National Business Daily*, and can be used as a reference for planning and designing farms in poor villages.)

2. The Xiaokang Institute's "Cadre Cultivation Program"

In the process of poverty alleviation and moving towards moderate prosperity (xiaokang), poor villages need a group of leaders who have the ability to develop the economy and a responsibility to serve villagers. These cadres should take the lead in becoming prosperous themselves, and then lead villagers to rise out of poverty. The cultivation of such personnel is an important component of alleviating poverty in all respects, and is achieved through the Xiaokang Institute's Cadre Cultivation Program. The following section will elaborate on the concept from the aspects of basic orientation, function, and value, as well as patterns and characteristics.

(I) The basic positioning of the Xiaokang Institute's Cadre Cultivation Program

General Secretary Xi Jinping stated in 2014 that the development of a poverty-stricken area depends on its internal driving force, and its development can only move forward with the combination of industry and labor forces. As mentioned above, farms are the basic organizational unit for the future development of poor villages, and are in effect a form of industry. There is now a need for labor, and for cadres who can lift poor people out of poverty and into prosperity. History tells us that to alleviate poverty in a sustained and comprehensive manner, the most important element is to support poverty alleviation cadres in poor villages.

The core task of the Xiaokang Institute's Cadre Cultivation Program is to train poverty alleviation cadres to work in poor villages, guided by the government and with the organizational support of social poverty alleviation associations and the "Golden Weaving" system.

a) Training target

The Xiaokang Institute aims to train poverty alleviation cadres in poor villages to become qualified farmers, farm owners, and "vendors." Cadres in poverty-stricken villages can be divided into two categories: members of the village Party branch committee and villagers' self-government committee (hereinafter referred to as the "two committees"), and those who are able to rise out of poverty and are willing to take on the responsibility of leading others towards a better life, such as the director-general of a specialized farmers' cooperative.

In eastern China, almost all candidates for the village committees are entrepreneurs with successful businesses. Many members of the two committees started out as entrepreneurs and later became village officials. However, the cadres in poor villages in western China are mostly not successful entrepreneurs. The rural collective economy is negligible. What's more, the village cadres themselves have restricted mindsets and ideas that lag behind. As a result, for a long time, poor villages have lacked leaders who understand the economy and management, making it difficult to form a strong team to boost economic development. Although governed by the villagers themselves, the rural areas (including the farms to be built in the future) are the foundation stone of the whole nation. For the Xiaokang Institute's Cadre Cultivation Program, the cultivation and education of the members of the two committees should come first. It is only when these members are motivated, energetic, and capable that they will be able to promote the collective economic development of the village and lead the poor villagers out of poverty and towards prosperity. Therefore, it is necessary to accelerate the cultivation of poverty alleviation cadres through the new-type training system at the Xiaokang Institute, contributing to the building of a moderately prosperous society.

The goal of the Xiaokang Institute is to enhance the sense of social responsibility and the sense of mission of poverty alleviation cadres in all poverty-stricken villages, enhancing their abilities in industrial development, business development, and leadership. The Institute also aims to become a new version of the historic Whampoa Military Academy, cultivating the main force of the battle against poverty alleviation in the last mile.

b) Training methods

The Xiaokang Institute's Cadre Cultivation Program is province based. It works with provincial poverty alleviation offices and local colleges (priority is given to local agricultural colleges) to establish local branches of the Institute. Participants must strictly follow the recommended selection process to ensure that the best candidates receive training.

• PARTICIPANT SELECTION PROCESS

Potential leaders of poverty-stricken villages are mainly recommended by the supporting enterprises, and the supporting enterprises are recommended by the local poverty alleviation offices together with the local agricultural committees, agricultural departments (bureaus), and organization departments. It should be noted that whether the selection of participants is accurate depends to a large extent on whether the supporting enterprises are responsible and whether the selection is precise and reasonable. Therefore, each local supporting enterprise should strengthen its organization and management so as to lay the foundation for the appropriate selection of trainees.

• Methods of cultivating leaders of poverty-stricken villages

To cultivate poverty-stricken village leaders, the Xiaokang Institute combines classroom education and development when they return to their hometowns. Both are given equal importance and promoted in parallel.

One strand of training is aimed at those who are interested in becoming farm owners. The training period is arranged according to the number of participants, distance, and structure. The training is divided into theoretical study, practical training in enterprises, and business planning.

Theoretical study involves trainees doing research at the Xiaokang Institute, while expanding their professional vision through communication with the supporting enterprises. They can also formulate business ideas and engage in entrepreneurship. There is also practical training in enterprises, in which participants attend actual training in enterprises with the intention of twinning support. Trainees gain a comprehensive and systematic understanding of the whole process of enterprise management, and clarify their own business projects.

For business planning, participants will return to the Xiaokang Institute to discuss and analyze the problems they encountered in their training. They will write and evaluate farm development plans under the guidance of their trainer and supporting enterprises. On completing intensive training, participants can also log on to the Xiaokang Institute's online system to receive regular and continuing distance education. After face-to-face training, the participants will return to their hometowns to start their own farms.

There are currently two development pathways for the participants, namely cooperation with supporting enterprises, and independent business development. These things have been elaborated in the implementation of the "Million Farms in Thousands of Counties and Ten Thousand Villages" plan, so will not be repeated here. Continuous supervision and evaluation are required. Participants should report the progress of their farms through the Xiaokang Institute's WeChat platform every month. During a certain period of development in their hometowns, they should make a mid-term summary report on their entrepreneurial projects, and then choose a time to make a year-end summary report. According to the actual development of farms in each region, the Xiaokang Institute will commend the participants who have performed exceptionally. Meanwhile, for those who wish to become "vendors," in addition to the above training, specialized courses also focus on e-commerce knowledge. The specific training methods are described below.

(II) The role and value of the Xiaokang Institute's Cadre Cultivation Program

At this new historical juncture, the opening year of the 13th Five-Year Plan and the first year in the war against poverty, the Xiaokang Institute's unprecedented Cadre Cultivation Program has far-reaching significance for today and for the future.

a) The reason for building the Xiaokang Institute

The author of this book was responsible for creating "Lectures for Chinese Village Cadres" (an advanced training course offered by Renmin University of China), and participated in the design of the "Training Project for Entrepreneurial Leaders in Poverty-stricken Villages" and the "Training Course for Entrepreneurial Volunteers (Mentors) in Poverty-stricken Villages" directed by the Poverty Alleviation Office of the State Council. He has also traveled widely to investigate the entrepreneurial practices of the participants after they return to their hometowns. On the whole, the participants often have ideas but no solutions, and many complementary conditions are not connected in an orderly manner. Although the national top-level design is a closed-loop design for the whole industrial chain, there are still gaps in the grassroots practice, and the participants still encounter problems of various kinds when they return to their hometowns. The need to solve these problems was the reason the Xiaokang Institute was built. It was designed closely around these issues, and the organizers and hosts will be the ones to address the problems. This way, development issues can be addressed in a very targeted manner, and development potential can be explored.

The main problems that need to be solved at present are:

- Insufficient material support in terms of capital, technology, and land

A lack of resources such as capital, technology, and land is a major constraint on the growth of cadres in poverty-stricken villages. Building farms and the promotion of industrialized agriculture business are signs of poverty alleviation and development in poverty-stricken villages, and is also a proven way for cadres to lead poor families out of poverty. To promote industrialization in villages, factors such as land and technology are crucial, and all these elements require financial support. A survey was conducted among 213 leaders of poverty-stricken villages. When asked to identify the biggest problem they or their group encountered in the process of starting a business, the top five most frequently selected factors were: lack of capital (58.9%); lack of human resources (27.8%); insufficient policy support (26.9%); lack of professional skills (26.3%); and lack of land and housing needed for starting a business (22.8%). This shows that the lack of material factors such as capital, technology, and land is a significant constraint to the development of cadres for poverty-stricken villages.

It is particularly noteworthy that the shortage of capital has become the biggest roadblock for cadres in poverty-stricken villages. According to the summary of the third session of the "Training Project for Entrepreneurial Leaders in Poverty-stricken Villages" directed by the Poverty Alleviation Office of the State Council, the difficulty of obtaining loans for business start-ups has been highlighted by the participants. The most crucial issue in the implementation of the "Million Farms in Thousands of Counties and Ten Thousand Villages" program is the availability of effective policy support and financial backing. The leaders of poverty-stricken villages often do not have the required collateral for bank loans, so they are unable to obtain them. As mentioned above, in 2014, the Poverty Alleviation Office of the State Council issued a document that declared plans to develop micro-credit and provide preferential financial policies for the development of industries by poor households with established records. Banks would provide unsecured credit loans of up to 50,000 yuan per household for a term of up to three years, and financial institutions would provide loans at the national benchmark interest rate, with subsidies for poverty alleviation from the central and provincial governments, as well as county-level risk compensation funds and micro-credit insurance for poverty alleviation. However, in practice, there is a lack of lubricant for linkages, and training institutions need to be involved.

- INSUFFICIENT SHARING OF SUPPORTIVE ENVIRONMENTAL FACTORS SUCH AS HUMAN
  RESOURCES AND ACCESS TO INFORMATION

Among the 213 leaders of poverty-stricken villages surveyed, 27.8% of them considered "lack of human resources" to be the most significant factor influencing their entrepreneurial development, ranking second only to "lack of capital." Modern society is geared towards sharing and win-win cooperation, and human resources – especially private enterprises with cooperative relationships – are of even greater significance to the poverty alleviation cadres. Since they have lived in the countryside for a long time, leaders in poverty-stricken villages have a relatively weak hold over human and information resources, and these resources are precisely the crucial references for making major decisions about the scale of their farms and the weight of their investments. This calls for a training platform to pair them up.

• LACK OF EDUCATION, VOCATIONAL SKILLS, AND MANAGEMENT SKILLS

It is no longer enough for the leaders of poverty-stricken villages to possess simple agricultural abilities such as performing manual labor all day in the fields. It is more important that they have vocational agricultural skills and modern management ability in order to adapt the existing factors and forms of production in order to gain more opportunities for development. According to the data, the urban-rural dichotomy determines the huge education gap between urban and rural areas, the insufficient and unbalanced investment in rural basic education, as well as the marginalization of the education of the migrant population (mainly migrant workers and their accompanying children). As a consequence, the education level of cadres in poverty-stricken villages is generally low, with most having only junior high school or high school education, and only very few having received higher education (college degree, bachelor degree or above). Low education levels, lack of vocational skills, and weak management ability will certainly limit their capacity to lift the poor out of poverty. Using certain examples, it is possible to identify that most leaders of poverty-stricken villages are aware of and regret their lack of knowledge. Due to their own lack of comprehensive abilities, they have paid a lot of "school fees" and taken a lot of detours in the development of poverty-stricken villages. All of this determines the real space for the Xiaokang Institute to cultivate leaders of poverty-stricken villages.

b) The current and long-term value of the Xiaokang Institute

Currently, the Xiaokang Institute is an effective vehicle for solving the shortage of intellectual factors in poverty-stricken villages. In the long run, it will help to adjust the personnel structure in rural areas and help to consolidate and expand the Party's governing base in rural areas, which is of both practical and long-term significance.

(1) The Xiaokang Institute is a cradle for nurturing poverty-stricken villages to rise out of poverty and become prosperous. In the 13th Five-Year Plan period, the pace of poverty eradication in China has accelerated significantly, and there are unprecedented demands on the capacities of leaders of poverty-stricken villages. Working on the front line, these leaders are the most important actors in the fight against poverty, acting as a bellwether to activate the internal power of poverty-stricken villages. The Xiaokang Institute was created to focus on their development needs, providing them with tailor-made training courses, and creating an appropriate environment for them to earn money when they return to their hometowns. In this case, it is possible to fully unlock the function and value of poverty alleviation policies, which will ensure that poverty-stricken villages rise out of poverty and become prosperous.

(2) The Xiaokang Institute is a significant tool for winning the battle against poverty. The "Decision of the CPC Central Committee and the State Council on Winning the Fight Against Poverty" states plans to:

Increase the implementation of vocational skills through developing plans as well as education and training projects for poor households; guide enterprises to combine poverty alleviation with vocational education; encourage vocational colleges and technical schools to recruit students from poor households; ensure that workers from poor households acquire at least one skill to become wealthy, so as to alleviate poverty successfully by practicing skills.

From an external perspective, the key to poverty alleviation in poverty-stricken villages is to increase investment and work on the principle of giving more. From an internal perspective, the key lies in following a people-oriented approach, focusing on the development of human resources in poverty-stricken villages, and cultivating a group of leaders in poor villages with proper knowledge and skills and strong moral compasses. As the most passionate, energetic, and hopeful people in poverty-stricken villages, these leaders must be cultivated as a matter of national importance in order to win the war against poverty. The building of the Xiaokang Institute is in line with this need for training, and will serve as a powerful tool for the government to train leaders to become educated, skilled, good at running businesses, and strong in management, so as to contribute to leading people out of poverty and into a moderately prosperous society.

(3) The Xiaokang Institute is an effective way to consolidate and expand the Party's governing foundation. Nowadays, in disadvantaged villages, most young people who are able to work will leave to find jobs elsewhere. Those who remain are mostly women, children, the elderly, and the disabled. In addition, since China's industrialization, the dualistic social structure of emphasizing the city over the countryside and labor over agriculture has influenced the overall mentality. Young adults who stay in disadvantaged villages are often labeled as losers. To rise out of poverty and become wealthy is the most typical, actual, and urgent need of the people who stay in poor villages. The establishment of the Xiaokang Institute caters to the demands of these young people who are unwilling to accept the status quo and are keen to earn money. The Institute offers training platforms to help them start their own businesses, and provides support to cultivate their vocational and entrepreneurial skills so that they can become leaders in poverty-stricken villages and fulfill their ambitions in life. By training the leaders of disadvantaged villages to

alleviate poverty and promote prosperity, the Xiaokang Institute will help young and middle-aged people to stay in villages and develop local advantages. This is of great significance to the consolidation and expansion of the Party's governing foundation in poverty-stricken villages.

(III) The model and characteristics of the Xiaokang Institute

The Xiaokang Institute is led by the government and implemented by a combination of the financial system and social poverty alleviation organizations. It is specifically envisaged that it will be guided by the Poverty Alleviation Office of the State Council, co-run by the China Association for the Promotion of Voluntary Services for Poverty Alleviation, the China Development Bank, and the Agricultural Development Bank, and hosted by local poverty alleviation offices and local universities and colleges.

a) The model for the Xiaokang Institute
The Xiaokang Institute is structured according to the "headquarters + branch" model (see diagram below). The main institute is located in Beijing, and operates

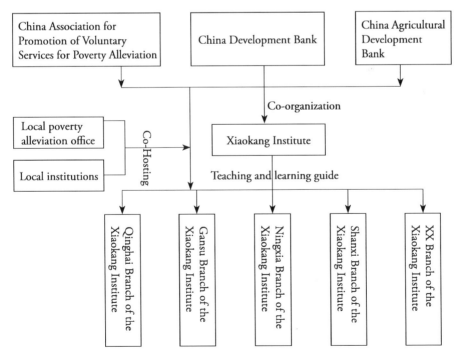

Structure of the Xiaokang Institute

under the direct guidance of the Poverty Alleviation Office of the State Council. The branches are set up in accordance with the distribution of poverty-stricken areas and the cultivation needs of each province, district, and city. In principle, there is no subordinate relationship between the main institute and the branch institutes, but rather one of teaching and guidance. The main institute can adjust the teaching materials according to the situation and provide services to promote the development of teaching and training. The branch institutes are set up with the support of local universities, and the teaching is provided by schools.

The teaching at the Xiaokang Institute is closely aligned with the development needs of the participants, offering online and offline, home-based and localized teaching content, through the tripartite "face-to-face + internet + mobile" format. This allows participants to carry their course with them so that they can learn at any time and anywhere, while providing a diversified and exclusive interactive platform for constant communication.

b) Basic features of the Xiaokang Institute

Firstly, in terms of the authority of the organizational structure, the original purposes of establishing the Xiaokang Institute were to closely integrate the development demands of the participants and to unite the various departments and institutions responsible for production factors to participate in training, so as to promote education and development. The trainees are leaders of disadvantaged villages – the main force in the building of farms – and this in itself requires help from the government, the financial sectors, social organizations, and institutions. Therefore, the Xiaokang Institute comes under the overall guidance of the Poverty Alleviation Office of the State Council, with the China Association for the Promotion of Voluntary Services for Poverty Alleviation, the China Development Bank, and the China Agricultural Development Bank as the organizers, and local poverty alleviation offices and local universities as the hosts, giving it the authority it deserves.

Secondly, the courses are designed to be highly practical. The curriculum is divided into two categories: public courses and specialized courses. The public courses focus on the general policies of the country to combat poverty, while the specialized courses fully reflect the specific requirements of the participants' development, and focus on practicality.

Thirdly, as for the flexibility of teaching practice, during the training period, offline activities can be held on campus, such as communication and matching forums for project ideas, and design competitions for entrepreneurial projects. While online, students can learn to participate in e-commerce sales by promoting local high-quality agricultural products through WeChat circles, QQ groups, or on information service platforms such as Farm Box and No. 1 Shop for Poverty Alleviation, ensuring flexibility in online and offline teaching practice.

Fourthly, to ensure the precision of industry matching, the Xiaokang Institute insists on the principle that class teaching and development practice are of equal importance, but places more emphasis on practice. The training is closely integrated with the participants' farm development plans, and provides precise help to match them with the leading enterprises in the fields of planting and breeding.

3. The "Trillion-yuan Financial Policy Dividend Program"

The author has taught the equation of poverty alleviation through industry on many occasions, and believes it to be applicable:

$$f \text{ (poverty alleviation through industry)} = a \text{ (project)} + b \text{ (staff)} + c \text{ (funds)} + d \text{ (market)}$$

Alleviation that relies on industrial development is the leading measure in the battle against poverty, and among its many elements, the core is capital. The "Trillion-yuan Financial Policy Dividend Program" uses the national financial support policy for poverty alleviation to solve the bottleneck of capital in order to realize poverty alleviation and development. The essence of this program is to design a PPP (public-private-partnership) model, that is, a model for the cooperation of government-social capital. With the leverage of the government's financial policy, it is possible to stimulate more social capital to participate in poverty alleviation. The "Decision of the CPC Central Committee and the State Council on Winning the Fight Against Poverty" states: "Play the main and leading role of government investment in poverty alleviation and development, and open up new funding channels for poverty alleviation and development, ensuring that the government investment in poverty alleviation is commensurate with the task of poverty alleviation and development." It is certain that in the next five years, the government will release huge financial policy dividends in the field of poverty alleviation, which will create the ideal environment for social capital development. This is the policy basis for the design of the "Trillion-yuan Financial Policy Dividend Program."

(I) Design principles of the "Trillion-yuan Financial Policy Dividend Program"

To truly play the role of financial policy in supporting the economic development of especially disadvantaged areas, it is necessary to learn from the lessons of past financial poverty alleviation projects, and carry out systematic and reasonable program design, in order to profit and avoid making the same mistakes.

a) Market-based promotion

This involves using market-based approaches to alleviate poverty with state funds. In the past, the state financial funds for poverty alleviation have often adopted approaches such as policy-based support and unconditional one-off investments, since there was no concern about cost. The situation led to many local governments falsifying and siphoning off state funds for poverty alleviation. The implementation of market-based promotion means that the design and operation of the "Trillion-yuan Financial Policy Dividend Program" enables the use of market-based approaches to poverty alleviation with state funds. By adopting conditional funding approaches, financial institutions can pursue profits while improving the living standards of the poor through market-oriented methods, ensuring the effectiveness of the investment of national financial resources.

b) Activating the initiative

This means that the national financial resources for poverty alleviation should be conducive to sparking the motivation of the poverty alleviation target. It is a two-way relationship between those who help the poor and those who are helped. Only when both ends are active can good results be achieved. Through the design and operation of the "Trillion-yuan Financial Policy Dividend Program," it is possible to change the situation in which only the government is active, avoiding poor households' expectation of waiting, relying on others, and asking for help, while leveraging the initiative of the poverty alleviation target. At the same time, through the Xiaokang Institute's training and cultivation program, it is possible to consistently improve the self-development ability of the disadvantaged areas and achieve stable poverty alleviation and development.

c) Insisting on precise matching

This refers to the point-to-point operation of national financial funds for poverty alleviation. Through the design and operation of the "Trillion-yuan Financial Policy Dividend Program," the effectiveness and precision of poverty alleviation can be improved by changing the former diffusion of state financial resources to help the poor. In the implementation of the financial policy dividend program, financial institutions select customers through effective targeting, and then provide corresponding financial services according to need. Through the person-to-person and peer-to-peer operation mode, input costs are saved and lifting truly impoverished families out of poverty is achieved.

d) Government-led development

This means that the operation of national financial funds for poverty alleviation is conducive to two-way development in both supporting advantageous industries and helping leading enterprises in disadvantaged areas. Through the design and operation of the "Trillion-yuan Financial Policy Dividend Program," the financing channels of advantageous industries can be broadened, and through the advantage of capital and effective credit system, strong support can be provided for the industrialization of disadvantaged areas. This way, the investment of national financial funds for poverty alleviation can help the development of farms, create more employment opportunities, and fully exploit the development of local industries with specific advantages, achieving the goal of fundamentally eliminating poverty.

(II) Top-level design of the "Trillion-yuan Financial Policy Dividend Program"

The top-level design of the program mainly gives macro guidance on the absorption and operation of the financial investment. The financial system for poverty alleviation will be set up through the implementation of this program. The function of policy finance, commercial finance, cooperative finance, and government coordination will be fully utilized.

a) The scale of the "Trillion-yuan Financial Policy Dividend Program"

At the national level, there are two agreements projects. The first is the "Agreement on Cooperation in Development Finance for Poverty Alleviation" signed between the Poverty Alleviation Office of the State Council and China Development Bank on May 16, 2015, which explicitly grants 1.7 trillion yuan of loans for poverty alleviation to 592 national major poverty-stricken counties. The second is the "Policy-based Finance for Poverty Alleviation Cooperation Agreement" signed between the Agricultural Development Bank of China and the Poverty Alleviation Office of the State Council on September 8, 2015, which specifies that the cumulative credit allocation for poverty alleviation should not be less than two trillion yuan. The financial scale of these two agreements amounts to nearly four trillion yuan. These four trillion policy-based poverty alleviation funds will release huge dividends.

b) Investment of the "Trillion-yuan Financial Policy Dividend Program"

(1) According to the planning and arrangement of the Poverty Alleviation Office of the State Council, the China Development Bank will increase financial support for poverty alleviation in four aspects:

First is the development of specific industries, focusing specifically on rural planting, breeding, ethnic handicrafts, the processing of agricultural products, and tourism. Leading enterprises and rural cooperative organizations will be strongly supported.

Second is the improvement of infrastructure, including small projects such as safe drinking water, farmland water conservation, rural roads, and health care systems, as well as the rebuilding of dilapidated houses in poverty-stricken villages, relocation projects, and the construction of new towns in poor areas.

Third is the development of education, supporting two kinds of poor students (laborers from poor families who graduated from junior and senior high school and failed to continue their education) in vocational education and starting a business after graduation, and expanding the coverage of student loans.

Fourth is the creation of major projects, mainly key projects in line with national development planning as well as the industrial and environmental protection policies.

(2) According to the planning and arrangement of the Poverty Alleviation Office of the State Council, the China Agricultural Development Bank will increase financial support for poverty alleviation in the following four aspects:

First is poverty alleviation through relocation. Policy credit support will be provided for the relocation of impoverished people who have established a record, including the building or purchase of housing for poverty alleviation and other supporting facilities directly related to the relocation of the poor, such as the building of infrastructure and public services.

Second is establishing photovoltaic power stations, focusing on supporting the building of ground photovoltaic power plants using barren mountains and slopes in poor counties with good conditions for developing the photovoltaic industry, and construct small village-level power plants in counties with conditions that suit the development of photovoltaic power generation.

Third is the development of tourism, focusing on supporting 1,000 scenic spots and their major surrounding villages to alleviate poverty, helping these poor villages and households to alleviate poverty and become prosperous.

Fourth is the development of infrastructure in poverty-stricken areas, focusing on supporting the building of environmental facilities, public service facilities, supporting convenient commercial facilities, and new urbanization in poverty-stricken areas.

c) The application of the "Trillion-yuan Financial Policy Dividend Program"

The "Trillion-yuan Financial Policy" is a huge dividend pool. The purpose of the "Trillion-yuan Financial Policy Dividend Program" is to ensure that this huge dividend pool works effectively. The first step is to build an industrial information platform for poverty alleviation in conjunction with the talent cultivation program at the Xiaokang Institute, so that information on the building of farms and industrial development needs will be shared in disadvantaged villages. Moreover, information should be shared on the advantages and intentions between supported enterprises, providing links to policies and financial support for poverty alleviation for supported enterprises. Secondly, through the training of leaders in disadvantaged villages and volunteers in poverty alleviation enterprises, China implements hand-in-hand industrial poverty alleviation design, so as to achieve more accurate capital application, ensure the investment efficiency of poverty alleviation enterprises, and reduce the investment risk of national policy finance. Thirdly, through follow-up support after the training of leaders in disadvantaged villages and volunteers at poverty alleviation enterprises, the operation of industrial projects of poverty alleviation will be evaluated in a timely manner to avoid the misappropriation of national poverty alleviation funds and to ensure the healthy development of industrial projects of poverty alleviation.

d) Financial prevention within the "Trillion-Yuan Financial Policy"

Poverty alleviation funds have been described in Chinese as "the flesh of a Tang Dynasty monk," (i.e. a large bonus or benefit that is pursued at any cost), firstly because it is good to eat, and secondly because it is difficult to supervise. From a horizontal perspective, poverty alleviation funds come from too many sources and are managed by multiple departments, often involving departments and units such as the Ministry of Finance, the Development and Reform Commission, the Poverty Alleviation Office, the People's Committee, the Forestry Department, the Department of Agriculture, and the Federation of the Disabled. These departments are not subordinate to each other, and information is not mutually available, so it is difficult for them to monitor each other. From a vertical perspective, the authority of approval for poverty alleviation projects is decentralized to each county, and the provincial and municipal government departments are responsible for supervision. However, some of the national poverty alleviation funds require local finance departments to offer a certain amount of matching funds, and some simply cannot afford it. If there are no matching funds after the special funds come down, in order to complete the project, local governments have no choice but to make false matches. In these cases, some departments tend to have city- and county-wide collusion at the upper and lower levels, and supervision is in name only.

In reality, the most effective way to eliminate corruption is to conduct supervisory audits, but this has shortcomings of its own. Audit supervision often comes after the fact, and although evidence of the use of funds is easy to obtain, when it comes to project establishment and fund allocation, it is often difficult to obtain detailed and complete first-hand information. It is difficult to prevent in advance and correct in a timely manner. The low cost of breaking the law also makes many people desperate enough to take risks.

If the difficulty of supervision is the systemic reason why poverty alleviation funds are often diverted and misappropriated, then the low cost of breaking laws makes many people unscrupulous. According to the 2011 "Measures for the Administration of Special Fiscal Funds for Poverty Alleviation," civil servants who misrepresented, fraudulently claimed, intercepted, and squandered special fiscal funds for poverty alleviation will be punished according to the "Regulations on Penalties and Punishments for Financial Violations." The punishment decreed by this regulation is to return the fiscal funds and illegal proceeds within a certain period of time, and the organization at which the violator works will be given a warning or notification of criticism. The supervisors and personnel who are directly responsible within the organization should be marked with a major demerit; in more serious cases, they should be punished with demotion or dismissal. When the violation is flagrant, they will be punished directly with dismissal.

These abovementioned acts constitute crimes, and the violator will be held criminally liable, but on the whole, the intensity of the punishment does not stop some officials trying to misuse poverty alleviation funds illegally. Ouyang Weihong, Director of the Second Division of the Commissioner's Office of the Ministry of Finance in Hubei Province, has said that those who embezzle national poverty alleviation funds should be sent to the judiciary for serious punishment, but this is not the case in reality. Some local officials protect each other, so the punishment is lighter than it should be. Some departments even deal with these cases only with a comment such as "Never again," and reduce penalties. Many departments even take merely writing a self-criticism letter as a form of administrative punishment. Some serious offenders are not referred to the judiciary for investigation and punishment. These punishments hardly serve as a proper warning, and the economic penalty for individuals is not very high. These shortcomings are the factors that the "Trillion-yuan Financial Policy Dividend Program" tries to avoid.

(III) *The need for government support in the "Trillion-yuan Financial Policy Dividend Program"*

The implementation of the "Trillion-yuan Financial Policy Dividend Program" requires the resolution of information asymmetry for financial institutions. This is the condition for appealing to the government for support. To study this more closely, we first set the basic symbols and assumptions:

1. Assume that poor households face inter-period choices between the present and the future, defined as $t = 1, 2$, the consumption in period 1 and period 2 are defined respectively as c_1 and c_2, and the time discount rate is set to 0 for the purpose of the study. The utility function of poor households can be expressed as: $U = U'(c_1) + U''(c_2)$, where $U' > 0$, $U'' < 0$.

2. Assume that the income that poor households can obtain in periods 1 and 2 is y_t, which consists of two components: constant base income y_b and variable temporary income e_t, and $e_1 = -e_2$.

An increase in current income will reduce the same income in a future period. Changes in the income of poor households due to certain factors in the present will be counteracted by the opposite effect in a future period, leading to changes in the opposite direction, thus completely offsetting the effects in the present. Without considering the effect of the time-discounting factor, it can be assumed that half of the shocks and impacts of poor households occur in the present and the other half occur in a future period, and such shocks and impacts follow a $[0, 1]$ distribution. When there is no financial institution, poor households lack access to savings and borrowing, and the utility function of these households is:

$$Ue = U'(y_b + e) + U''(\bar{y} - e)$$

When financial institutions exist to provide credit services, poor households are positively influenced and can use them to save their increased income. Poor households that suffer a negative impact can receive loan support. Financial institutions charge poor households a fixed service fee (f) to cover the fixed costs of doing business. The poor household makes a choice according to the magnitude of the impact (e) and the service fee (f), decreasing consumption (s) in period 1 and increasing consumption (s) in period 2. The utility function of poor households becomes:

$$U = U' (\bar{y} + e - s - f) + U'' (y_b - e + s - f)$$

This equation shows that the optimal choice for an individual poor household is when s can fully offset e. Thus, the overall utility function of every impoverished household participating in the financial system is:

$$U = 2U (\bar{y} - f)$$

An impoverished household will choose to bear the fixed cost only if it observes that it is likely to be affected by a large influence and impact, otherwise it will choose not to participate in money lending to avoid bearing the service fee. Therefore, when the fixed service fee (f) is certain, there is a threshold of impact (e*), and only poor households with influence and impact greater than the threshold (e*) will choose to participate in money lending.

$$U' (\bar{y} + e^*) + U'' (\bar{y} - e^*) = 2U (\bar{y} - f)$$

In the first case, the government does not support financial institutions, but instead provides direct financial support to poor households, thus increasing their basic income (y_b). Since the government does not know the specific situation of each poor household, it is difficult to distribute funds to those who are most in need. In the second case, the government supports financial institutions through means such as financial subsidies and tax incentives. This will compensate for some of the fixed costs of financial institutions and reduce the transaction costs in the operation process.

The mathematical model analysis shows that due to the information asymmetry and transaction costs in the real-life credit market, the government cannot know exactly when and how poor households are affected by external shocks, so direct financial support to the poor households often cannot optimize their consumption and production across time. In the context of poverty eradication, the government supports financial institutions to reduce transaction costs and to serve poor households more effectively. This indirect financial approach is more efficient than directly supporting the poor households.

4. The "Social Action Plan for Poverty Relief Through Consumption"

This plan aims at alleviating poverty through promoting consumption at a social scale with a scientific design. This includes the design of consumer goods in poor areas and the design of consumer paths to promote the participation of the whole society in poverty alleviation through consumption.

(I) The implication and essence of poverty alleviation through consumption

As soon as human beings became aware of using and consuming materials, the process of consumption began. Consumption accompanies us from birth all the way to death. People are not born producers, but they are consumers at birth. Within the socialist market economy system, the essence of consumption has exceeded possessing goods, using materials, and enjoying services to a significant link between economic, cultural, and social activities. In regard to poverty relief, the means of consumption can lead poor people towards prosperity, embody the culture of consumption, and promote traditional culture.

a) The implication of poverty alleviation through consumption

In China, the word "consumption" first appeared in the Han Dynasty. No society has been able to stop consumption at any time. The essence of it is to use and consume natural resources and artificial materials to meet people's needs. Poverty relief through consumption – in other words, consumption with regard to relieving poverty – differs from other forms mostly in that it involves quality agricultural products from concentrated poor areas, such as high-quality meat, eggs, fish, and shrimp products. Consumers buy whatever they need in a customized way to help poor families make money.

There is a distinction between production consumption and personal consumption (or living consumption), and the same distinction can be made between consumption and poverty alleviation. The future layout of China's rural areas will be a combination of urban communities and farms. The agricultural products produced by farms are either needed for daily life or for the reproduction of raw materials by enterprises and other market players, which are in turn needed for production. Regardless of needs, the primary concern of consumption for poverty relief is to promote the concept of win-win or multi-win, rather than just giving charity. Agricultural and sideline products from poor areas have great potential for exploitation and economic benefits. At the same time, people's desire to consume agricultural and sideline products from poor areas is not only limited to the functional value of the products themselves, but also a sense of responsibility for social poverty alleviation and a desire to be recognized by society.

b) Poverty relief through consumption

This can be condensed into several segments: businesses into villages; managers into households; pairs into groups; and mutual aid. Businesses into villages refers to the aforementioned farm plan, which maps out businesses to bring advanced production methods and business models to promote sustainable economic development in poor areas. Managers into households refers to the use of a consumption concept that advocates for consumers (managers) to connect directly with poor villagers without the interference of middlemen.

Pairing into groups emphasizes targeted, one-to-one poverty relief that can foster the development of a whole area. Mutual aid refers to help between consumers and farmers that benefits both parties by bringing health into cities and wealth into villages.

(II) The attributes and features of poverty alleviation through consumption

As well as being a form of consumption, poverty alleviation through consumption is a new social relationship and a cultural form that has its own attributes and features.

a) The attributes of poverty alleviation through consumption

The national aim of building a moderately prosperous society through poverty alleviation makes poverty alleviation through consumption a social activity with multiple attributes that combine economic, social, and cultural aspects.

First are economic attributes. Marx wrote in his *Introduction to the Critique of Political Economy* that "consumption creates the power of production." The emergence of a new consumption point or hotspot can often boost or even revitalize the development of a certain or several corresponding industries. Similarly, if the agricultural products of a poor area become a consumption hotspot, it will revitalize local industries, help poor families, offer job opportunities, and increase income levels. The economic attributes of poverty alleviation through consumption should come first for poor areas.

Second are social attributes. The biggest distinction between humans and animals is that humans have social attributes. People buy products from poor areas both as a natural act and as a social process of helping others. People buy things according to their own preferences in terms of aesthetics and taste, which means they help different providers of such products accordingly.

Third are cultural attributes. In some sense, poverty alleviation through consumption is a form of culture. In modern societies, people's consumption of farm products from poor areas is likely to raise the income of several impoverished families. As increasing numbers of social groups take part in such consumption, they form a cultural phenomenon that will contribute to national poverty relief. These distinctive farm products are important carriers of culture, and can even become symbols of specific meanings that people accept or express.

b) General features of poverty alleviation through consumption

On November 23, 2015, the State Council issued the "Opinion on Promoting the Leading Role of New Consumption and Accelerating the Cultivation of New Supply and New Impetus" (abbreviated to the "Opinion"). It emphasizes the fact that the Chinese consumption structure is undergoing profound changes. Consumption upgrades consisting mostly of new hotspots and modes will lead to the rapid growth of corresponding industries, infrastructure, and public service investments, and will explore new territories in the future. The "Opinion" makes it clear that the six areas of consumption (service, information, green products, fashion, and quality) will be major domains and directions of the overall consumption upgrade.

Since China entered the new era, its national economy has grown fast, its people have gained a solid material foundation, and its fields of consumption have continued to expand. Its consumption ability has significantly increased, and its consumption mode is undergoing changes. Poverty relief through consumption will certainly create new consumption hotspots, and they will have the following features:

First, consumption tends to be customized. Modern society offers a wide range of commodities, and is more open and tolerant than before. People generally have more freedom and equality compared with the strict uniformity of the past. People pursue individuality, and they buy products according to their own tastes to demonstrate their understanding and support of the concept of poverty relief. Especially in the critical period of poverty alleviation, now and within the next five years, poverty alleviation through consumption will be a mainstream strategy for people to support it while gaining recognition for their self-identity. Modern society appeals for people to recognize the concept of poverty alleviation through consumption, and calls for individualized, customized consumption. The world's richest people are rich in the same way, while poor people are poor in different ways. It is this difference that laid the foundation for customization.

Second, the consumption model is innovative. Poverty relief through consumption involves high-quality agricultural specialties from poor areas. However, the immaturity of infrastructure in poor areas regarding water, electricity, roads, and networks poses great challenges to meeting the needs of consumers. Poverty relief through consumption needs to address this problem in an innovative way to reduce intermediate processes and ensure product quality to help increase the income of poor families.

Third, consumer demand is becoming more diversified. Nowadays, when materials are extremely abundant, people consume both for survival and for higher pursuits. Their desire for safe and healthy consumption, and the sense of accomplishment, belonging, and identity brought about by consumption have become significant contents and formats of consumption today. In the past, most urban consumption was of food, while at present it is more of enjoyment. For example, people buy rural houses, and family farms, and attend fruit-picking festivals. Needs that differ from cities to countryside, from east to west, and from the coast to inland areas put forward higher demands on agricultural products of poor areas, namely distinction, high quality, and shortage.

Fourth, consumption is multi-leveled, since income and consumption levels differ among ethnic groups and regions. Differences in ethnicity, region, income, age, sex, and education level result in a divergence in consumption needs. In turn, these differences lead to different habits of poverty alleviation through consumption accordingly.

Fifth is the aestheticization of consumption. People today care both for the use-value of goods and their symbolic value. Goods from poverty-stricken areas have labels like "organic" and "nutritious." Buying such products increases people's moral merits by contributing to the country's poverty alleviation through consumption plan. Poverty relief through consumption enables consumers to obtain aesthetic and emotional enjoyment, happiness, satisfaction of needs, and the realization of their imagination.

(III) Pathways and attempts at poverty relief through consumption

There are various pathways for poverty alleviation through consumption, including online and offline practices. Online practice combines e-commerce with poverty relief, building a large e-commerce platform called "Tian Box." Offline practice has platforms such as the "Agricultural Carnival Marketplace Festival." Whether it is online or offline, hand-in-hand poverty alleviation through consumption is the basic pathway.

a) Hand-in-hand poverty alleviation through consumption

Poverty relief through consumption is a social action that calls for successful cooperation between consumers and poor households, precise connection, reduced intermediate processes, and education that satisfies individual consumer requirements.

On the afternoon of October 16, 2015, the 2015 High-level Forum on Poverty Reduction and Development, and Rural Development took place as scheduled at the Beijing International Hotel Convention Center. The forum was hosted by the Forum Organizing Committee and co-organized by the Policy and Regulations Department of the Poverty Alleviation Office of the State Council and the China Association for the Promotion of Voluntary Services to Alleviate Poverty. The main purpose of this forum was to help the poor take action. Liu Yongfu, Director of the Poverty Alleviation Office of the State Council, visited the forum and led the signing ceremony for poverty alleviation enterprises and villages. Outstanding enterprises

Launch ceremony for the Hand-in-Hand Action for Poverty Relief

such as Beijing Juchayuan Network Technology Co., Ltd. and Lingyang Street Village Enterprise Group from Ju County in Shandong Province signed 12 "Paired Assistance Agreements" on site. According to preliminary predictions, these agreements are expected to benefit more than 20,000 poor families as a poverty alleviation project.

b) Juchayuan's innovative attempts to help the poor

Among the contracted assistance projects, Beijing Juchayuan Network Technology Co., Ltd. (hereinafter referred to as "Juchayuan") connects tea plantations worldwide to benefit millions of tea farmers. The company makes use of the Internet to connect tea farmers with factories and consumers, providing substantial assistance. At present, Juchayuan has completed the first phase of a 3,000-mu tea plantation, with an average income of 3000–6000 yuan per mu (666.7 m^2), which can help more than 2,000 poor families rise out of poverty.

There are 14 concentrated and contiguous poverty-stricken mountainous areas in China, of which 11 mainly grow tea. Nearly 50% (or about 276) of the national key poverty-stricken counties are located in the eight major tea-producing areas. Juchayuan's CEO Wang Xiaotian and his team recognized a problem: the main reason why tea farmers are poor in the mountains is that their best tea is trapped there and cannot be sold at good prices. Tea farmers have no time for branding, nor do they promote their tea. They can only sell hard-planted tea to dealers at a low price. The dealers ask for more from customers, who have to pay for middlemen.

To solve this problem, Wang Xiaotian's team acted quickly and established Juchayuan, which was fortunate to be the first poverty alleviation through consumption project in the hand-in-hand action scheme. Operating under the concept that one should not refrain from good deeds just because they are insignificant, the Juchayuan method helps tea farmers rise out of poverty by encouraging the consumption of tea from confirmed poor areas.

Juchayuan has gathered resources from all sides to help the poor, with the support of the Poverty Alleviation Office of the State Council, the guidance of the Institute of Rural Development of Renmin University of China, and the help of industry leaders in brand planning and Internet brand promotion. It integrates the tea industry of 276 national key poverty-stricken counties, and sets up "tea shops" at the county level, backed by 128,000 village-based teams in poor areas to maintain progress. It invites tea experts and marketing executives to make plans for local tea development and establish local brands. As a fair trading platform, Juchayuan relies on the innovative model of "poverty relief + Internet + tea," connecting tea plantations all over the country, and benefiting millions of tea farmers in the process. It aims to increase tea farmers' income, reduce the burden for the public, and enable everyone to drink good tea at a reasonable price.

As of 2013, there were more than 37 million mu of tea plantations in the country. The output of tea that year was more than two million tons, worth more than 300 billion yuan, of which poverty-stricken areas accounted for nearly half. China's tea market has huge potential, and yet tea farmers are generally poor. According to statistics, in 2013, the output value of tea plantations per mu in China was only 3,489 yuan. Tea farmers got even less, with most of the money going to middlemen. Consumers have to pay extra for tea. The Juchayuan consumption model allows the sales of one mu of a tea garden to effectively help a household get out of poverty. One person buys one jin, and one hundred people help one household. Juchayuan also encourages people to subscribe to tea plantations and give tea farmers a modest income. It integrates tea resources and designs tea plantations of different sizes for people to subscribe to. Buying three tea bushes can help the poor, and buying one mu of a tea plantation can help a tea farmer rise out of poverty. Juchayuan fixes the price with the "tea price = tea leaves purchase price + frying cost + packaging" formula, using the Internet model for the public, but also to benefit tea farmers. People only need to pay a minimum of 50 yuan to subscribe to a tea plantation. As a fair trade, tea farmers give them high-quality tea.

The contribution of Juchayuan's hand-in-hand poverty alleviation model lies in the connecting of quality and low cost. Juchayuan is free to use for farmers, which is useful since tea farmers in poor areas generally lack brand awareness, and the ability to integrate the marketing resources of all parties is low. Tea farmers on their own are weak in the market. Juchayuan is based on local tea houses, and relies on village-based groups to recommend reliable, high-quality tea factories. The tea factories purchase high-quality greens from the tea farmers in the surrounding areas, and follow the market. Each tea farmer has a file and card that include the members of his or her family, the previous year's annual income, the size of the plantation, the annual output, and annual tea-green income. Every transaction between the tea farmer and the factory is recorded, and annual information is written down. The data is published on Juchayuan's official website. Tea farmers strictly follow the poverty relief guide, planting, fertilizing, and picking the tea. Tea greens that do not meet the requirements will be recorded in the farmer's file. After two negative incidents, the farmer will be put on a blacklist. Each batch of finished tea is sent for quality inspection, and will be archived. Tea experts go on secret visits to spot test each procedure before, during, and after delivery to ensure quality. The tea farmers' identity files make it easy to monitor the quality of finished tea and trace the origin.

They also help village-based teams, poverty alleviation offices, and agricultural bureaus to collect data. The franchising and selection of tea factories also follow a set of processes that prioritize quality and production ability. Tea farmers compete in terms of the quality of tea, while tea factories compete for purchase prices and production capacity. All parties on the Juchayuan platform are in a virtuous cycle of competition, which ultimately benefits consumers.

Juchayuan's hand-in-hand poverty alleviation action connects tea farmers, tea factories, and consumers. It creates a virtuous cycle in which the three parties can all benefit. Its logic can be widely applied.

CHAPTER 4

The Strategic Direction of the Final Battle

The key to advancing the "Four Major Plans" is to grasp the strategic direction and focus on the strengths. This is the only way that can China accelerate the pace of securing a decisive victory in 2020. This chapter focuses on revitalizing the existing poverty alleviation resources, leveraging the difficulties of poverty alleviation, and striving to find the final strategic solution for poverty alleviation, focusing on the four key points of revitalizing the "hat-trick," seeking wealthy supporters, cultivating vendors, and establishing the Tian Box initiative.

1. Revitalizing the "hat-trick"

The "hat-trick" began in 1858, when cricketer H. H. Stephenson scored three consecutive goals and was awarded a hat. The term "hat-trick" was later widely used in sports competitions, and was also used to describe three consecutive successes. Here, we use it to refer to poverty alleviation by understanding, making use of, and finally removing the poverty "hat."

(I) Understanding the "poverty hat"

In April 2014, the Poverty Alleviation Office of the State Council issued the "Work Plan for Poverty Alleviation and Development and the Establishment of Documents and Cards." The plan passed strict application and approval procedures to record information such as the basic conditions of the poor and the causes of poverty.

Through calculation and evaluation, the plan identified poor counties, villages, and households. Since then, they have put on the poverty "hat." Of course, these targets are subject to change, and the identifying strategy is constantly being adjusted. Through more than a year of statistical investigation, 832 poor counties, 128,000 poor villages, 29.32 million poor households, and 70.17 million poor people have been identified as being below the poverty line.

Poor groups lack funds, technology, management, and information, and thus they are typically vulnerable. So, what benefits can they get by wearing the poverty "hat"? It should be said that they have been given the greatest care and support in all aspects. For the convenience of description, we only briefly describe the financial services of poverty relief. As analyzed before, the lack of funds is the biggest obstacle for poverty relief. To meet the financial needs of poor people, China encourages and guides financial institutions to participate in financial poverty relief, which consists of inclusive and preferential financial support.

Inclusive financial support refers to support for transport, safe drinking water, relocation, and special projects. In 2014, China implemented 10 key poverty alleviation services, namely transport, safe drinking water, power supply, renovation of old houses, income increase for special industries, rural tourism, education, health and family planning, cultural construction, and technology building in poor villages with more than one trillion yuan. The support was both unprecedented and effective. In 2015, the Poverty Alleviation Office of the State Council signed nearly four trillion yuan's worth of financial poverty alleviation service strategic cooperation agreements with the China Development Bank and the Agricultural Development Bank of China, mainly for relocation, photovoltaic poverty alleviation, and poverty alleviation through industry. In the next five years, the country will relocate 10 million poor people with a total investment of about 600 billion yuan. The "Benefit For All Plan" implemented by the state will file and provide 3,000 yuan per year per student for poor children who received secondary and higher vocational education. During the 13th Five-Year Plan period, the state took the lead in waiving school fees for children from poor families in junior and senior high schools. It also subsidized the training of entrepreneurial leaders for poor villages. All in all, the state's inclusive financial support covers many fields and is very strong.

Preferential financial support refers to special financial support services that tackle insufficient funds, such as microfinance, community development fund support, and cooperation of poverty alleviation funds in poor villages. For example, in December 2014, the Poverty Alleviation Office of the State Council, the Ministry of Finance, the People's Bank of China, the China Insurance Regulatory Commission, and the China Banking Regulatory Commission jointly issued the "Guiding Opinions on the Innovative Development of Poverty Alleviation Microfinance." It stipulates that households should be provided with microfinance products and services below 50,000 yuan, which should be mortgage-free and non-guaranteed, and enjoy benchmark interest rates and a fiscal discount within three years. The "Decision of the CPC Central Committee and the State Council on Winning the Fight Against Poverty" further clarifies a series of policies for poverty alleviation during the 13th Five-Year Plan period, and pointed out the great potential advantages of poor people. Understanding and transforming the implications of the "poverty hat" can continue to create new prospects for poverty alleviation.

(II) Wearing the "poverty hat" well

Since the "poverty hat" contains so many potential advantages, how should it be worn? The author believes that it should be guided by the market. Wearing a market-driven hat can mix the potential advantages of poverty with the market to make it abide by the rules of the market.

a) The significance of a market-driven "poverty hat"

According to the state's overall design, besides the 20 million poor people who are completely supported by the state, the remaining 50 million will rise out of poverty mainly through developing industries, relocating to other places, ecological compensation, and developing education, all of which require sensible participation in the market management system. For example, to promote the building of modern farms, it is possible to distribute poverty alleviation funds to poor individuals as their market shares. The moneylender will have shares in the enterprise while the latter operates in the market according to modern standards. In this way, the poor will become shareholders of the enterprises. They can work for the enterprises, and help to manage them. They get paid both for work and share income. The benefits of this set-up are manifold:

(1) It improves labor productivity and eliminates poor people's tendency to wait, rely on others, and ask for help. Industry is the root of poverty alleviation and development. Market participation in poverty alleviation and development resources will integrate poverty alleviation resources with industries, generating mutual profits, helping enterprises to balance costs and benefits, and guide and encourage poor

groups to participate in production. This realizes the standardized management of industry while improving labor productivity, eradicating the inertia of the poor, and reducing their reliance on others.

(2) It sparks the inner motivation that promotes sustainability. Enterprises can help increase sustainability, reduce costs, and increase the income of poverty alleviation by working with poor people. At the same time, this kind of positive interaction can in turn improve the productivity of poor people, which is beneficial to enterprises.

(3) It helps to resolve conflicts in cooperation and promote equal status. Enterprises are always seeking profit, and can dominate cooperation with poor people. That is why conflicts sometimes occur. However, if enterprises can guarantee the income of poor groups within a reasonable range and bear the risks, conflicts will be naturally resolved. At the same time, enterprises indirectly cultivate capable people who can help more poor families rise out of poverty. This kind of interaction can ensure equal status for both sides, and demonstrate social justice.

b) The function of the market-driven "poverty hat"

This mechanism changes the traditional passive mode of poverty alleviation and dramatically strengthens an active mode. It achieves this by:

• IMPROVING THE NATIONAL POVERTY ALLEVIATION MECHANISM

Poverty alleviation and development in China have long been a government-led prospect. The three-pronged scheme of special poverty alleviation, poverty alleviation through industry, and social poverty alleviation are exclusively led by the Party and government. It is an active practice that has given rise to many cases of poverty alleviation. A market-driven "poverty hat" is beneficial to the positive relationship between the government and the market.

• AMPLIFYING THE EFFECTS ON RESOURCES OF POVERTY ALLEVIATION AND DEVELOPMENT

Government-led poverty alleviation and development is prone to corruption, and can lead to idleness among poor people. Conflicts arise when poor groups need a lot but resources are limited. Market allocation of poverty alleviation resources must be more effective at combining the advantages of resources such as market capital, technology, and information, to magnify the effect of these resource with an active approach.

- Accumulating the effects of poverty alleviation

Generally speaking, poor groups lack the basic skills needed to participate in market operations. As a result, the rate of lapsing back into poverty after getting out of it is very high. Market allocation of resources for poverty alleviation and development is an effective way to seamlessly connect resources such as capital, assets, and labor of poor groups with market operation projects.

c) Putting on the market-driven "poverty hat"
- Poverty alleviation through industry

Industry is the most important aspect of poverty alleviation and development. Key to its success is the appropriate planning of industrial modes. Currently, the main mode of poverty alleviation through industry is the joint-stock cooperative system where the government, enterprises, professional cooperatives, financial institutions, and poor households jointly design joint-stock cooperative companies. This model is manifested in the large-scale development of planting and breeding bases in poor areas. Special handicrafts and rural tourism are also employed. Primary, secondary, and tertiary industries are combined to help the poor.

- Poverty alleviation through consumption

This method provides a channel and a market for quality agricultural goods produced in poor areas. Under the premise of mutual benefit, consumption subjects (mainly including enterprises, social organizations, and individuals) consume the agricultural and sideline products of poor families in a personalized way, which can meet the unique needs of consumers, accumulate merit and goodwill, and increase the sales income of poor groups. Both sides get what they need, thus promoting sustainability in cities and wealth in villages.

- Other forms of poverty alleviation

Within the market mechanism, there are many ways to allocate resources for poverty alleviation through the market to help the poor earn more money. For example, poverty alleviation can be conducted through science and technology, education, collaboration, and finance. Each method has its focus, but also influences the others. The goal is to help the poor become wealthy.

(III) Removing the "poverty hat"

The purpose of putting on the "poverty hat" is ultimately to remove it, which relies on the country and the market.

a) The national "hat"-removal mechanism

In China's existing poverty alleviation and development policies, poor counties are often able to receive financial transfer payments, project funding arrangements, and the development of infrastructure. Therefore, the "poverty hat" is regarded by some poor counties as a "cash cow," and they are subsequently reluctant to take it off. At the same time, some poor counties rely on it for their financial expenditures to function properly, so they are also reluctant. In 2015, during the Central Conference on Poverty Alleviation and Development, 22 provinces signed responsibility letters for poverty eradication, and agreed on a schedule for "hat" removal. In response to the phenomenon that some regions are reluctant to remove their "hats," the state has introduced another policy guaranteeing support, including financial rewards for individuals and counties that seek to alleviate poverty. The policy has been functioning well.

b) The market "hat"-removal mechanism

The core of the market "hat"-removal mechanism is to use the "hat-trick," the core of which is to achieve continuous success. The first thing is to allow the potential advantages to penetrate the market. For example, it is possible to issue a special loan for poverty alleviation as an enterprise investment and gain the first income by a fixed dividend. Secondly, the poor can use the income to participate in the operation of the enterprise, to get their second source of income. This way, the poor can accumulate wealth as well as improve their abilities.

■ **Case Study**

In July 2015, the Department of Finance of Gansu Province collaborated with banking and financial institutions in the province to create exclusive financial products tailored for the province's 970,000 households with 4.17 million poor people on record. The department launched a special loan project for targeted poverty alleviation. The project ran from 2015 to 2017, with a total scale of 40 billion yuan, and a loan amount of 10,000 to 50,000 yuan per household with a term of one to three years. In the process of implementation, the city of Wuwei innovated loan mechanisms that were both corporate-supported and self-initiated, based on records of poor people's wills and their productivity. To help impoverished farmers with a lack of experience and skills and high risk of loan repayment, loans were granted to local high-quality leading enterprises. The enterprises were responsible for repaying the capital, and the impoverished farmers received regular dividends.

The female workers at Diyuan Computerized Embroidery Garment Co., Ltd. in Gulang County, Wuwei City, are mainly left-behind women from poor families who have undergone technical training. The company concentrates on using special loans for more than 20 poor households, taking at least one person from each household into employment. The enterprise returns 3,000 yuan per year to the poor employees, who are paid more than 2,000 yuan per month for their work. In this way, impoverished households are guaranteed dividends, and also receive financial subsidies, wages, and income from the land transfer.

Wuwei Gulang Oasis Ecological Migrant Poverty Alleviation Industrial Base works with the model of "company + base + ecological migrant" to lift poor households out of poverty. At the same time, impoverished workers on the industrial base transfer their original land to receive rent, obtaining three incomes – "wage income + dividend at the end of the year + land rent."

Of course, the use of the "hat-trick" in poverty alleviation needs to have individual policies to suit different people and households. The same goes for the "hat"-removal mechanism. "If you grow tea at home, develop tea; if you raise sheep at home, expand that work; if you want to learn skills to work, enroll at training institutions." This was the original intention of the state in creating "poverty hats," and it relies on the market. The "hat trick" can be used to achieve the "hat"-removal mechanism.

2. Seeking wealthy supporters

This policy directly connects poor people with supporting corporations, social organizations, and individuals. The two sides sign contracts and work together.

(I) Who are the supporters?

The supporters we are talking about here are relative to the disadvantaged poor groups, and refer to the actors involved in poverty alleviation and eradication. From the perspective of China's current poverty alleviation and development practice, supporters mainly include all kinds of private enterprises, social organizations, and individuals, and are the main body in the general pattern of social poverty alleviation and eradication.

Private enterprises: The participation of private enterprises in poverty alleviation is contractual, with the poor groups as the main body of the enterprises. This is mutually beneficial. Cooperation can promote the integration of the poor groups into the market operation, and through the market operation mechanism, effectively improve the ability to get out of poverty independently and achieve long-term and stable poverty alleviation. The participation of private enterprises in poverty alleviation is conducive to poor people learning to develop special industries according to market demand, and using the "support" of the leading enterprises to improve the degree of organization and specialization of production of the poor groups in the market, seeking market advantages and benefits.

Social organizations: The participation of social organizations in poverty alleviation and eradication is a kind of public welfare, supporting poor groups through social organizations. The participation of social organizations in poverty alleviation and eradication can make up for the shortcomings of government and market mechanisms, and fully mobilize social forces to participate in poverty alleviation. It guarantees that poor groups will enjoy all the rights of poverty alleviation and eradication, enjoy basic public services and equal rights in society, and share the fruits of development.

Individuals: Individual participation in poverty alleviation and eradication fully mobilizes affluent individuals in society to join the cause, helping poor individuals improve their livelihoods. China's affluent population is expanding, and this group is a force that cannot be ignored in poverty alleviation and eradication.

(II) Why are supporters needed?

The 13th Five-Year Plan period is the decisive era for poverty eradication. Poverty alleviation and development has been elevated to a key project within the national "First Centennial Goal," as it had become the biggest roadblock in building a moderately prosperous society. The current task of poverty alleviation is no longer the basic goal of providing food and clothing, but of quickly raising the income level of poor groups, enhancing their self-development, and helping them rise out of poverty and become moderately prosperous as fast as possible. The preferred way for impoverished people to achieve this goal is to take advantage of private enterprises and the market to rise out of poverty and earn a living as quickly as they can. Therefore, it is particularly important to encourage private enterprises to participate in poverty alleviation and development. Innovations in this field are thus crucial.

a) Supporters reflect the concept of national poverty alleviation and development in the new era

The "Decision of the CPC Central Committee and the State Council on Winning the Fight Against Poverty" states:

> Encourage support for private enterprises, social organizations, individuals to participate in poverty alleviation and development, to achieve effective docking of social support resources and targeted poverty alleviation… Improve the system of identifying leading enterprises for poverty alleviation, and enhance the ability of enterprises to motivate poor households to increase their income.

This is the basis of the supporter system, and embodies its basic concept. Since the 18th National Congress of the CPC, an atmosphere of promoting agriculture with industry and helping the countryside through cities has been formed. Therefore, private enterprises should become an important force in poverty alleviation and development. Enterprises seeking development should connect with the poor groups with the strongest desires to develop, to strive for co-development.

b) The supporter system stimulates the market and sustainable development of poor areas

Private enterprises in poor areas can carry out one-way public welfare and target specific characteristic of these areas, helping them to develop resources and cultivate industries. Industrial clusters are established through large-scale production, modernized management, refined division of labor, and industrialized operation, leading to new economic cooperatives in poor areas. Private enterprises also carry out training for the poor labor force, or directly employ impoverished people to help them improve their abilities.

c) The supporter system as a win-win practice

Private enterprises can develop various forms of large-scale operation and build a new model of poverty alleviation and development that combines intensification, specialization, organization, and socialization. Poor people can acquire dividends from the poverty alleviation funds they receive through the national poverty alleviation policy. Assets such as land and houses can increase in value, and they can also be employed to increase their wages. This aligns with the policy orientation of ensuring people's livelihoods and stability.

(III) How to get supporters

The ideal result of having supporters is to encourage poor farmers to achieve a high degree of agricultural industrialization. Poor farmers at an absolute disadvantage in the industrial chain become shareholders, investors, and even owners of the supporting enterprises. If the supporter's system is not designed properly, it is easy to blur the property rights of poverty alleviation funds, resulting in a loss of status for the poor.

a) The enterprise-driven model

The enterprise-driven model consists of "enterprise + base + farmers." It is led, organized, approved, and supervised by the government. Enterprises and poor households jointly undertake loans, and enterprises are responsible for repayment. This mode of poverty alleviation takes enterprises as the main body, and these enterprises operate independently. The operation mechanism covers the government, financial institutions, enterprises, and poor farmers, with enterprises as the leader, guiding impoverished farmers to enter the market, linking all aspects of agricultural production with market mechanisms, and promoting agricultural production and farmers' income. With this model, enterprises are bundled together with the government, banks, and impoverished farmers as a whole. Enterprises are fully stimulated as they operate independently, while the government intervenes administratively, so that farmers can enter the overall market cycle and realize the development of poverty alleviation within the operation of the market mechanism. Thanks to the government's protection policy, enterprises can enter industrialization and the market cycle with low risk. Project funding mainly comes from a variety of reimbursable poverty alleviation funds, some of which is self-financed by the enterprise. Enterprises are responsible for loans and repayments. This mode of poverty alleviation plays a significant role in improving the ability of poor groups to go to the market.

For example, the building of farms can develop according to this model. Poverty-stricken farmers receive microcredit for poverty alleviation through the "hat-trick" on the premise that the ownership belongs to them. The bank invests these funds in specific farm projects, which are jointly developed by the impoverished farmers and enterprises. The farms that are built expand the scale of the enterprise's production base and guarantee poor households a fixed return on their income. The enterprise is responsible for repaying the loan at maturity. There are two points to note here: first, the ownership of the micro-credit for poverty alleviation belongs to the impoverished farmers to avoid unclear property rights after cooperation; second, the bank will directly allocate the loan to the enterprise to avoid allocating money to farmers that will be difficult to recover. In the new era of poverty alleviation, the "enterprise + base + farmers" model has been given a new implication. The enterprise belongs to the farmers, the base is composed of the farmers, the enterprise operates according to the shareholding system, and the benefits are shared with the poor farmers, creating a way for impoverished farmers to rise out of poverty and earn a living.

b) The industry-driven model

This refers to the economic pattern led by supporting enterprises (focusing on leading enterprises), leading specialized breeding bases and intermediary organizations to contact thousands of households, and realizing one-stop services for breeding, service, processing, and operation. Industry-led poverty alleviation is mostly based on local resources, and focuses on factors such as supporting local leading industries, and reorganizing land, capital, and labor. It drives the development of agriculture, the processing industry, and the service industry with leading industries, and then cultivates new large-scale enterprises to lift poor rural areas out of poverty and into prosperity.

■ Case Studies

The city of Jinjiang in Fujian Province has more than 200 industrialized agricultural business organizations, including two at the national level, 11 at the provincial level, and 23 at the municipal level. With their obvious advantages, they promote the optimization of the agricultural industry's structure to raise both the efficiency of agriculture and farmers' income. For example, the economic development of Qiancai Village in Anhai Town is lagging, so the Fuyuan Company has carried out twinning activities with village enterprises and formed a driving mechanism consisting of three iterations of 80%. This way, 80% of the villagers participate in enterprise investment shares, 80% of the employees of the enterprise come from the village and surrounding areas, and 80% of the income of the villagers comes from the enterprise. The implementation of this scheme has improved the village, strengthened its financial status, and helped residents to become wealthy. In 2012, the total industrial and agricultural output value of the village was 450 million yuan; the per capita net income was 11,000 yuan, and the tax revenue was more than 40 million yuan. The formerly impoverished village has become moderately prosperous, and its name is known far and wide.

Another example is the village of Heqingsi in Nanhai District, Foshan City, Guangdong Province. It has taken the lead in helping Shanglin County in the Guangxi Zhuang Autonomous Region to carry out entrepreneurship training for leaders in poor villages, and to develop a smart fish-farming industry. After the completion of the project, nearly 10,000 poor families in Shanglin County will be lifted out of poverty, with an average annual income of 20,000 to 100,000 yuan per household. Elsewhere, Shandong Dongju Solar Energy Co., Ltd. is helping to develop the photovoltaic industry in the village of Sanyi in Lintao County, Gansu Province. This project has a total investment of 270 million yuan, and will build a 25 MW photovoltaic power station, a 5.9 MW distributed power station, and 400 greenhouses. When the project is completed, it will lift 1,000 local poor families out of poverty who are unable to work, and help 400 poor families with working ability to engage in farming and breeding, with an average annual income of 60,000 yuan.

c) Driven by capable people

This refers to capable individuals from private enterprises helping the poor move towards prosperity. In recent years, more rural grassroots cadres have been cultivated, and many of them have become village leaders, setting up factories and building enterprises. Through their own efforts, these capable people have consistently expanded the scale of their enterprises. As well as becoming wealthy themselves, they help villagers make money as well, and play a pioneering and exemplary role. Private enterprises run by capable people can absorb farmers into factories as workers, and provide employment opportunities for the villagers. They can also raise villagers' consciousness, encouraging them to emulate capable people in terms of mindset and lifestyle, pursuing self-reliance through independent poverty alleviation, learning about and participating in market operation, ceasing to rely on the government alone, and joining the process of poverty alleviation and prosperity.

■ Case Study 1

The state-recognized Linyangjie Village in Linyang Town, Ju County, Shandong Province, is a national advanced village. It is one of the "Top 100 Villages" in China, and "The Most Beautiful Leisure Village," and also functions as a base for scientific education. Its development can be summarized as enriching agriculture with industry, promoting industry with agriculture, developing with culture, and benefiting people through tourism.

In the 1980s, Linyangjie Village was infamous for its poverty, with residents not even able to afford food and clothing. At that time, Ma Xianfu, Secretary of the village's Party branch, utilized Party policies to become wealthy by doing business abroad, but the sight of the villagers living in poverty made him uncomfortable. In order to help Lingyang become wealthy as quickly as possible, in 1984, Ma Xianfu donated his three enterprises to the village. With the Reform and Opening, the enterprises in Lingyang Street Village soon grew from three to 13, and the industrial output value exceeded 100 million yuan in 1993. In the 1990s, based on the advantages of the local Lingshang vegetables, Linyangjie Village built three joint ventures with Korean and Hungarian businesspeople, including Rizhao Dongju Fruit and Vegetable Food Co. Now, the village has a refrigerated processing area with a storage capacity of 100 million kilograms of fruits and vegetables at a time. It has developed a 10,000-mu green melon and vegetable export base, and built a wholesale market of nearly 10,000 square meters for melons and vegetables. Its watermelons, tomatoes, zucchini, ginger, and green asparagus are recognized by the China Green Food Development Center, and the trademark of the Lingshanghe brand has been registered to sell products in China and abroad. In 2014, the total annual industrial and agricultural output value of the village exceeded three billion yuan, the collective economic income exceeded 26 million yuan, and the per capita net income of farmers reached 25,600 yuan.

After the development of enterprises in the village, Ma Xianfu led the village's two-committee team (the "two committees," namely the village Party branch committee and the villagers' committee, are the Party's grassroots organization in rural areas and the villagers' self-governing organization) to develop cultural undertakings and special industries based on the village's natural features. Linyangjie Village is the location of the Linyang River site of the Dawenkou Culture, where the earliest Chinese writing was born, advancing Chinese civilization by 1,500 years. The world's earliest brewing vessels were unearthed there, making it the true birthplace of wine culture. In order to excavate and promote Linyang River culture, Linyangjie Village and the Institute of Archaeology of the Chinese Academy of Social Sciences (CASS) cooperated to build the Southeastern Shandong Archaeological Research Center and the Linyang River Cultural Museum. This was the first time that CASS had cooperated with a village collective.

At the same time, Linyangjie Village is building a high-end agricultural industry focusing on osmanthus. This flower has a rich heritage in China, and its scent is enjoyed around mid-autumn time. Since 2003, Linyangjie Village has been cultivating an osmanthus industry, creating a northern hub, and hosting an osmanthus event every year at Mid-Autumn Festival, using it as a medium to attract business. In 2014, the Linyang Osmanthus Festival was announced by the Shandong Provincial Festival Advisory Committee as a key even in the region. According to Ma Xianfu's philosophy, "One person's prosperity is not true prosperity, but everyone's prosperity is real prosperity; one village's prosperity is not true prosperity, but all the rural areas' prosperity is real prosperity." Therefore, after Linyangjie Village has become rich, it will insist on helping one or two poor villages every year to achieve common development.

■ **Case Study 2**

Hualiang Dressing Factory in Yongfeng Town, Xinghua City, Jiangsu Province, is a joint-stock private enterprise that was put into operation in 1999. It had assets of 1.6 million yuan and 48 employees, and achieved an output value of 1.8 million yuan, with a profit tax of 250,000 yuan (a profit of 150,000 yuan and tax of 100,000 yuan) in 2000. This factory an example of those who attain prosperity helping others to become wealthy too, advocated by the Association for the Promotion of Old Areas in Yongfeng Town. In 2001, the average annual net income per capita reached 4,000–5,000 yuan with a high of 8,000 yuan and a low of 3,000 yuan.

The impoverished people who went to work at the factory generally reflected: "The factory director leads us to rise out of poverty and earn a living, and is a caring person." Song Zhiliang, the factory director, is a farmer by birth, and is highly ideological. He is very enthusiastic and passionate about poverty alleviation. He says, "When I started to become rich, I could not forget the Party's leadership and the poor folk." He took the initiative to participate in social poverty alleviation, solving problems for the Party and the government, and helping impoverished people to become wealthy. His approach is to help the poor get jobs in his factory, placing the right person into the right role.

In encouraging poor people to get jobs in the factory, workers are offered education about ideology and political goals, following the Party line in terms of the requirements of open governance. Between 1999 and 2000, residents from 12 villages and 22 households were given jobs in the factory. Among them, three were disabled, two were widowed, two were impoverished due to illness, six were single, and nine were in specific hardship. The scheme received praise from the general public.

Roles are assigned according to the needs of each person. The main products of the Hualiang Dressing Factory are tampons and cotton balls, which are semi-finished products. Product sales are very good. Work is reasonably distributed and wages are paid monthly. Director Song Zhiliang says that he will continue to help the poor who are working in his factory, and will expand his assistance to 20–30 poor households in the future.

d) E-commerce driven

This is a mode that uses e-commerce to help the poor. With the popularity of the Internet, especially in the past five years, e-commerce in China's urban and rural society has shown rapid development, entering the era of "Internet +." With the help of the Internet, supporters integrate special agricultural and sideline products from poor areas into the market so that they become popular. This practice benefits both farmers and consumers. This is driven by e-commerce. Agricultural and sideline products in poverty-stricken areas are monitored from the farm to the dining table through the Internet, so that customers can consume them with confidence. This leads poor farmers to increase their incomes, and also benefits consumers.

The Tea Garden project is a typical case of e-commerce-driven poverty alleviation. E-commerce enables customized purchases that benefit the farmers.

There are many supporters in the current process of poverty alleviation. There are several problems worthy of notice in the process of attracting supporters. First, market entities such as private enterprises should build their own brands and motivate impoverished farmers to participate in their development. Second, institutions such as the government and banks should assist impoverished farmers and give the green light to help enterprises. Third, impoverished farmers must be enriched through skill training to help them cope with risks more effectively. Fourth, there is a danger of exploitation of the interests of impoverished farmers by social capital. Thus, it is necessary to clarify the rights and obligations of both sides in the form of contracts, standardize the design of the model, and leverage the role of supporters.

3. Cultivating vendors

In the past, in remote rural areas, it was common for vendors to go from village to village. The sound of their rattles was accompanied by their sales patter: "One stretcher and two baskets, three or five in a group going in all directions. The drums jingle; the buckles and the shoelaces are the same. The sun rises over the mountain and dawns again; the sound of hawking makes life seem busy." The figure of the itinerant vendor was a common scene in the countryside. However, with the progress

Itinerant vendor in the countryside   A village vendor's stall

of the times and the rapid development of supermarket docking for farmers, the traditional vendor has gradually faded from view.

With the advent of the "Internet +" era, rural e-commerce has become the next prize in the eyes of many e-commerce giants. It also brings a breakthrough in terms of speeding up the pace of poverty alleviation in poor areas. However, in the rapid layout of rural e-commerce, its development in rural areas is facing a lack of human resources. Therefore, guiding and cultivating rural e-commerce personnel is a key link in the development of rural areas and in accelerating the pace of poverty alleviation in poor regions.

The vendor plays a significant role in poverty alleviation. At present, most poor areas function using a 38–61–99 model (38 for women, 61 for children, 99 for the elderly). It is not feasible to transfer the urban Internet development model to poor villages. It is therefore the duty and mission of the vendor in the new era to help villagers buy and sell, to receive express deliveries, and to sell natural, non-polluting, and high-quality agricultural and sideline products from the villages in the cities. This way, rural products can go out, and urban products can come in. Therefore, vendors in the new era have a triple role of administrator, courier, and broker, and they are the key to closing the "last mile" of poverty alleviation through rural e-commerce.

(I) Background of vendor cultivation

The cultivation of vendors has a favorable background in terms of policy and the market.

On August 21, 2015, the Ministry of Commerce and 19 other departments jointly issued the "Opinions on Accelerating the Development of Rural E-Commerce," which introduced a number of measures to support the development of rural e-commerce by various types of capital, such as e-commerce, logistics, commerce, and finance.

Premier Li Keqiang hosted an executive meeting of the State Council on October 14, 2015, and made the decision to: improve the compensation mechanism for universal broadband telecommunications services in rural and remote areas; narrow the digital divide between urban and rural areas; expedite the development of rural e-commerce, and promote consumption and people's livelihood through the growth of new business models; and to determine measures to promote the development of the express delivery industry and foster new growth points in the modern service industry.

The "Micro Report on County E-Commerce Talent Research" jointly released by Ali Research Institute and Taobao Business School points out that the demand for e-commerce personnel in the next two years will exceed two million people in county-level online business, and there will be a huge shortage of personnel in operation promotion, artwork design, and data analysis.

In order to strongly develop rural e-commerce in poor villages, it is necessary to select and cultivate a group of "e- vendors" with a certain degree of rural experience and professional skills. This is crucial if poor villages and poor households are to rise out of poverty and earn a living.

(II) Cultivation orientation of vendors

Vendors in the new era should understand agriculture, rural areas, farmers, e-commerce, management, and the development needs of poor rural areas. They need to be enthusiastic about identifying the cause of poverty alleviation and the enrichment of poor groups, and will eventually become the leaders of the enrichment of poor villages in poverty-stricken areas.

a) E-commerce administrators in poor villages

Rural e-commerce is a systematic project that involves the selection of agricultural and sideline products, planting and breeding, promotion, and after-sales service. All of these things require a great deal of work from vendors. At present, agricultural and sideline products and services are mainly sold on B2B, B2C, and C2B platforms. In recent years, mobile client sales have gradually become a major business segment, requiring vendors to be proficient in operating and using these platforms. E-commerce is different from traditional business thinking, which requires vendors to consider the development of agricultural and sideline products from the perspective of customers. All of these things require vendors to have the qualities of a general manager of rural e-commerce.

b) Couriers in poor villages

For the development of e-commerce in poor rural areas, the most significant infrastructure development encompasses transport and networks. Although the transport conditions in poor areas have improved significantly with the promotion of urban-rural integration, there are still large spans of village roads that have not yet been repaired. Poor traffic conditions directly hinder the transport of goods. At the same time, low network coverage in poor areas leads to the slow development of rural e-commerce. Therefore, vendors must also play the role of rural couriers, bringing the wealth of cities into villages and the ecology of the countryside into cities.

c) Brokers for farmers in poor villages

The vendors that are cultivated will undertake the work of buying on behalf of impoverished farmers. They also help to sell the farmers' products. Special and high-quality agricultural and sideline products and their services in poor areas should be promoted through the Internet, and vendors should be able to conduct surveys and statistics on the market demand for various agricultural and sideline products, as well as being aware of commercializing packaging and creating their own brands for various agricultural and sideline products. The vendors are the spokespeople and brokers of poor village farmers.

■ Case Study

Jingdong (JD.com) is responsible for the birth of the thousandth rural promoter. Li Xiaogang, a resident of a remote village in Chaohu, Anhui Province, is quietly changing his focus in 2015. His wish is now different from previous years: to allow villagers to enjoy the convenience of online shopping. Li Xiaogang's change of direction comes from Jingdong Group's "e-commerce to the countryside" scheme, in which he became the thousandth rural Jingdong promoter.

Li often thinks about how to make sure villagers enjoy the convenience of having large electric appliances delivered to their doorstep, and how to extend e-commerce to the remote village of Chaohu in Anhui Province. "I have a lot of plans in mind to take advantage of the return of young people to their hometowns during Chinese

Li Xiaogang – the thousandth rural Jingdong promoter

Rural promoter Li Xiaogang talks to villagers every day about Jingdong and online shopping

New Year. I'll be promoting Jingdong Mall's top-quality inexpensive goods to every household, and improve the living configurations of villagers' homes."

What Li Xiaogang didn't expect was that he would become the thousandth rural promoter of Jingdong Group nationwide. From watching the news, he learned that national leaders had approved Jingdong's services for the rural market, and this spurred his enthusiasm for entrepreneurship. As Premier Li Keqiang stated, "People in villages should enjoy the same consumer services as people in cities."

Rural promoters were an important starting point for Jingdong Group's channel sinking in 2014, through the incentive mechanism. Since then, rural consumers who know about online shopping, and have good connections and influence are invited to join the Jingdong e-commerce team in the countryside, and become its main force.

These "neurons" are managed, trained, and evaluated by rural service centers, which form the centralized management system for Jingdong Group's e-commerce in the countryside. It is a multi-business bearing model. The management staff includes the distribution station manager and village supervisor, the latter of whom trains and manages local rural promoters, who are not only salespeople, after-sales service providers, logistics staff, and delivery personnel, but also Jingdong Group creditors.

(III) The principle of cultivating vendors

It may well be the case that the direction and maturity of e-commerce development in poor villages are determined by the number and ability of vendors in the new era. The cultivation of vendors is a complicated system that is mainly composed of the Xiaokang Institute, and requires the cooperation of many parties such as the government, associations, enterprises, and schools to gradually establish a vendor cultivation system that is adapted to the specifics of e-commerce demands in poor rural areas.

a) Treating introduction and cultivation equally

To cultivate vendors efficiently, it is necessary to embrace the principle that "introducing" and "cultivating" are equally significant, and also to deal with the relationship between introducing personnel and cultivating staff. The reason is that staff cultivation cannot be achieved overnight, and requires a certain period of time, but China is pressed for time when it comes to hardcore poverty alleviation. Therefore, introduction and cultivation need to go hand in hand. The key to introduction is to bring in far-sighted personnel that understand the e-commerce circles of big cities and are aware of the latest development trends. Meanwhile, cultivation involves nurturing down-to-earth personnel who are familiar with the actual situation of rural e-commerce and are able to integrate and explore the resources of agricultural and sideline products in poor villages.

Poverty-stricken areas have inherent advantages in introducing personnel. According to statistics, by the beginning of 2015, the number of people dispatched to poor villages nationwide by government agencies reached 430,000, including 170,000 first secretaries assigned to 128,000 poor villages, achieving full coverage of poor villages. The aim of this is to help poor villages develop rapidly and rise out of poverty. These first secretaries are the "brought in personnel" who should be given priority in the cultivation of vendors, and they should then select people to lift their villages out of poverty as the focus of cultivation.

b) Cultivating personnel through practice

Vendors should be trained and cultivated based on practice. It is an objective fact that there is a contradiction between the supply and the demand of vendors. Based on this challenge, in addition to making full use of the advantages of the first secretaries engaging in e-commerce businesses, it is also necessary to pay more attention to cultivating local vendors through practice. For example, through leveraging poor villages' own resources in the process of cultivation, it is possible to arrange various flexible exchange lessons such as online business club salons and mutual enterprise visits, to cultivate personnel through practice and communication.

c) Cultivating personnel according to market demands

All rich regions in the world develop in a similar manner, while poor regions vary. This difference requires an insistence on nurturing rural e-commerce personnel in a market-oriented way with a greater emphasis on diversity. As brokers for farmers, vendors need to master operational skills as well as management and market research knowhow.

In general, vendors in the new era are village administrators, couriers, and farmers' brokers, and need to be reasonably designed and cultivated according to the specifics of local industry and market demands.

d) Emphasizing practical cultivation

When cultivating vendors, it is necessary to focus on the long-term development of poor villages and cultivate practical personnel targeting e-commerce there. In essence, the resources of poor villages are similar to those of urban communities, but they are very different in another way. While resources in urban communities emphasize consumers, farmers are both consumers and producers in poor villages. Farmers need the goods that urban people need, and the crops can be supplied directly to end-consumers at the market as well as to the merchants. This extends the supply chain and provides a two-way supply and demand relationship between poor rural areas and vendors. Therefore, from the perspective of long-term development, China must focus on practicality and pertinence when cultivating vendors. It is necessary to rely completely on the traditional local business of poor villages as well as leveraging the advantages of the Internet in information services, in order to truly cultivate the practical personnel needed for poverty alleviation.

4. Establishing the Tian Box platform

At the National Poverty Alleviation Work Conference held at the end of 2014, e-commerce poverty alleviation was formally brought into the national poverty alleviation policy system and work plan for the first time. It is so significant that it has become one of the 10 targeted poverty alleviation projects of the Poverty Alleviation Office of the State Council. Needless to say, e-commerce is a new field for many full-time poverty alleviation personnel, and also an unprecedented way out of poverty for farmers in poor areas. The author believes that the key to alleviating poverty with the

The No.1 Poverty Alleviation Store concept

help of e-commerce is to build purchasing and selling platforms for agricultural and sideline specialties in poor areas, which are directed by the government and widely adopted by enterprises and society – that is, to build a Tian Box platform.

Tian Box is a metaphor for the process by which agricultural and sideline products from poor areas are packed in a box resembling the Chinese character 田 ("tian," meaning field – see image below) after certain processing procedures, before being sent to city markets for consumption. One or several Tian Boxes can represent all of the agricultural and sideline products of a county. Generally speaking, the agricultural and sideline products from poor villages on the Tian Box platform are sold in a personalized way, so the material of the box, the design, and the product types are all based on actual demand. At present, the Poverty Alleviation Office of the State Council is promoting the construction of the Tian Box platform and cooperating with major e-commerce enterprises to build the No.1 Poverty Alleviation Store.

(I) Institutional background of the Tian Box platform

In March 2015, Premier Li Keqiang introduced the "Internet +" action plan in a government work report. In May 2015, the State Council issued the "Opinions on Developing E-Commerce to Accelerate the Cultivation of New Economic Dynamics," which put forward the opinions that e-commerce should appear in rural areas and that rural e-commerce should be developed. In September 2015, the Ministry of Commerce and 19 other departments jointly issued the "Opinions on Accelerating the Development of Rural E-Commerce," which proposed that several rural e-commerce demonstration counties should be cultivated as leaders within five years. Rural e-commerce involves agricultural economic development, the development of infrastructure, rural logistics, employment of farmers, and improvements to quality of life, and has become a significant entry point for enhancing economic vitality, promoting industrial restructuring, and changing the path of economic development.

At present, with the accelerated penetration of the Internet into rural areas, rural e-commerce is gradually expanding from the consumer field to the production field. Attention from policy-makers, the development of the mobile Internet, and the decline of industrial products and rise of agricultural products will further stimulate the potential of the rural e-commerce market. E-commerce giants will also focus their attention on counties, which will be an opportunity to improve the rural e-commerce infrastructure and to drive industrial development.

Poverty alleviation through rural e-commerce is a practical way for the Chinese government to alleviate poverty successfully, targeting and promoting the development of local industries by e-commerce, such as helping the poor open online stores. It is also an innovative method of alleviating poverty in the Internet era.

Signing ceremony for strategic cooperation between the Poverty Alleviation Office of the State Council and Jingdong Group's E-commerce Targeted Poverty Alleviation Strategy

The Poverty Alleviation Office of the State Council has incorporated e-commerce into its poverty alleviation and development system, and it is also strongly promoting e-commerce poverty alleviation projects, to positive effect. At present, provinces such as Shandong, Gansu, and Hebei have issued documents on poverty alleviation through e-commerce, which will send advantageous products from poor areas to the market by setting up experimental bases for e-commerce poverty alleviation in poor villages and adopting methods such as "platform + park + training."

In January 2016, the Poverty Alleviation Office of the State Council and JD.com (Jingdong) signed the "Strategic Cooperation Framework Agreement on Targeted poverty alleviation through E-Commerce" in Beijing. The agreement stipulates that JD.com will join with the China Association for the Promotion of Voluntary Poverty Alleviation Services and the executive association of the Poverty Alleviation Office of the State Council to build the No.1 Poverty Alleviation Store.

Based on the advantageous resources of 832 poverty-stricken counties in China, the No.1 Poverty Alleviation Store will explore sales channels for high-quality agricultural and sideline specialties in poverty-stricken areas, as well as channels for people in poverty-stricken areas to alleviate poverty through consumption. The two parties plan to set up the No.1 Poverty Alleviation Store on JD Mall, working together to make a buying and selling system for standardized and traceable agricultural and sideline products, and forming a nationwide famous brand as quickly as possible.

(II) The functional positioning of the Tian Box platform

The concept behind the Tian Box platform is to establish a platform for trade, exchange, and information. On it, commodities can be exchanged between urban and rural areas, green products can enter cities, and villagers will become richer. Social resources for poverty alleviation can be exchanged between supporters and recipients, and the national policies for poverty alleviation can be understood, increasing poor people's awareness that Tian Box can help them become wealthy.

When establishing the Tian Box platform, it is necessary to highlight its transaction and exchange functions as well as its simple and convenient operating system. It should be designed to fully consider the application needs of mobile clients so that data entry, querying, and platform operation can be carried out through cell phones.

According to the transaction records on the platform, a "merit book" should be established to quantify the poverty alleviation results of organizations and individuals, and a database should also be formed to commend them according to their rankings, to so stimulated their sense of honor and enthusiasm.

The Tian Box platform should also be fully integrated with the design of the poverty alleviation system. For example, the teams and the first secretaries working in villages can carry out poverty alleviation work and record everything they do through the platform. This will provide a reference for assessing the work of the teams and the first secretaries in villages.

(III) The inherent advantages of the Tian Box platform

a) The increasing popularity of e-commerce

The development of e-commerce has a lot of benefits today, and is increasing in popularity. The wider the strategic layout of county-level and rural e-commerce, the more beneficial it is to the building of the Tian Box platform. Data from many field research and e-commerce platforms show that in many poor areas, although there is only a small proportion of people currently using e-commerce to sell products online, a certain number are already using e-commerce to shop online and gain direct experience of buying and selling this way. It is the modus operandi of the Tian Box platform to "buy it, buy it right, and buy it cheap." Moreover, the increase in the scale of online shopping can also cultivate people's awareness of e-commerce, promote the building of e-commerce infrastructure in specific regions, and spread logistics, creating better conditions for the poor to participate in the buying and selling of products online.

b) Boosting platform-building practices

Although the government is still piloting the top-down promotion of platform building by formulating policies, the practice of bottom-up platform building in society and the market has already been developing. The explosive growth of many e-commerce villages has helped the poor gain confidence in the poverty alleviation function of e-commerce platforms, which has laid a realistic foundation for Tian Box.

c) A poverty alleviation project listed by the Poverty Alleviation Office of the State Council

Since 2014, poverty alleviation through e-commerce has been highly valued by national governments and poverty alleviation offices at all levels, and has been listed as an intensive poverty alleviation project by the Poverty Alleviation Office of the State Council. Local governments have also shown great enthusiasm for poverty alleviation through e-commerce. Some leaders have stated their requirements as the pilot of e-commerce poverty alleviation to the national poverty alleviation authorities; some places have combined e-commerce with the amount of poverty alleviation to make deployments; some have explored many methods of poverty alleviation through e-commerce. This all provides assurance and support for building a comprehensive Tian Box platform.

In summary, building the Tian Box platform is a realistic choice in the fight against poverty. The basic conditions are already in place, and the platform is facing a rare opportunity for development.

(IV) Ways of building the Tian Box platform

a) Government support and social participation

The support of local governments is indispensable for building the Tian Box platform. At present, major e-commerce giants have set "channel sinking" as a major strategy, and have started to cooperate with local governments. Poverty-stricken regional governments should seize this opportunity to revitalize the agricultural economy of their local region and find new highlights for poverty alleviation as well as a new engine for economic transformation and upgrading. At the same time, they should also leverage the role of social forces such as industry associations, cooperatives, village committees, and leading poverty alleviation enterprises, and explore the high-quality agricultural and sideline specialties of specific regions by setting up public service institutions. The Tian Box platform is built by the government and social forces, with the government promoting and providing guidance, and social forces taking the initiative to dock with comprehensive e-commerce service providers such as JD.com to jointly develop and build the platform.

b) Service centers in villages and networks in counties

During its development, the Tian Box platform should be closely integrated with JD.com's "One Village, One Product, One Store" poverty alleviation project, and the implementation of the "One Million Farms in One Thousand Counties and Ten Thousand Villages" plan. Relying on these projects and programs, each poor village should establish a village-level e-commerce service center, taking the administrative village as a unit. Thus, a county-level e-commerce service network covering the whole of a poor county can be further established to realize the two-way communication of green products into the city and wealth into the village.

The village-level e-commerce service center can provide online shopping services for poor villagers, particularly in the current situation whereby many elderly people left behind in poor rural areas lack internet access and technology. For example, they can purchase daily necessities and agricultural materials online, sell local agricultural and sideline specialties, pay phone bills and electricity bills, and receive training in science and technology.

The county-level e-commerce service network is mainly dedicated to the building, maintenance, and management of logistics systems in poor village by combining with poverty alleviation system resources to set up logistics and distribution teams. It collects information from each village e-commerce service store to build a network terminal database, in order to grasp the business dynamics of each site at any time.

c) Continuous innovation based on local situations
To build the Tian Box platform, it is necessary to focus on poor counties first. Through connecting with model villages and households, the platform will continue to help and encourage the local community to form a conducive environment for developing e-commerce. The effect of targeted poverty alleviation can be achieved by connecting poor households and the disabled directly with recipients. By supporting the leading enterprises engaged in the e-commerce business, subjects such as online business brokers, wealthy individuals, breeding households, and professional associations, it is possible to promote the selling of agricultural and sideline products and the employment of poor households.

d) Focusing on cultivating personnel and providing long-term support
The key to poverty alleviation through e-commerce is staff. The lack of personnel has become the biggest obstacle to the development of rural e-commerce. The introduction and cultivation of a new era of vendors can provide lasting support for the building of the Tian Box platform, upon which the author will not elaborate further.

Building the Tian Box platform can help expand the development radius of poor villages, lower the market access threshold, and gather sporadic market demands, which will bring significant development to poor areas. Therefore, by seizing the opportunity of building the Tian Box platform, constantly introducing and nurturing new vendors in a market-oriented way, and at the same time implementing the building of comprehensive and affordable infrastructure covering the whole area, impoverished regions will be able to overtake the curve.

CHAPTER 5

Putting a Team Together for the Final Battle

ood governance at the county level is the foundation of a peaceful country. Since ancient times, China's counties have played an essential role in governing the country, as well as promoting social development. General Secretary Xi Jinping has repeatedly emphasized the significant role of county-level institutions in poverty alleviation efforts during his talks with outstanding secretaries of CPC County Committees nationwide. He has pointed out that within the organizational structure of the CPC and the political structure of the state power, the county level is the key link between the top and the bottom, and is an important foundation for economic development, safeguarding people's livelihoods, and maintaining stability, as well as a basic training base for cadres to start up their businesses, practice, and grow. The "Decision of the CPC Central Committee and the State Council on Winning the Fight Against Poverty" also emphasizes that county-level CPC committees and governments must assume the main responsibilities in poverty alleviation and elimination. In short, in order to win the decisive battle against poverty by 2020, county-level CPC committees and governments are the basic team, and should play a central role.

1. The key links in the fight against poverty

At present, there are 832 poor counties in China, including 592 national-level poor counties. The absolute impoverished population accounts for about 10% of the total. The central government must build a "five-level linkage" comprising provinces, cities, counties, towns, and villages in order to solidify the organizational basis of poverty alleviation. This organizational design determines that the county-level committees and governments will become the key links.

(I) *The final link: Party and government organs*

The "Decision of the CPC Central Committee and the State Council on Winning the Fight Against Poverty" delineates the responsibilities and work points of each level. Provincial CPC committees and governments play the main role, being responsible for setting targets, issuing projects, allocating funds, organizing and mobilizing members, as well as supervising and assessing the work. The roles of municipal CPC committees and governments are linking the top with the bottom, regional coordination, supervising and inspecting work, and encouraging poor counties to take off the "poverty hat." Party committees and governments at the county level should take responsibility for making progress, implementing projects, using funds, and deploying manpower, and pushing forward implementation. The reason why the central government has divided the responsibilities in such a way is determined by the characteristics of the final links of the county-level party committees and the government.

China's administrative organization is divided into six levels, from the central government to governments of provinces, cities, counties, towns, and villages. Among these six levels, the county level is the lowest, with complete departments. Towns and villages do not have complete departments. They only take corresponding personnel responsibilities. Therefore, the main responsibility for promoting and implementing the policies and decisions of the central, provincial, and municipal committees and governments naturally falls on the final link – the county-level committees and governments.

County-level committees and governments are the most basic level of all in China, and they are also the most complete final link of the organizational structure and functional configuration. The functions of county-level committees and governments determine that they can fully activate political, economic, cultural, and service-related resources to alleviate poverty, which are not available at the township and village levels. Provincial and municipal support measures on poverty alleviation funds, policies, and project introduction ultimately depend on the work of county-level committees and government leadership teams to be put in place. Therefore, county-level committees and governments are the final link in poverty alleviation work, and the most important one. In some cases, it is possible to see the importance of county-level committees and governments as the final link of the Party and government system.

Some deviations in poverty alleviation work in China at the present stage are reflected in divergences in the implementation of some specific policies by the administrative organizations at the county level. For example, in order to obtain the status of a poverty-stricken county and obtain more policy support, some counties falsely report their financial status. Some do not meet the criteria for a poverty-stricken county, but they claim the title in order to enjoy subsidies, which is a waste of national financial resources, and also causes inaccuracies in poverty statistics and decisions. Some counties adopt a non-cooperative game approach, which seriously compromises the effectiveness of the national poverty alleviation policy. In addition, for the sake of momentary political achievements, some counties have built vanity projects that do nothing to improve local poverty, and invoke complaints from the poor. This illustrates the fact that if county-level committees and governments fail to implement and carry out favorable state policies for poverty alleviation and the allocation of funds for poor areas, the pace of poverty alleviation will be seriously affected.

On the contrary, China has seen many county-level leadership teams that make full use of the favorable policies and funds given by the state, planning and designing for the poor, carrying out effective and targeted poverty alleviation work, and obtaining many achievements. For example, some counties use specially allocated financial funds to carry out poverty alleviation projects, using the government as the main guarantor to provide small loans with interest discounts to poor people, promoting local people by giving them projects and ideas to start their own businesses, which greatly increases income. With precise financial support as the foundation, they attract leading enterprises, and high-productivity, labor-intensive, or resource-intensive projects to invest in poor areas, which improves their economic development, greatly increases the income of poor people, and realizes the basic concept of transforming from a "blood transfusion" to a "blood generation" model relying on internal power as advocated in the general pattern of poverty alleviation. For example, some counties have changed their concepts and made comprehensive use of all their quality resources, and have made a set of combinations to help farmers with funds, policies, and services.

Therefore, it must be understood that county-level committees and governments are the final link for all county-level and government organs, carrying out all the central, provincial, and municipal policies and funds to alleviate poverty. Whether these policies and funds can be implemented, and whether they can be implemented well, all depends on the work of county-level leadership teams. County-level party committees and governments must be responsible to the central government, be determined and dedicated, and live up to expectations.

(II) The chief link in the battle against poverty

National statistics on poverty-stricken areas use counties as the highest statistical unit. Such a statistical distinction is in line with the reality of China's poor areas. In the 832 poor counties and 592 national-level poor counties alike, the leader and the chief link in the battle against poverty is the county-level Party committee and government.

This link is determined by many things. Firstly, the manpower of the organizations at town and village levels is limited, because there is no sound institutional setting, and the leadership of the organizations at township and village levels to fight poverty is insufficient, meaning that they are unable to plan, organize, coordinate, and implement. Secondly, the financial resources of the organizations at township and village levels are limited – national finance is connected to county finance, and the expenses of the organizations at town and village levels come from county finance. Poor financial circumstances also exacerbate the inability of organizations at the town and village levels to deploy funds to implement poverty alleviation work. Third, the capacity of organizations at the village and township levels is limited. Their policy level and ideology are relatively backward because of obstructions to transport, backward public facilities, information blockage in poor areas, and their grassroots position. The state of the organizations at town and village levels makes the role of the head of the county Party committee and government extremely significant.

As the head of poverty-stricken counties, county-level Party committees and governments must establish a strong sense of responsibility and mission, and dare to take charge and take the initiative. As General Secretary Xi said, they should focus on poverty alleviation and eradication without distractions, and unite the general public to eradicate poverty as soon as possible through hard work. As the chief link, county-level Party committees and governments play the leading role. They should think about how and why they are poor, and identify the exact root of poverty. They should consider their advantages, think about how to become wealthy, and choose a scientific path. They should remain open minded, make a good overall plan, and understand which projects can be accomplished by self-reliance and which ones require the help of others. Thus, they can build on strengths and avoid weaknesses, and enhance the initiative, efficiency, and permanence of poverty alleviation.

The chief link should play an exemplary role in leadership and demonstration. First, the ideological understanding and working attitude of county-level Party committee and government staff should be corrected. They should study the speeches of General Secretary Xi on poverty alleviation and understand their essence, guide poverty eradication projects, and meticulously implement the policies of the Party Central Committee and the State Council. They should also build confidence in poverty alleviation and accelerate its development, following the concepts of self-reliance and hard work, and working hard to change the status quo. Secondly, they should clarify the objectives and focus of each stage, because only when the objectives are clear can the working direction and operation run smoothly. They should improve the target responsibility system, and reconstruct the work performance assessment system according to the requirements of General Secretary Xi Jinping and the central government for poverty alleviation and elimination. Based on the actual situation, county departments should first negotiate the progress and target requirements, and clarify the overall target of poverty alleviation to be accomplished within a certain period of time, and then analyze it layer by layer so that the overall target can be delegated to each department and finally implemented by individuals. Through this system, the responsibilities of each department and each staff member are clarified so as to inspire enthusiasm and creativity in all personnel.

(III) The intermediate link between the top and the bottom

The five levels of provincial, municipal, county, town, and village linkage are the mechanism and method of the 2020 battle against poverty, which aims to drive the development of comprehensive poverty eradication work through top-down integrated supervision. In this way, each link can play its role in winning the battle.

The middle of the linkage is the county-level Party committee and government. As mentioned earlier, county-level Party committees and governments are the end of the administrative system from the central government to the counties, and also the head of the system from the counties to the villages, functioning as the intermediate link between the top and the bottom. From the perspective of the poverty eradication system, only the county-level Party committees and governments are both the focus and the point of poverty eradication in poor counties. As General Secretary Xi Jinping has stated, "A county Party secretary must visit all of the villages; a municipal Party secretary must visit all of the towns; a provincial Party secretary must visit all of the counties, districts, and cities." The ultimate goal of poverty eradication is to lift everyone in poor villages out of poverty, which is within the purview of the county-level Party committees and governments. Provincial and municipal Party committees and governments are mainly responsible for planning, formulating policies, mobilizing funds, providing guarantees, and guiding directions, while county-level Party committees and governments need to carry out all of the above policies and implement them in towns and villages. Thus, county-level Party committees and governments are the basis for poverty alleviation, economic development, protection of people's livelihoods, maintenance of stability, and promotion of long-term national security, and they play a significant role in the whole five-level linkage system.

County-level Party committees and governments are in the middle of the link, connecting the top and the bottom. They have to be responsible for both sides – the policymakers and the general public – to ensure the implementation of higher policies as well as high-quality grassroots services. To this end, county-level Party committees and governments should position themselves accurately, striving to build the link, and playing a positive role in connecting the top and the bottom.

They have to be politically aware by constantly acquiring theoretical knowledge, intensifying theoretical training, and keeping pace with the Party Central Committee in terms of ideology, politics, and action, remaining dedicated to their duties in the battle against poverty. They must also maintain fairness and ethics, not using power for personal gain or to harm the interests of farmers. They should do their jobs in a down-to-earth manner, make friends with town and village cadres, sum up the lessons they learn, and identify suitable methods to alleviate poverty in towns and villages together. They must speak for poor farmers, put themselves in their position, and think about the practical problems facing peasants in the same way. They should communicate with impoverished farmers, and patiently explain the policies to win poor people over and gain their support and understanding.

2016 was the opening year of the 13th Five-Year Plan, and the first year in the process of winning the battle against poverty. County-level Party committees and governments must do the following things in order to play the role of connecting the link: First, county-level leadership teams should assess the completion of poverty alleviation and eradication in the 12th Five-Year Plan period, clarify the status quo, and identify gaps and problems in order to lay a good foundation for the fight against poverty in the 13th Five-Year Plan period. Secondly, they should accurately grasp the overall requirements for the 13th Five-Year Plan at the county level, clarify the work direction, and combined with the actual situation of poverty in their county, connect with higher departments to ensure that more industrial poverty alleviation projects can be included in higher-level planning. Thirdly, while promoting the work of poverty alleviation, they should select some main and key projects, and intensify the efforts of poverty alleviation so that they can become the leading industries in the county and drive the rapid development of the county's economy and society in order to promote the effective implementation of poverty alleviation planning. Fourthly, they should carry out in-depth research and make plans for poverty eradication in order to lay the foundation for connecting the link. Research is the premise and basis for clarifying the ideas behind poverty alleviation. How to fight poverty, build a moderately prosperous society, deepen reform, undertake industrial transfer, and get project support must all be researched and analyzed if they are to be accurately grasped when planning poverty alleviation work. Fifthly, the awareness of the county-level Party committees and governments of the military order must be strengthened, the ideas and attitudes of the leaders must be corrected, and all deviations in thinking must be eliminated to ensure the effective implementation of poverty eradication and contribute to all five levels of the joint poverty eradication campaign.

2. The "front-line command" of the battle against poverty

According to General Secretary Xi Jinping, the "front-line command" is a metaphor for county-level leaders. He has stressed the importance of county-level power in the governance of the country, pointing out that "county committees are the front-line command of the Party in ruling and enriching the country." County-level power is taking on increasing responsibilities, especially in terms of building a moderately prosperous society, deepening reform, comprehensively ruling the country, and strictly leading the Party. In particular, it plays a significant role in the process of the "Four Comprehensives," namely, building a moderately prosperous society, deepening reform, ruling the country by law, and strictly leading the Party. The role of the "front-line command" is fully in line with the specifics and essential requirements of county-level Party committees and governments in poverty eradication.

The following section will elaborate on the role and function of the "front-line command" in poverty eradication from three aspects: the dual subject responsibility system of the "front-line command," the dual people-in-charge system, and the general commander of the "front-line command."

(I) The dual subject responsibility system of the "front-line command"

The "Decision of the CPC Central Committee and the State Council on Winning the Fight Against Poverty" states that county-level Party committees and governments take the main responsibility, which proves that in the decisive battle against poverty, the county committee and the county government are the two key subjects of responsibility, and the battle is carried out using a dual-subject responsibility system.

The dual responsibility system is an accurate reflection of China's county-level political system, and also shows the superiority of China's county-level political system. China is under the unitary leadership of the CPC, and the CPC Central and Party committees at all levels are the leading core of the state and power at all levels. Meanwhile, the State Council and governments at all levels exercise power under the unified leadership of the CPC Central Committee and the Party committees at all levels. In the battle against poverty, The "Decision of the CPC Central Committee and the State Council on Winning the Fight Against Poverty" specifies that county-level Party committees and governments assume the main responsibility, which ensures that the superimposed effect of the dual subjects of county committees and governments can be fully utilized.

First, all factions should adhere to their duties. The "Decision of the CPC Central Committee and the State Council on Winning the Fight Against Poverty" specifies in the basic principles of the battle against poverty that the county Party committee has overall responsibility for the battle, leveraging the leading core role of the county Party committee in coordinating all parties. The county government guides the battle against poverty, strengthens the government's responsibility, and leads the market and society to make concerted efforts, which proves that the county-level Party committee must leverage its leadership role in the battle against poverty, insist on integrated coordination, maintain the direction, and control the overall situation. The county government must follow the overall arrangement of the battle against poverty, take the lead in the implementation of plans, coordinate manpower, deploy funds, arrange projects, promote industrial development, and make sure that each project is completed according to the timeline.

Secondly, the division of labor and cooperation is necessary. The county-level Party committee and county government are both the subjects of responsibility according to the "Decision of the CPC Central Committee and the State Council on Winning the Fight Against Poverty," both undertaking the mission and responsibility of leading the county out of poverty. Therefore, it is necessary to insist on the division of labor and governance, making joint efforts, neither overstepping authority nor shirking responsibilities, and cooperating and adapting activities so that people can make concerted efforts to alleviate poverty.

(II) *The dual people-in-charge system of the "front-line command"*

The implementation of the dual responsibility system of county-level Party committees and governments in the battle against poverty necessitates having two people in charge. The "Decision of the CPC Central Committee and the State Council on Winning the Fight Against Poverty" clarifies that they are the secretary of the county-level Party committee and the county governor.

In other words, the first person responsible for the county Party committee is the secretary, and that of the county government is the county governor. These two people undertake the historical mission of poverty eradication together.

Of course, this does not mean that their responsibilities are halved. It can be implied from the responsibilities of the county Party committee and the county government that the responsibilities of the two roles are also clear, and that they should fulfill their mission according to their respective responsibilities – the county Party secretary is the leader cooperating with the county governor to jointly implement policies.

First, a practical attitude to work must always be maintained, proceeding from reality and making decisions based on the actual situation of the county. To seek truth from facts is to adhere to the local conditions and make use of them. It is necessary to digest and absorb cases of successful poverty alleviation in other counties rather than blindly following trends or rigidly copying others' paths to success. Seeking truth from facts also requires scientific decision-making, planning, and action, making full use of the laws of science, working according to regulations and procedures, bold exploration, careful verification, and innovation, so that all decisions and measures can withstand the test of time.

Secondly, a habit of learning and thinking must be maintained. Through continuous learning, the horizons of poverty alleviation can be broadened, and improve the ability to recognize, analyze, and solve the problems that hinder poverty alleviation. Those in charge must genuinely understand all of the instructions and concepts of alleviating poverty from higher institutions such as the Party Central Committee and the State Council, and learn from the successes and failure of other counties and regions, so as to seize the opportunity and position the county's poverty alleviation in the general environment, within the general trend, and in the big picture. China must think about the present from a long-term perspective, and consider the work done from a more universal perspective. It is necessary to weigh the pros and cons from the perspective of sustainability when making decisions, take the opinions and suggestions of all parties, develop poverty alleviation work in a more foresighted way, and eliminate situations in which decisions deviate from the general policy of the Party Central Committee and the actual situation of the county.

Thirdly, a passionate entrepreneurial mindset must be maintained towards work. China has been in three overlapping periods of reform, conflict, and economic transition. This is also a critical turning point in the development of the CPC and the nation overall. Many new situations, problems, and trends are challenging the strategic vision and thinking abilities, the understanding of their historical status, and the sense of responsibility of county Party secretaries and county governors. In such a period, county Party secretaries and county governors bear the great historical mission of working for the welfare of the general public in poor areas. They must maintain their enthusiasm, see themselves as hard-working and practical people, devote all their time and energy to poverty eradication and entrepreneurship, and also use scientific methods to promote these things. They must go deep into the rural grass-root level and into poor households to carry out research, summarize the basic tasks of poverty alleviation, and enhance their ability to analyze and solve problems. The problems of poverty alleviation must be approached, coordinated, and supervised in person so as to truly seek benefit for the poor.

Fourthly, efforts must always start with the poor, and must include them. Both the county Party committee secretary and the governor must always bear in mind where their power comes from, and what they use it for. They should respect the power given to them by the public, and remember the teachings of General Secretary Xi. "Take a walk in their shoes. Don't treat your people badly, because you are one of them." They should always bear in mind the fundamental purpose of the CPC, serve the public wholeheartedly, and always put the interests of the people first. No matter how trivial something may seem, it is a big deal when it comes to people's affairs. No matter how difficult something is, it is necessary to do it well. The people are a family. Only when this concept is established can a county's first secretary truly treat the affairs of the poor as their own family affairs. They must hear the opinions, suggestions, and demands of the masses, fully understand their needs, take the will of the general public as the basis for decision-making and deployment, and ensure that all decisions on poverty alleviation are made in accordance with people's wishes.

Fifthly, a sense of crisis must be maintained. General Secretary Xi once said in an interview that China is a large country with a large population and complex conditions, so leaders should uphold a sense of awareness of their actions. They must remember that the interests of the public are paramount, and that their responsibilities are extremely heavy. They must not slacken in the slightest, nor let their standards drop, and must be on duty and work diligently at all times. Xi also stressed that leaders should undertake their responsibilities, because only in doing so can they make great achievements. As the "front-line command" in the battle against poverty, the county Party committee secretary and county governor must fulfill the requirements of the "Three Strictures and Three Realities," remembering the four traits of Jiao Yulu-type county Party secretaries proposed by General Secretary Xi, and never neglecting their duties. The county Party secretary should take the lead, maintain the correct ethos, and gather the power to lift the county out of poverty and drive economic and social development.

(III) The "commander-in-chief" of the "front-line command"

General Secretary Xi Jinping has emphasized that the county Party secretary is the "commander-in-chief" of the front-line command. In the battle to end poverty and build a moderately prosperous society, the county Party secretary undertakes a combination of political and social responsibilities, and is in an extremely critical position, playing the role of a knot. In *Up and Out of Poverty*, Xi wrote that if China is a net, then the 3,000+ counties within it are the knots. A loose knot will cause a turbulent national political situation, while firm knots will lead to a stable condition. The tightness of the knot is determined by the county Party secretary – the "commander-in-chief" of the front-line command. The county Party secretary plays a decisive role in determining whether the battle against poverty can be won, whether the central policy can be implemented, and whether the county's predicament can be solved with scientific planning, reasonable deployment, and steady command.

Loyalty to the Party is the premise of a good "commander-in-chief" of the "front-line command"; the key is having the courage to take the charge; the root is honesty. The county Party secretary is the core of a county's poverty alleviation efforts, wielding the power to deploy and decide on the development of people, money, and materials across the whole county. Therefore, the secretary's political quality and awareness are a personal issue as well as a matter of the direction of county-wide poverty alleviation. County Party secretaries should remember the General Secretary's teachings, that is, "to consider the Party, the people, the responsibility, and the precautions." They should be politically sensitive in leading the battle against poverty, caring for the poor, and guiding their team. For the poor to achieve moderate prosperity, county Party secretaries must maintain their position, do their job, undertake full responsibilities, and try their best no matter how great the difficulties are. To undertake the responsibility of seeking benefit for the poor, they must always maintain political consciousness, be loyal to the Party, and live up to the trust granted to them by the Party and the people.

A good "commander-in-chief" of the "front-line command" must be confident about winning the battle against poverty, and must have a sense of political responsibility and historical mission when facing the strenuous task of poverty alleviation. The battle can be won as long as confidence is established. The CPC Central Committee and the State Council have made clear arrangements for the new era of poverty eradication, proposing the ideas of "Four Practices," "Five Batches," and "Six Precisions." As the "commander-in-chief" on the front line of the battle, the county Party secretary must consider the actual situation of the county, and implement the decisions and the concepts of the CPC Central Committee and the State Council according to their own conditions. He or she must improve their own ability to take charge, and strengthen the battle against poverty to achieve the final victory.

A good "commander-in-chief" of the "front-line command" must establish a new view of the political performance required to win the battle. However, in the current environment of poverty alleviation, there are still many problems with the style of some county Party secretaries. Since they hold the power of the public, money, and materials, and lead the Party committee, government, NPC, and CPPCC, so many county Party secretaries commit corruption that cases of bribery, embezzlement, and lifestyle indiscretions are frequently reported in the news. The problems of formalism, bureaucracy, hedonism, and extravagance have not been completely solved. There are also some county Party secretaries who are eager for quick success and instant benefit, and unilaterally emphasize superficial projects without considering social values and ecological consequences. Some other county Party secretaries seem to be busy all day long but work with low efficiency. They do not listen to the suffering and difficulties of poor people, and they are reluctant to go to remote impoverished places with inadequate access to transport for research. Their flippancy means that poverty alleviation cannot be carried out. These problems must be overcome, their ideas must be reformed, and a strong belief in serving the poor and leading them out of poverty must be instilled. In short, county Party secretaries should adhere to the basic value of alleviating poverty and achieving prosperity in the county, reflect on themselves, and live up to the honorable title of "commander-in-chief" of the "front-line command."

A good "commander-in-chief" of the "front-line command" must plan and design poverty alleviation work according to the actual situation of the county. In the new era, new situation, new projects, and new environment, China must plan to complete the task of poverty alleviation and build a moderately prosperous society. The 13th Five-Year Plan will be implemented in the next five years. All the tasks of poverty alleviation should be arranged in close accordance with its requirements, with a clear understanding that development is the best way to alleviate poverty, and that the full and reasonable use of market laws is the most effective method. China must pursue development through innovation, coordination, environmental awareness, openness, and sharing, as pointed out by General Secretary Xi Jinping in the 13th Five-Year Plan period, taking into account actual local situations, and upgrading the industry on the basis of the former "blood transfusion" model of poverty alleviation. It must improve industrial efficiency, leverage internal power, and transform invested capital into real productivity. Thus, the former "blood transfusion" model can be transformed into the "blood generation" model according to the actual situation of poor villages, and each impoverished household will be provided with a livable income.

A good "commander-in-chief" of the "front-line command" must make full use of a county's natural resource advantages so as to form an industrial base in poor areas. History has proved again and again that no improvement to productivity can be achieved in poverty-stricken areas without industrial development, and no sustainable wealth acquisition and accumulation can be achieved without improvements to productivity, and thus poverty alleviation becomes empty talk. Industrial development can create exceptional conditions and environments, infinite possibilities, and continuous vitality for targeted poverty alleviation. In the current stage, the basic conditions of poor areas in China have generally improved, the building of infrastructure support is gradually improving, and many places now have an industrial base.

For the "commander-in-chief" of the "front-line command," the key to poverty alleviation in the future lies in choosing the correct industrial project in accordance with the actual local situation, finding a way to become wealthy in line with local specifics and public opinion, and combining and making full use of the market to improve production efficiency and internal power. To ensure sales and services in the new era, they must look for exceptional county-level enterprises to invest in, provide capital and employment opportunities for poor people, and use industry to promote poverty alleviation. They should put together a professional team of personnel to help solve their county's poverty alleviation problems, and seek a poverty eradication mechanism that aligns with local development. The resources of the entire county should be integrated into a platform, and all available resources should be used to improve the effectiveness of poverty alleviation and eradication there.

At the same time, as the "commander-in-chief" of the "front-line command," the county Party secretary also has to play a service role. Firstly, they must serve the poor and think on their behalf; secondly, they must serve enterprise projects, and provide full support and assistance for these enterprises and projects to the greatest possible extent in order to provide good environmental conditions for industrial development, reduce market transaction costs, and accelerate the pace of marketization in the county. They should guide industrial restructuring, emphasize ecology and environmental protection, and reduce the number of small backward enterprises with high energy consumption and low efficiency, to achieve the goal of sustainable development of resources. All forces must be united and encouraged to promote poverty alleviation and place it in the most significant and practical position. All departments must pay close attention to forming a linkage between the upper and lower levels, creating an overall poverty alleviation pattern of joint management.

3. The command strategy of poverty alleviation

General Secretary Xi has repeatedly stated that the basic strategy for poverty eradication lies in precision, as proven by the practice of poverty alleviation and eradication since the 18th National Congress. The basic requirement of the Party Central Committee for targeted poverty alleviation and eradication is to achieve the "Six Precisions" – precise objects, precise project arrangements, precise use of funds, precise measures taken in households, a precise First Secretary of the county, and precise results. The key is to solve a series of problems such as who to help, who can help, how to help, and how to return, as well as the correct implementation of the targeted poverty alleviation and eradication strategy. From the current analysis of the specific situation of poor counties, to implement targeted poverty alleviation and eradication, it is necessary to also implement the command strategy of "Three Insistences," that is, insisting on making breakthroughs with industrial development, insisting on a national poverty alleviation framework, and controlling the overall situation from the forefront.

(I) Insisting on making breakthroughs with industrial development

Economic indicators are among the most significant ways to measure poverty. The poorer the area, the more blind it is to finance. As enterprises participate in poverty alleviation by changing their original production and operation methods, they are gradually seeking business opportunities. These so-called business opportunities do not mean how much money can be earned from the farmers or how much benefit can be obtained. Instead, according to the needs of the enterprise's own development, the first link in the industrial chain is delegated to the farmers. The farmers are thus driven by the project, and their income will be returned to the enterprise so as to achieve win-win sustainable development. Therefore, it has become the command strategy of the "front-line headquarters" for targeted poverty alleviation and eradication to attract people through the industry and support industrial development, to improve the economic conditions in poor areas and increase the income of poor people.

According to economics, poverty is the deprivation of the well-being of the public, in which individuals and families do not have enough income to meet their basic needs. At the same time, people generally believe that poverty is a form of inferiority, and if the situation is not radically improved, the living environment will get worse for everyone. Therefore, increasing income and eradicating poverty have become the main expectations of anti-poverty efforts. However, the inherent thinking of the poor is to expect others to help eliminate poverty, benefiting from the "blood transfusion" model of poverty alleviation. Within such an ideology, the psychological expectation of the poor is to rely on government support to solve the problem of poverty, but this can never be satisfied in terms of operational feasibility and sustainability. Therefore, economically speaking, the most effective way to improve the internal power of poor regions is to adopt a "blood generation" developmental approach to poverty alleviation, and to leverage the role of market mechanisms. The "blood generation" model means increased consumption capacity for the market, a more stable society, and a more equitable distribution mechanism for the government.

County-level Party committees and governments must grasp the command strategy of industrial breakthrough. They must accurately map out the overall base of each town and village in the county, and understand how large the local impoverished area is, how many people are in poverty, how poor it is, what the causes of poverty are, and what the potential resource advantages are. In this way, they can make individual poverty eradication plans according to the needs of the poor towns, villages, households, and people. In order to ensure that the work of poverty alleviation and eradication is transparent, and to make sure there is data to rely on and check, indicators for each year's work in the next five years have been set up in a scientific way, with details of each time point.

For some counties and regions with serious poverty, the work of poverty alleviation may have to be carried out first by "blood transfusion" – to improve infrastructure, stabilize the political and economic environment, change the ideology of the poor, and lay a good foundation for attracting industrial investment, in preparation for the implementation of "blood generation" measures such as industry introduction and implementation. It is necessary to focus on "blood transfusion" in the early stage, both "blood transfusion" and "blood generation" in the middle stage, and finally "blood generation" in the later stage. For counties with low poverty rates, it is necessary to change gradually from the mode of classifying poverty by income to the concept of looking at poverty through industrial capacity and development. According to economics, there is no output without input.

County-level Party committees and governments should do everything possible to increase investment in the alleviation and eradication of poverty through industry, to increase the investment of financial funds, and also to coordinate the input of projects, technology, personnel, and policies.

It is necessary to: use the reform and innovation of investment and financing systems as the driving force; increase investment in poverty alleviation and eradication through industry by multiple channels, multiple means, and multiple ways; strive to intensify the input mechanism of industry departments; intensify the supported input of social forces; encourage market entities, social organizations, and individuals to participate in poverty alleviation and eradication through industrial development; explore the establishment of capitalized investment and financial mechanisms for poverty alleviation and eradication resources; and intensify the mechanism of asset-based income for the poor. Poverty alleviation personnel should make full use of specific local resources in poor areas, as well as resources under the collective ownership of the poor, and the potential resources held by the poor so that the poor can obtain income from them. On the basis of who to support and how to support, personnel must find the best way to increase income steadily within industries, and alleviate poverty steadily in counties.

The effectiveness of county-level Party committees and governments in poverty alleviation and relief work is limited by the scale of resource input, and also depends on the structure and way of such input. Choosing the right industrial method for targeted poverty alleviation and eradication can improve the allocation efficiency of poverty alleviation resources. For example, if the problem of poverty alleviation and eradication is placed into the market mechanism, the market will provide the most effective way of resource allocation.

Therefore, it is vital for county-level Party committees and governments to establish mutually beneficial relationships and cooperations with the market, which is the lever of funds and resources. This is also needed for targeted poverty alleviation and eradication, to leverage and use the role of market mechanisms in the development of industries for targeted poverty alleviation and eradication. It is necessary to: gain motivation through attracting market players; seek vitality through attracting market mechanisms; form poverty alleviation and eradication industries to stimulate market potential; and promote the market-oriented allocation of resources for poverty alleviation and eradication, in order to maximize and optimize the benefits. The greatest benefit of making full use of the market to allocate resources and alleviate poverty is to enable poor groups to better integrate into the market and create their own value once they have risen out of poverty, so as not to fall back into it.

Neijiang County in Sichuan Province took the local situation into consideration in its targeted poverty alleviation work. It created innovative financial poverty alleviation mechanisms to support micro and small enterprises, and launched a series of credit products such as small loans for small enterprises, supplier loans, and personal business credit loans to support small and micro enterprises to start their own business development, thus driving the regional economic development. The approach is that the government and the financial service center take the lead to establish a team dedicated to serving small and micro enterprises, and activate a rapid response mechanism to improve their ability to adapt to the market, which efficiently solves the problem of financing for small and micro enterprises.

At the same time, it also provides tailor-made service programs for small and micro enterprises, which strengthens their supervision and helps their development. The microfinance institutions in Neijiang county have simplified the financing process for micro and small enterprises, and are committed to providing one-stop financial services. Working for their benefit, they have contributed greatly to the development of the county's industry-based poverty alleviation. By the end of October 2015, the loan amount for small and micro enterprises in the county reached 202 million yuan, with the total support of more than 200 customers.

(II) Insisting on a national poverty alleviation framework

Currently, poverty in China mainly occurs in villages and towns, but the poverty-alleviation work of county-level Party committees and governments cannot be considered solely from the perspective of county development. County Party secretaries, county governors, and various departments of county committees and governments must think about the major social issue of poverty alleviation and eradication in counties from a higher level and with a longer-term perspective. They must learn about and implement the national positioning and ideas on the bigger picture of poverty eradication, focusing on the overall national situation based on the actual situation in counties. They must also coordinate and implement poverty alleviation and eradication work through county-wide industrial development.

Sociology regards poverty as a phenomenon of social exclusion – a disconnection between individuals and groups, especially vulnerable groups such as the elderly, the weak, the sick, and the disabled who do not have sufficient civil rights to participate in economic and social activities. Thus, social inclusion policies become a significant tool within anti-poverty policies Sociologists have analyzed poverty from the point of view of the vulnerability of individuals and families in society, and believe that poverty is divided into deprivation and social exclusion. The concept of deprivation refers to poverty caused by a lack of resources, while the concept of social exclusion refers to the disconnection of poor individuals from society as a whole, such as a lack of skills, loss of health, and housing problems, which prevent them from having equal access to public resources, the labor market, and basic public services – essentially, a lack of equal civil rights. So, how can county-level Party committees and governments use the broad strategy of targeted poverty alleviation and eradication to solve these problems?

County-level Party committees and governments should understand that it is the government's responsibility to alleviate and eliminate poverty, and that all citizens have equal rights; the poorer the population, the more help they need. Targeted poverty alleviation and eradication require precision, so a county's poor population must be classified according to the causes of poverty, and special treatment given to those in specific conditions of poverty. Specifically, for those who are deprived, the government should invest resources according to the actual situation. Some places may be rich in material resources but lack labor, technology, and development funds, so the county Party committee and government should take the initiative to attract these resources. For the excluded, the goal of poverty alleviation should be to implement the "Two Worry-frees" and "Three Guarantees" to ensure equal rights for the poor.

General Secretary Xi Jinping has repeatedly stressed the importance of education in poverty alleviation and eradication, pointing out that "helping the poor must help the wise." Education must never be reduced no matter how poor you are, and wisdom is needed to alleviate poverty. Education is fundamental to cultivating wisdom, and is also a significant way to pull out the roots of poverty and stop intergenerational transmission. Xi also repeatedly stressed that China must not let the children of poor families fall behind at the start. It is a significant element of poverty alleviation and development to provide children in poor areas with a good education. The Party committees and governments in poverty-eradicated counties should seek ways to promote the integration and utilization of county educational resources based on national, provincial, and urban educational resources. They should make full use of existing educational resources, and accelerate the development of new educational resources to cultivate children, so as to improve their own abilities and reserves for creating social value in the future. For the poor labor force in counties, the Party committee and government should integrate with education and training resources outside of the county. They should organize and intensify special professional knowledge and skill training, and improve the skills and social capital of the poor labor force, so that they can integrate more effectively into society and the market, and enjoy public resources and basic public services.

For the poor supported by social security, it is necessary to promote the implementation of the national standards for rural poverty alleviation and rural low-income security, and increase the efforts of other forms of social assistance. It is necessary to implement national medical insurance and medical assistance, and new rural cooperative medical care and major medical insurance policies, as well as: constructing a complete county social security system; improving the county-level primary medical care system; favoring the poor; protecting the basic rights of impoverished disabled groups to access medical services; promoting the effectiveness of county-level poverty alleviation work; and preventing the occurrence of poverty due to illness.

(III) Controlling the overall situation from the forefront

To be at the forefront in poverty alleviation means focusing on the poor. Compared with the previous crude poverty alleviation and eradication model, the current pattern is targeted, which means that it helps the very poorest and neediest. It is only by eliminating poverty for these critically poor people that poverty eradication can truly be considered to be working. To achieve precision, county-level Party committees and government leaders must go deep into poor households, listen to and understand the demands of the poor, and grasp their actual situation.

In previous attempts at poverty alleviation, some counties and districts have experienced shortcomings to varying degrees. For example, more often than not, they have been helping farmers rather than the poor. As a result, the target of assistance has been middle- and high-income farmers rather than the neediest and poorest. The main reason for this is that the work has not been based at the forefront; the situation of the target population has not been well understood, the policies and funds have not been directed appropriately, and the targeting has not been precise enough. Therefore, they are not alleviating and eradicating poverty for the truly impoverished. Targeted poverty alleviation and eradication consists of applying scientific and effective procedures for precise identification, precise assistance, and precise management of targets, according to the actual situation for poor villages and farmers. The work of poverty alleviation must be led by the government, encouraging the participation of the market and resources from all echelons of society, and formulating optimal support and plans in line with local situations, so as to achieve the purpose of self-development within poverty alleviation. It is only when the most pressing problems are solved (especially the problem of industrial development) that the stability of county society, the long-term political situation, and the development of culture and education can be guaranteed. Therefore, the targeted poverty alleviation work of county Party committees and governments must be based at the forefront, and must serve the poorest people effectively.

To be at the forefront in the battle against poverty, it is also necessary to control the overall situation of poverty alleviation and eradication in counties, and promote it as a whole. 2016 is the key year for deepening reform. As the "front-line headquarters," county-level Party committees and governments must implement policies and strategies that are consistent with the major policies of the Party Central Committee. It is necessary to grasp the symbolic, leading, and pillar reform tasks, take the initiative, and work closely and accurately.

As for county reforms, it is necessary to implement the tasks deployed by the Party Central Committee, and also to explore and innovate. On the premise of adhering to the "one country" principle, China must determine the focus, the pathway, the sequence, and the method of reform, and creatively implement the initiatives of the Party Central Committee, so that the reform can dovetail more accurately with the needs of poverty alleviation. It is necessary to understand the idea behind the "Decision of the CPC Central Committee and the State Council on Winning the Fight Against Poverty," and develop and improve the implementation mechanism, basing work on reality and the specific problems, and solving the outstanding problems so that poverty alleviation can take effect.

Put simply, there are both opportunities and challenges in the battle against poverty. County-level Party committees and governments should play the role of "front-line command," making full use of the five levels of linkage, which is a top-down system of poverty eradication. They must base their work at the forefront, with the very poorest people, and control county-wide poverty alleviation efforts. They must coordinate and implement policies precisely, seize the moment, and strive to create a new status quo for poverty eradication.

CHAPTER 6

The Main Instigator in the Final Battle

The fact that impoverished Chinese villages have gained prosperity proves that external help does play a significant role in poverty alleviation. However, in the long run, the decisive factor is an internal one. The external factor is the condition of change, while the internal factor is the basis of change. The external factor can only work through the internal factor. Cases have proved repeatedly that only with the joint efforts of village leadership teams can external help become effective, and only then can a country really become wealthy. The once-poor villages that have been lifted out of poverty all have strong village leadership teams, and their exemplary leadership in the fight against poverty has been proved by practice. The "Decision of the CPC Central Committee and the State Council on Winning the Fight Against Poverty" points out that it is necessary to intensify the building of rural Party organizations in poverty-stricken areas, so that they can become a strong basis to lead the people to become wealthy. Undoubtedly, in this five-level linkage of provinces, cities, counties, towns, and villages, and in the battle to eradicate poverty across the country, the village leaders are the front-runners and main faction.

1. The status of the main faction in the battle against poverty

Whether a village is rich or not depends on its leadership team; whether the team is strong or not depends on its leader. This is a summary of the status of the rural two-committee team. For poor villagers to rise out of poverty and earn a living, a leadership team comprising two committees that is led by the first secretary of the village Party branch serves as the main instigator on the front line, in an irreplaceable position.

(I) The "front-line commanders" in the battle against poverty

A village's two committees are at the forefront of the fight against poverty. All of the policies and decisions made by the Party and the government in the fight against poverty depend on the village's two committees for their implementation. They are the commanders who understand the reality of poverty-stricken villages and take off the "poverty hat" one household at a time. In the five-level linkage of the poverty alleviation system, the village's two committees have the most say in the actual situation of each household. The most substantial and fundamental questions – namely how to fight, where to fight, who comes first, who comes second, and whether it is possible to win – are ultimately for them to decide.

In the current decisive battle against poverty, the core leadership position of village leadership teams will be raised to a new height. Their historical status is determined by China's specific national conditions. Eliminating poverty and achieving common prosperity are the essential requirements of China's socialist system. Since Reform and Opening, China's government-led poverty alleviation and development project has made remarkable achievements, successfully reducing the number of impoverished people by nearly 700 million, and becoming the first country in the world to achieve the UN's "Millennium Development Goal" of halving the number of people in poverty. As the bridge and bond between the Party and the government at the top and thousands of households at the bottom, the leaders of poverty-stricken villages propagate and implement the policies and measures made by the Party and the government in the fight against poverty, becoming the direct commanding force on the front line. The success of dismantling the label of poverty and helping impoverished people earn a living is the result of rural two-committee leadership teams' efforts and wisdom, as they serve as the irreplaceable "front-line commanders" in the fight against poverty.

(II) The official leader of the battle against poverty

A village's two committees are the heads of public affairs in that village. The fight against poverty in a poverty-stricken village involves all of the impoverished people, as well as agricultural development, rural improvement, environmental transformation, pensions, medical care, and education. Managing all of these complicated matters is the responsibility of the person in charge.

The fight against poverty is a seesaw, requiring the leaders of poverty-stricken villages to fully understand both sides, one of which is the policies and guidelines of the Party and the government, and the other is the actual situation of the village and the thoughts and ideas of the impoverished people, so that two sides can connect. In terms of working methods and approaches, it is recommended to: stay ahead, grasping the actual situation, making sufficient preparations, and capturing the initiative to win the fight against poverty; never wait for or rely on others, be self-motivated, be one step ahead of others, and strive to be the leader in lifting impoverished villagers out of poverty and towards prosperity; speaking of working principles, insist on being fair in all activities, be it the arrangement of funds for poverty alleviation, the adjustment of an agricultural project, or training personnel; treat it objectively without any family-related preferences; be responsible, innovative, self-disciplined, and decent.

(III) The wealth manager in the battle against poverty

Those who are in charge should manage the wealth of the village. In the fight against poverty, there will be a lot of funds and materials to support poor villages in terms of environmental improvement and public services. Whether the corresponding funds and materials are well managed and used to bring benefits lies in the village's two-committee leadership team.

The wealth management status of the two-committee leadership team is determined by the specifics of poverty alleviation and development work. In China, poverty alleviation and development work is both a political and an economic act. The Party and the government will activate a large number of human, material, and financial resources for this work in poor villages, and the village's two-committee leadership team serves as the most direct and final organizer, manager, and implementer. Throughout history, the Party and the government have always insisted that policies should be targeted at each specific village, household, and person in poverty alleviation and development work. Both funds and projects should be implemented for each poverty-stricken household and person.

Indeed, poverty alleviation institutions and supporting organizations of all levels play a major part. However, the village's two-committee leadership team is most familiar with the local situation. It knows the majority of poor families, and can play a precise management role in grasping the situation, proposing projects, and using funds. Thanks to its experience of poverty alleviation and development work, the wealth manager is extremely significant in lifting poor villages out of poverty and into wealth. The effectiveness of poverty alleviation can only be improved with careful calculation, good management, and proper use of each fund invested by the Party and the government, plus all human, material, and financial resources.

■ **Case Study**

The administrative village of Changying in Heilongjiang Province is located in the western part of Mianpo Town in Shangzhi City. More than 40 years ago, Changying was the city's typical "Three Reliances" village, spending money on loans, living on relief, and surviving by counter-purchase. Nowadays, Changying is one of the country's top 500 villages, with fixed assets of more than 200 million yuan, and a per capita income for farmers of more than 20,000 yuan. Changying's eradication of poverty and becoming better-off can be seen as the result of the hard work and courage of the two-committee leadership team of the village under the guidance of the village branch secretary Zhang Xiulin.

At the beginning of Zhang Xiulin's tenure, the village's collective account contained just 3.46 yuan, and its external debt was 170,000 yuan. He and two branch members scraped together 600 yuan to repair a broken tractor, and acquired five tons of diesel on credit. At the start of winter, Zhang went to Weihuling forest in Laojieji with the village accountant and two drivers to collect wood. They divided into two groups, and took day and night shifts, keeping the vehicle running. The Oriental Red tractor had no cab, so Zhang and his colleagues were freezing cold, their hands and faces numb. After a few days, their hands were cracked and swollen, and their faces were black with frostbite. When they returned to the wood-carved house at night, their shoes and feet were frozen together, and they could barely get them off. That winter, the four of them earned 18,000 yuan through hard graft. The following year, they spent 9,800 yuan on a 28-type rubber wheel tractor, and went up to the mountains, where they earned more than 50,000 yuan. With this snowballing method, they accumulated funds little by little, and set up village-run enterprises such as a transport team, a nail factory, a sieve factory, and an agricultural machinery repair factory. In 1976, they finally paid off their debts. By 1978, a brigade headquarters was built in an enclosed four-sided courtyard, and their collective savings reached more than 1 million yuan.

In 1983, when the contract responsibility system was implemented, Zhang Xiulin was forced to sell the headquarters compound, locomotives, and factories, or else he would be made to look bad. However, he was very determined, and insisted on keeping it. In 1986, the two-committee leadership team of the village set up the province's first farmers' cooperative foundation with the capital accumulated in the village-run enterprises, and put together a transport team, developing 66 professional transport households. In 1993, they took over the task of transporting 36 kilometers of earth and rock on the 301 National Highway. The village's building fleet of more than 100 vehicles worked on the site, earning 13 million yuan for the village in two years.

In order to fix the skewed proportion of people and land, the village's two-committee leadership team engaged in intense debate and finally decided to focus on the building of ditches and ponds on the Hasui Railway. The deepest of these ponds is more than seven meters, and the shallowest is more than five meters. At that time, many people opposed filling in the ponds to make fields, saying that it was a daydream and a waste of money. Some people even put up large-character posters on telephone poles with the slogan "Down with Zhang Xiulin! Changying can be rich," and some even put them on the gate of the town government. However, Zhang Xiulin believed that land was the lifeblood of farmers, and there was too little of it in Changying. He had faith in this conviction, and made up his mind to fulfill it. In this way, the two-committee leadership team led the villagers to start the project of filling in the ponds to create the field. They set up a 100-meter-long plastic shed on the site, where dozens of people lived and ate. During the day, they went to the hillside five kilometers away to extract soil with a cannon, and at night, they flattened the ground. When they were tired, they slept in the hut, and when they were hungry, they had limited mouthfuls of dry food and vegetable soup. Once, Zhang Xiulin fainted and fell headlong into a five-meter-deep puddle, almost drowning. When he fainted for the second time, villagers took him to hospital, where he was diagnosed with heart disease and diabetes. His partner wept and said, "If you won't think of me and our children, you have to think of your mother and father! They are old. You cannot put your life at risk!" The villagers who came to see him filled the ward. Some of them came directly from the building site, with their clothes and shoes full of mud. Whenever he thought of this, Zhang Xiulin's eyes would fill with tears. In the end, he was not hospitalized. Instead, he went back to the building site and took charge. In 13 years, they invested 7.86 million yuan, transported 3.68 million cubic meters of soil off-site, and artificially created more than 1,480 mu of high-yielding paddy fields. This doubled the village's land area, which is 110 mu more than the original, equivalent to creating another Changying.

Zhang Xiulin was awarded an impressive title by the Heilongjiang Provincial Government – the "Yu Gong of his Generation," after a character in Chinese mythology who was tenacious and unafraid of difficulties. In the process of filling the ponds and creating fields, he was diagnosed with two more incurable diseases, but the village earned the capital it needed to develop. By then, the residents of Changying had no more worries about food and clothing, but the work of the village's two-committee leadership team did not stop. In 2001, Zhang Xiulin made more than a dozen trips to Northeast Agricultural University. Professor Jin Xueyong was moved by his sincerity, and visited Changying with another three professors. When he saw their artificial field, Professor Jin immediately agreed to cooperate with them, and set up the province's first village-level high-tech rice research institute. In 2003, on the basis of the artificial field, they leased 8,820 mu of arable land in six villages around them, and established a modern agricultural park in Shangzhi City, which has an area of 10,300 mu. In 2008, Changying invested more than 4.8 million yuan to acquire the former Shangzhi Seed Company, and registered five million yuan to establish Heilongjiang Changying Seed Industry Co. It has formed a seed industry that integrates scientific research, experimentation, demonstration, production, promotion, and sales.

However, public participation in seed growing is limited. In order to make more villagers wealthy, the two-committee leadership team aimed at high efficiency, and recognized the obvious advantages of the local berry crop. However, the villagers were hesitant. To convince them, Zhang Xiulin chartered three buses and took the village's more than 100 residents to the province's berry production area five times. Once provided with seedlings, cement piles, and steel wires, 60 households reluctantly agreed to plant raspberries. However, the crop needed two or three years to yield benefits. In the spring of the following year, 47 households pulled up all of the raspberry seedlings and planted corn and soybeans instead. Watching the raspberry seedlings being destroyed, Zhang Xiulin was so upset that he wept. Only villager Zhang Shouyi and several members of the village Party persevered with the raspberry growing, along with some of the village cadres. Two years later, Zhang Shouyi's berry income reached 100,000 yuan – 10 times higher than planting a large field. He is now rated by the city as a major raspberry grower, with an annual income of more than 600,000 yuan, and a more prosperous life. Today, the local berry planting area has grown to more than 10,000 mu, with 840 households from six villages.

In order to increase the benefits for farmers, the village's two-committee leadership team decided to build their own processing plant in the village, and created a one-stop station for production, processing, and marketing. Where did the millions of yuan come from? Zhang Xiulin led the way, mobilizing members of the village's two-committee leadership team to raise 100,000 yuan each. The meeting lasted until midnight. When he returned home, he stayed up all night and went to sit outside of his friend's house at 5am. At 7am, he borrowed 700,000 yuan from his friend. Halfway through the project, the money ran out. The fruit was going to be picked in early April, and if the factory could not be built, it would rot in the fields. By that time, their money had been wasted, and the two-committee leadership team's credit and image were in tatters. Finally, with the help of the municipal government and the municipal Party committee, the company coordinated a bank loan of five million yuan, and finally built the freezing plant, which was put into operation the same year. Today, Changying Food Company has developed into a frozen processing enterprise with more than 40 million yuan of assets.

Thus far, the village of Changying has formed five pillar industries (seeds, berries, transport, cattle, and tourism), and has seen the establishment of Heilongjiang Changying Food Co., Heilongjiang Changying Farming Co., Heilongjiang Changying Forestry Co., Changying Logistics and Transportation Company, Heilongjiang Shangzhi City Changying Modern Agriculture Park, and Haerbin Changying Rice High-tech Research Institute. It has a cooperative with 58 large farming machines, a dairy farm with a feeding capacity of 1,000 animals, and 12,680 mu of artificially planted forests.

While developing industries, Changying is also intensifying the development of infrastructure and public welfare, building 7,200 meters of white pavement, 14,400 meters of cement side ditches, 686 cement bridges, 3,600 meters of masonry retaining walls, 50,000 green trees, 20,000 square meters of lawns, 10,000 square meters of flowerbeds, 10,000 meters of iron fences, and 686 sets of standard iron gates for each household. The living environment has also been greatly improved with an investment of 2.65 million yuan, and a 1,800-square-meter comprehensive service building with offices and facilities for training, culture, sports, and entertainment has been built. It is equipped with TV sets, VCD players, computers, and multimedia projection equipment. A village library has been built, and more than 1,222 books have been purchased to enrich the cultural life of the villagers. The comprehensive service building has become a place for villagers to participate in science and technology training, cultural activities, and entertainment. A village recreation square of 8,000 square meters, a basketball court, a village health clinic, a family planning service room, and a new residential building of 4,800 square meters have been built, greatly improving living conditions for village residents.

At the same time, for many years, the village has been implementing measures to benefit the public, giving subsidies of 5,000 to 10,000 yuan to villagers who build new houses or purchase apartments. Senior citizens over 60 years old are given a certain amount of pension according to their age. When a villager dies of disease, he or she is given a funeral allowance of 500 yuan. A subsidy of 500 yuan per semester is given to a villager's child who goes to university. Elderly cadres of the former village are given an annual payment of 1,000 yuan.

The individual portion of the new rural cooperative medical care is borne by the village. According to the income of the collective economy, a certain amount of money is proportionally distributed to the villagers. Collective public welfare undertakings require villagers to work, and they are paid according to their workload. Villagers must contribute to the part involved in the village policy discussion, which is paid by the village collective. The village committee supports the residents to expand the raspberry planting area. If there is a shortage of funds for villagers' wealth-making projects, the village committee will help coordinate loans so that the villagers can really benefit from the growing collective economy.

Zhang Xiulin has been awarded the title of "Exceptional Communist Party Member or Party Worker" by the provincial Party committee more than 10 times, and is a National Model Worker, a National Entrepreneurial Star, a National Cohesion Star, and a National "3-15" Gold Medal Winner. Zhang and the village's two-committee leadership team have worked more than 40 years in poverty alleviation, proving that if a poor village attempts to rise out of poverty and become rich, there must be a head of the family who dares to take responsibility, and a two-committee leadership team that dares to try. Practice tells us that to win the fight against poverty, the role of the village's two-committee leadership team is irreplaceable.

2. The role of the main instigator in the battle against poverty

As the main instigator in the battle against poverty, the village's two-committee leadership team has been rooted in the front line for a long time. It is most familiar with the poverty situation in the village, most aware of its root causes, and most effective at applying policies to households and people. The implementation of the objectives and tasks of the fight against poverty in the village and among the people fundamentally depends on the practice of the two-committee leadership team. As the main instigator, the role of the team in the fight against poverty is most fully reflected in the core combat effectiveness, basic creativity and backbone cohesion of the fight against poverty.

(I) Core combat effectiveness

General Secretary Xi Jinping has said that to enhance the inner power of poverty alleviation, the key is to stimulate the fighting power of all poor people to alleviate poverty. The village's two-committee leadership team is the core fighting force, and its strength determines whether a poor village can win the fight against poverty.

Combat effectiveness – the ability to complete combat tasks in the army – is reflected in the ability of the village's two-committee leadership team to fight poverty. The level of combat effectiveness is determined by the number of strikes or destruction of the opponent's target. China's current poverty alleviation and eradication work is an offensive battle, with the two-committee leadership team as the main fighter, leveraging the core combat effectiveness of poverty eradication and lifting all poor households and poor people in the village out of poverty. As proven by real cases, only the village's two-committee leadership team can play such a role.

■ Case Study

Dongbei Village, located in Dainan Town, Xinghua City, Jiangsu Province, was once a small fishing village where "the secretary was left with a table, the accountant was left with a poke, and the collective was left with an empty shell," as the saying goes. In 2014, Dongbei Village achieved a total social output value of 5.6 billion yuan, a collective economic income of 22.86 million yuan, and a per capita income of 46,000 yuan for farmers.

At the start of 1983, when 31-year-old Zhang Wende – an accountant from Dongbei Village – took over as the secretary of the village Party branch, the village collective account was more than 50,000 yuan in debt. Facing the expectant gaze of the village elders, Zhang Wende made a clear statement: "It is a fact to be poor now, it is a sin to be poor in the future." He promised the villagers: "Give me three years, and Dongbei will change dramatically. Otherwise the village's 'two committees' leadership team will collectively resign."

After the promise came action. Faced with the situation of having over a thousand pounds of grain, but no cash to distribute it, the village's two-committee leadership team came up with the idea of intensifying the village's industry. After many market surveys, the decision was made to start a metal products factory from scratch. Zhang Wende made several trips to ask the town leaders for help, and took a loan of 2,000 yuan from the Dainan Credit Union to open the factory. Lacking a plant, they vacated an office; lacking working capital, Zhang Wende took out all of his family's savings, and led a group of people to ask for help while working hard. Finally, the

Dongbei Village's enterprise: Jiangsu Xinglong Metal Products Ltd.

metal products factory hit the jackpot for Dongbei Village. With multiple rounds of technological renewal and product optimization, Jiangsu Xinglong Metal Products Ltd. became a leading enterprise in the city and later the country's world-leading stainless steel wire rope industry, exporting products to more than 50 countries and regions.

Dongbei became rich, and some villagers rose up in status. However, the village's two-committee leadership team was aware that some families with financial difficulties were still lacking economic resources. How could it be guaranteed that every household would become well-off? Zhang Wende suggested "a project for each home, skills for each household, income for each day, and a guarantee for each person" at a meeting of the village's two-committee leadership team.

In order to provide villagers with a good platform for employment and entrepreneurship, Dongbei invested in the construction of a 300-mu stainless steel scrap material market, which has absorbed more than 400 households into its business. For some villagers with family difficulties, the village's two committees recommended them for jobs at the enterprise, such as Zhou Lanxiang, who had some problems with her legs. The 12 other disabled people in the village who were able to work were also given jobs at Jiangsu Xinglong. Hundreds of villagers work in logistics services, earning a total of more than three million yuan a year in labor income.

Zhang Wende's cell phone was on 24 hours a day, and whenever a villager was in need, a call would be guaranteed to arrive within five minutes. He said, "If a villager contacts me, it must be an emergency. I am basically the police of Dongbei." At 9pm on New Year's Eve in 2009, Zhang Wende, who had been busy for days, had just gone to bed when his cell phone rang. It was a part-time worker, saying that the whole apartment building where she lived had suddenly lost power. Zhang Wende was sleepy, but managed to call the village electrician to repair the problem within five minutes, and even asked him to pull some strings to make sure they could watch the Chinese New Year Gala.

In the last decade, the village has invested 28 million yuan to build the province's first farmers' sanatorium, and a further 12 million yuan to build the first experimental elementary school, which is free of charge for all children of villagers and migrant workers. The village provides free medical checkups for residents once a year, and applies for pension, medical, property, and work injury insurance for each person. It also provides two levels of pension benefits for those who have reached the age of 65 and 75 respectively.

Village accountant Wang Songshan says, "Over the years, Dongbei's village collective had tens of millions of yuan of funds going in and out each year, but Secretary Zhang has never signed a single bill or invoice." This sounds unbelievable, but it turns out that it is the village committee director Zhang Mingrong who takes charge of all the financial affairs. Zhang Mingrong and Zhang Wende, who is 10 years older, have worked day and night for the village for three decades. To some extent, they have become inseparable. Dainan Town's Deputy Secretary of the Party Committee, NPC Chairman Bai Lei says that with Zhang Wende and Zhang Minrong's skills, they will become millionaires soon if they want to, but they enjoy serving the village and doing something practical to help the residents of Dongbei.

To make each Dongbei family wealthy, the village collective must also be wealthy. In March 2009, the village worked with the Xinghua Rural Cooperative Bank to set up the Golden Link Credit Union Company, with 196 enterprises in the village forming a credit union and obtaining a bank credit loan of 163 million yuan within a month. This made more than 30 million yuan for these enterprises that year, and the village collective also benefited from more than a million as the total guarantor.

In 1999, Dongbei village's two-committee leadership team invited experts to lay out plans and build new homes according to the requirements of a livable village. So far, they have built more than 500 villas and invested a total of more than 56 million yuan to build public facilities like roads and bridges, water supply and drainage, greening and lighting, and cleaning. Now, the village looks like a Chinese garden from afar – green and flourishing.

The layout of Dongbei Village   Townhouses in Dongbei Village

Dongbei Village   Dongbei Village

In 1996, Dongbei established the first village Party committee in Xinghua City. Zhang Wende took the initiative to resign from his position as deputy mayor of Dainan Town, and led the villagers to pursue industrial development. That year, a leading enterprise was set up in Dongbei Village – Jiangsu Xinglong Metal Products Ltd., with a market value of 65 million yuan. However, entering the 21st century, the village's enterprise capital chain broke. The bank demanded payment of the debt, and Zhang Wende faced mounting lawsuits. Six of the nine members of the village Party committee resigned to forge their own careers. Zhang Wende thought hard, and finally came up with an idea: – Jiangsu Xinglong Metal Products Ltd. should be reformed. Administrative staff and personnel should start their own plants and set up shops, turning the situation from one leading enterprise monopolizing the market to a private economy with entities in positive competition with each other.

Through reform and liberalization, encouragement, and guidance, Dongbei Village took advantage of Jiangsu Xinglong Metal Products Ltd. and developed 50 enterprises producing stainless steel wire. The village's stainless steel processing enterprises have grown to more than 100, and the industrial landscape is growing. Covering an area of more than 300 mu with more than 400 stores, Dongbei's stainless steel market has reached a turnover of 1 billion yuan annually, which has lengthened the industrial chain, thus promoting the linkage of secondary and tertiary industries. Jiangsu Dongbei Stainless Steel Imports and Exports Ltd. – a joint fleet of more than 40 stainless steel enterprises – entered the international market many years ago, and has gained a broader scope of development.

(II) *The role of basic creativity*

Some scholars have said the rich are alike all over the world, but the poor are poor in different ways. Faced with the more unusual causes of poverty, the key to applying policies to households and people lies in whether a village's two-committee leadership team can make use of creativity on the basis of existing resources. The leadership team is most familiar with the causes of poverty in each household, and also most aware of which resources can help poor households speed up their escape from poverty. Integrating existing resources and rearranging them is a basic kind of creativity. It helps maximize the desire of poor people to rise out of poverty, helps leverage the effect of external support, and helps amplify the effect of poverty alleviation and wealth accrual.

The biggest difference between creativity and other general abilities lies in its originality. It is an undirected and unconstrained way of thinking that explores the unknown from the known. According to the American psychologist Joy Paul Guilford, when divergent thinking is expressed as external behavior, it represents the individual's creative ability. Creativity means coming up with new thoughts and new practices in one's own way. In this era of mass entrepreneurship and innovation, the level of creativity of a village's two-committee leadership team (as the leader and the main combatant in the fight against poverty) determines the effectiveness of the fight in poor villages. This basic creative role of the leadership team has led to numerous examples of poor villages successfully escaping from poverty.

▪ Case Study

Yangjiayao Village in Kouquan Town, Datong City (South Suburban District), Shanxi Province, has been transformed from a barren land of ravines to layers of green terraces covered with fragrant with melons and other fruit. It has moved away from traditional agriculture to the initial realization of modern agricultural industrialization by zoning and clustering. It has changed from a dilapidated village

Yangjiayao Village in the past   Townhouses

to a green, livable, and attractive place to live, with rows of villas. From having no village-run enterprises, it now has 10 developing together. The per capita income used to be less than 1,000 yuan, but is now more than 30,000 yuan.

In just 10 years, Yangjiayao has realized an impressive transformation from a poor mountainous village to the best in northern China. There are multiple reasons for this transformation, but the success can mainly be attributed to the creativity of the residents.

Before 2004, Yangjiayao was widely known to be a backward village. Due to severe soil erosion, villagers could barely make ends meet throughout the farming year, and many of them went out to work. At that time, the Datong Coal Mining Group Co., Ltd. (Tong Coal Group) attempted to build a coal mine in Tashan. This involved land requisition and demolition, leading to many disputes and petitions from villagers. Yangjiayao thus gained a negative reputation. In 2004, Guo Zhanjun – the son of nouveau-riche parents – was running a family chemical company with an annual output of over 300 million yuan. When it came to changing Yangjiayao's fate, his superiors thought of him. Because of Guo's good reputation and appeal when he was living in the village, people were willing to listen to his advice. Guo Zhanguan, then aged 39, thought carefully – if he returned to the village, the family business would inevitably be damaged and he would be criticized from two sides if he failed to manage things in the village; if he did not do it, he would break the trust of his superiors, and would disappoint the villagers. Finally, he decided to return to the village as the Party branch secretary and chair of the village committee.

It is not easy being a village official. Straight away many villagers approached him for land acquisition compensation. Guo quickly convened a meeting of the village's two committees and representative assembly. He listened to the views and suggestions of all parties, and arranged equal land requisition compensation for each household. He safeguarded the fundamental interests of the majority of the people, and quelled petitions. In the village, Guo Zhanjun often said, "If you have problems to solve, you should come to me instead of petitioning. To petition alone is pointless. If the problem is beyond me, I will lead you to petition according to the law." Since 2004, there has not been a single petition in the village.

A series of village enterprises have been set up around the coal mine. The Tashan mine was built on the edge of the village, which in many people's eyes was a kind of "cannibalization" of the barren mountain village. However, in Guo Zhanjun's view, the Tashan mine provided good objective conditions for village enterprises. He decided to adopt the approach of managing the village by running businesses, and developing the village's economy by developing business, turning a roadblock into a stepping stone. In 2004, Guo and the village leadership team seized the opportunity offered by the Tashan coal mine, relying on it to benefit the villagers. By taking the form of sole proprietorship and joint venture, they financed 502 million yuan and built seven production and living projects, with the annual gross domestic product reaching 420 million yuan. Wolongguang Service Company, the first village-run enterprise, arranged for a team of villagers to transport carbonaceous, muddy, and sandy shale for the Tashan coal mine. With a total investment of five million yuan, the company uses a shareholding business model, with the village collective accounting for 51% of the shares and the villagers accounting for 49%. This boosts enthusiasm and provides jobs for 105 villagers. Wolongguang Service Company alone earned more than 50 million yuan a year, and the villagers felt that better days had finally come.

Since then, this innovative model of collective leadership, shareholding, and common prosperity has been tried and tested in other village-run enterprises, and has been widely adopted. In 2006, the village invested 40 million yuan to construct four buildings for Tashan staff apartments, which can accommodate and cater for more than 2,100 employees, increasing annual income by 4.5 million yuan. In 2007, a total investment of 170 million yuan was made to set up Qifeng Mountain Cement Co. In 2008, they invested 100 million yuan to set up Tongta Building Materials Co., Ltd. and cooperated with the Tongta Coal Industry Corporation to set up a sintering project for carbonaceous, muddy, and sandy shale, with an annual output of 200 million bricks, realizing the recycling of resources. In 2011, they invested 60 million yuan to build a small mixing plant and eight centralized service areas for the project department, increasing annual income by 10 million yuan. Nowadays, the villagers often say, "Relying on the mountain and making use of it is the scripture; serving the coal mine is the truth. Village enterprises are cooperating with each other; with mutual help and promotion, we will succeed."

Yangjiayao's comprehensive service building

A national first-class dairy base has also been built. The village successfully rose out of poverty and became wealthy, while the villagers' living standards have improved. Over the past few years, the village's two-committee leadership team has built a new first-class rural area on a provincial and national level, aiming at building a modern village that will be an example in terms of scientific development and farming culture. Using the income brought in by the village-run enterprises, they have invested 160 million yuan to build 178 sets of European-style villas and 190 sets of board-style residential buildings, with a broadband network, digital TV, and video surveillance all available in the area. The villagers' lives are absolutely first-class and enviable. At the same time, the village has built a 6,600-square-meter comprehensive service building and the 10,000-square-meter Mingxin Square, which provides a platform for cultural and sporting events.

Despite its success, Yangjiayao's two-committee leadership team has not stopped moving forward. Relying on the coal mine, the village will not have economic problems for the time being; however, in the long run, the mine's resources will be depleted. Only through transformation and sustainable development will there be a way out, so the village has begun to develop specialized modern agriculture. Guo Zhanjun has promoted large-scale breeding, investing 230 million yuan in Datong Sifang High-tech Agricultural and Animal Husbandry Co. The park breeds purebred Holstein cows, introduces advanced production lines from countries like Germany, and outsources corresponding management personnel with high salaries to create the largest first-class modern dairy farming park in the province. After the park is put into full operation, the total output value will be 160 million yuan, and it will employ 25,00 farmers from the surrounding area. At the same time, the 43,000 tons of cow manure produced in the park will be harmlessly treated to produce 35,000 tons of organic fertilizer, which will be used in gardening, flower growing, and planting.

In addition, Yangjiayao cooperates with Taiwanese businesspeople, investing 34 million yuan to build 20,000 square meters of single greenhouses, eight high-standard greenhouses, and a seedling research center specializing in rare Phalaenopsis orchids. With an annual output of 1.5 million seedlings, it is the largest planting base for this flower in North China.

(III) *The role of central cohesion*

A village's two-committee leadership team plays a central role in whether poverty-stricken groups can be brought together to fight the battle against poverty. It is only when the leadership team is strong and united that it can gather all forces, overcome difficulties, and finally win the battle. Therefore, the village's two-committee leadership team should first of all consistently enhance cohesion, improve relations, resolve disagreements, and eliminate internal conflicts. It should promote understanding and remove friction, building rather than destroying, and playing to its strengths in order to achieve the best possible performance.

On the front line of poverty alleviation, the village's two-committee leadership team is the bridge and link between the Party and the government and impoverished farmers. It shoulders the strenuous task of leading poor people to speed up poverty alleviation and prosperity. If the foundation is not firm, then the ground will be shaken. Despite the fact that the top-level design of the country has a thousand ways to fight poverty, there is only one way for the leadership team to alleviate it for villages. The working environment of the leadership team in poor villages is difficult. It is only by thinking with the general public on-site, working with them with the same goal, and pooling their strength that the leadership team will be able to achieve the goal of poverty alleviation.

■ Case Study 1
Luonan Village in Foshan City, Guangdong Province is located in the western part of Nanzhuang Town, Chancheng District, with an area of 4.75 square kilometers and nine village groups. It has a household population of more than 3,800, 153 Party members, and a foreign population of about 6,000. Under the leadership of Guan Runyao, secretary of the village Party branch committee, Luonan Village started with

50,000 yuan and developed an enterprise group with assets of more than a billion yuan.

The development of Luonan Village could not have been achieved without the political analysis and management abilities of the Party Committee. The ideas and measures of the Party Committee of Luonan Village are ahead of their time, reflecting public opinion and having a strong force and appeal among villagers. Taking into account the actual situation of Luonan Village, Guan Runyao has made the Party Committee and the Village Committee the leading core of modernization by strongly promoting the building of grassroots organizations and increasing the training of Party members and cadres. The Party Committee of Luonan Village insists on reporting and explaining its work to the village representatives and Communist Party members, accepting the supervision of the Party members and representatives, listening to the opinions and suggestions of the villagers' representatives, and playing the role of a bridge and link with public organizations such as trade unions, the Communist Youth League, and the Women's Union. By promoting scientific and democratic decision-making with the openness of government affairs, financial disclosure, information, and standardization, the village's two-committee leadership team fully reflects the villagers' right to know, to participate, and to supervise. The monthly income and expenditure of the village committee is examined by the financial management team and published on the bulletin board of the village committee and each village

Secretary Guan Runyao presides over the general meeting of Party members and village representatives

group. At the annual general meeting, the Party Committee announces the annual budget and final accounts to the Party members and village representatives, and holds villagers' meetings from time to time to disclose significant matters.

The Party Committee of Luonan Village sees the importance of legal education, and carries out various kinds of events to popularize the law, forming a social atmosphere of knowing, observing, and using the law. Fiber-optic camera monitors have been installed throughout the village, and dynamic security management has been implemented. Seventy-three security guards patrol the village 24 hours a day, forming a faultless security network. They insist on governing the village according to the law, perfecting and implementing the democratic management system, and ensuring the openness of village affairs. Seizing the opportunity of informatization, they have taken the lead in using an informatized rural management system, which has greatly improved the transparency of village affairs and financial disclosure.

Luonan Village's outstanding achievements have been recognized by higher levels. Its Party Committee has been praised for the "Development of an Advanced National Party Branch of a Rural Grassroots Organization" and named as a "National Advanced Grassroots Party Organization" by the Central Organization Department, a "Guangdong Red Flag Grassroots Party Organization" by the Guangdong Provincial Party Committee, and an "Advanced Grassroots Party Organization" by the Foshan Municipal Party Committee and the Chancheng District Party Committee. The village committee was named as a "Developed National-level Village," a "National Ecological Village," a "National-level Demonstration Village for Democracy and the Rule of Law," a "Developed and Advanced National-level Village and Town," a "National-level Advanced Mass Sports Unit," a "National-level Green Well-off Village," a "Guangdong Advanced Group," a "Developed Guangdong Village," a "Guangdong Ecological Model Village," and a "Guangdong Health Village," as well as being listed among the "Top Ten Villages of Guangdong Township Enterprises."

■ **Case Study 2**

Hailong Village was once incredibly poor. In 2001, it had a collective debt of more than 700,000 yuan; the villagers' annual per capita income was less than 1,600 yuan; 80% of the residents lived in scattered earth houses. Social relations were strained; collective petitions happened regularly, and crimes were frequent. When village cadres walked through the streets, people would roll their eyes, spit, and make rude remarks, full of resentment towards the "village officials." Eight years later, this poor village, which was in such a state of disarray and disorder, has been transformed: the annual collective income is 4.12 million yuan. The annual per capita net income is

9,643 yuan, which is more than double the per capita net income in Chongqing. The total amount of bank deposits is more than 100 million yuan. Many families have comfortable homes, but what is more commendable is that since 2002, there has not been a single threat to public security in the village, and not a single petition has occurred. What explains this dramatic change in just eight years, with the same piece of land and the same villagers? It was the village's two-committee leadership team with Yan Jing as the general secretary of the village Party branch that inspired people to overcome poverty in Hailong, leading and lifting the village from poverty to prosperity, and from chaos to governance.

It is only by uniting Party members that a grassroots base can be formed. Hailong Village planted the organizational network in the nerve endings of society, and built a new pattern for urban-rural integration of grassroots Party building, to create a friendly environment for scientific development. By doing more visible and tangible practical things, they greatly enhanced the cohesion of grassroots Party organizations.

Before Xu Ruijun founded Jing Yue Company in Hailong Village, he had never thought of joining the Party, and even resisted developing Communist Party members in private enterprises. What the boss did not like would naturally be refused by staff. Chen Kaiqun, a painter, had won third-class merit on the front line in Laoshan when he joined the army. A veteran Party member, he had weathered gunfire, but had been anonymous in the company, and became an underground Party member. Yan Jing believed that there can be no blind spots in organization building. It is only by organizing Party members that a grassroots fighting base can be formed. He said, "There are more than 400 people at the Jingyue Company, and we need to set up a Party organization." In response, Xu Ruijun was very dismissive. Yan Jing was not discouraged, and talked to Xu Ruijun several more times. He said, "The development of Party members is not only in the interest of the Party and the state, but also of the enterprise. When enterprises have a Party organization, Party members can be role models, creating a positive atmosphere; enterprises also have an additional channel of communication with the Party and the government." Xu Ruijun could not resist Yan Jing's earnest words, and eventually gave in. The six underground Party members then made their identities public and set up a Party branch. Chen Kaiqun was elected secretary.

There are many other cases like this. In the process of poverty alleviation, the sincere unity of the two-committee leadership teams in poor villages is a prerequisite. Gathering the villagers' strength, allowing them to play the main role, and improving their political participation will enhance their trust and recognition of the leadership team, as will enhancing their ability to rise out of poverty and earn a living, and improving their production and management organization. In this way, the village's two committees also become the basis for the Party and the government to unite the majority of social forces.

3. Poverty alleviation measures of the main instigators

It is not difficult to temporarily alleviate poverty, but maintaining sustainable poverty alleviation is a challenge. As the main instigators in the fight against poverty, the two-committee leadership teams work and live on the front line, and bear a heavy responsibility. At the same time, poverty-stricken villages often face substantial new problems that are tricky to solve. The two-committee leadership team must identify these problems, overcome their own shortcomings, and constantly intensify their ability to alleviate poverty.

(I) Hidden obstacles and phenomena

Poverty alleviation is a topic that is mentioned and discussed frequently. Currently, poverty is the biggest vulnerability in the building of a moderately prosperous society in all respects. To compensate for this shortcoming, China must first face up to the current outstanding problem that poor villages are experiencing.

a) The common phenomenon of "one high, one low, and one old"

Women, the elderly, and children compose the majority of the population that is left behind in poor rural areas. Most young adults who are well-educated and competent go out to work or start businesses, and are unwilling or unable to devote themselves to village affairs, leading to the phenomenon of "one high, one low, and one old" in the two-committee leadership team. "One high" refers to high age: in the two-committee leadership teams in poor villages, the aging of members is a relatively serious issue, and it lowers work efficiency. "One low" refers to low educational background: the proportion of members in the leadership teams who have higher than college or technical secondary education degree is very low. Most members have only primary or junior highschool education, which in some ways limits the ability of the group. "One old" refers to the members of leadership teams who have old-fashioned ideas and obviously insufficient capability. In short, the age, knowledge, and ability of the two-committee leadership teams in poor villages need to be optimized.

b) Relatively weak concept of democracy and law

Democracy and the rule of law are the internal requirements for building a rural political system and political guarantee for poverty-stricken villages to alleviate poverty. At present, the level of democracy and rule of law of the two-committee leadership teams in rural areas is not high, is even lower in the vast impoverished areas. Digging deeper into the reasons for this, the author believes that the first is lagging economic development. If even the most basic problem of food and clothing shortage cannot be solved in poor villages, the two-committee leadership team will not have time for issues such as democratic political rights. They are often so busy making a living that they have no energy to study legal matters. Economic difficulties make them ignore or de-prioritize the building of democracy and the rule of law. The second reason is backward historical traditions and customs. China has experienced more than 2,000 years of feudalism. In some poor villages with particularly weak economies as well as inaccessible transport and information, there are often regrettable incidents of village cadres bullying others, beating and scolding people at will. Village cadres usually have a lot of influence, and most poor people no not dare to stand up and resist. In other places, cadres in poor villages have huge family forces behind them, and their rules and regulations are cruel and strict, in many cases even replacing laws. The third reason is backward educational conditions. Having a relatively low accumulation of cultural and scientific knowledge, the two-committee leadership teams in poor villages are often unable to study independently and conduct in-depth research on laws and regulations; the idea of democracy and rule of law does not enter their minds through the channeling of knowledge. Even if they are given the opportunity to study law, they are often discouraged by their educational level. The fourth reason is anachronistic legislation and law enforcement. There are many legal vacuum zones in poor rural areas. For example, the burden on farmers and the building of rural grassroots political power are more prominent in poor areas. There are also a lot of problems in the administration of justice and law enforcement in poor villages, such as imperfect law enforcement institutions, low-quality law enforcement personnel, judicial corruption, and difficult implementation. These problems are the main reasons for the weak concept of democracy and rule of law in two-committee leadership teams in impoverished rural areas.

c) Financial management is generally opaque and un-standardized

At present, the two-committee leadership teams in some poor villages still have opaque and incorruptible activities, such as untimely financial accounting, non-standard account establishment, multiple reimbursements, false expenditure, and concealment of income. The reason for this is that ideological and political quality is the key factor. The Party Central Committee requires that all poverty alleviation funds be deposited in villages and implemented to households, while the two-committee leadership teams in some poor villages, especially the secretary of the village Party branch, actually practice fraud and fill their own pockets. Especially within major projects at the village level and the disclosure of village affairs and finance, they neither report to the superior Party committee and government, nor make disclosures to village residents. Unclear, closed, and opaque village-level finance has significantly affected the stability of poor villages and triggered petitions from residents. If these problems cannot be overcome, it is absolutely impossible to alleviate poverty.

(II) Analysis of the causes of the problems

There are many reasons for the above problems facing the two-committee leadership teams in poor villages, and they cannot be generalized. There are both historical and practical factors.

a) The concept of elections is not integrated with local culture

Compared with China's thousands of years of local traditional culture, elections – the core element of modern political culture – have only been introduced into rural society relatively recently, and have not yet become accepted. Traditional local societies form a network based on the clan name, which is ideologically expressed as the exclusive concept of clan and family. It shows a lack of democratic consciousness and conception, and even contradicts them. Clan forces exert influence in the whole process from nomination to voting during changing terms of office, and also exert pressure in the form of public opinion and voting on the decision making of the newly-elected two-committee leadership team. Therefore, the rural social culture still greatly affects the process and quality of the democratization of the two-committee leadership team, as well as affecting its ability to govern.

b) The weakness of the collective village economy

Since the implementation of the household contract responsibility system, the collective economy has weakened in most villages. Moreover, some villages have no collective economy whatsoever, and are heavily in debt. According to the data that is available, the annual collective economic income of many poor villages is almost zero. The disposable income of village-level collective economies is very small, and the two-committee leadership teams face the dilemma of having no food and no money. For one thing, the conditions for the leadership teams in poor villages to do practical things for the general public are limited, and there will be no tangible benefits for a long time. For another thing, village residents lack a sense of identity, and do not trust the two-committee leadership team. This greatly inhibits their enthusiasm and initiative for work, resulting in difficult selection, handling, and retention of the two-committee leadership team. Another factor is the low economic treatment of the members of the leadership team. In the battle against poverty in China, many wealthy entrepreneurial leaders have emerged. Their vision and practice have greatly inspired poor people to become entrepreneurs themselves. While others are trying to develop their own industries, the members of two-committee leadership teams are paid cheaply according to the number of working days, which affects their motivation. In addition, with rising prices, it is more difficult to retain members of leadership teams with the same treatment year after year.

c) A lack of training, selection, and appointment for members of two-committee leadership teams

In some poverty-stricken areas, village-level Party committees and governments lack a sound mechanism for the training, selection, and appointment of the two-committee leadership teams, resulting in distorted elections and even the phenomenon of throwing good money after bad. Some villages focus more on the use of the two-committee leadership teams rather than their training, and do not pay enough attention to education and cultivation. Besides, the insufficient investment of funds and energy have made it difficult to build high-quality leadership groups in poor villages.

(III) Forging the ability to fight poverty

With the acceleration of the national fight against poverty, cadres in poor villages will face a new round of challenges. Building two-committee leadership teams that are qualified to complete the task of poverty alleviation in the new era, as well as forging their ability to acquire wealth and guidance, have become the crucial measures to achieve prosperity in poor villages.

a) Improving the methods of voting and appointment

To improve the selection and appointment of the two-committee leadership teams in poor villages, it is necessary to grasp the following points: first, controlling the candidates' political quality as the main priority. When choosing Party members and cadres in poor villages, it is necessary to carry out various forms of examination and assessment for applicants, together with strictly controlling the population in order to preserve the progressiveness and purity of the leading groups from the source. Second, team structure must be optimized. Focusing on optimizing the leadership structure of the two-committees leadership team, when allocating its branch team, it is necessary to consider the age and cultural structure (mainly those aged about 40 and above with high school education), and bear in mind the advantages conducive to the formation of age brackets and culture. Third, selection channels must be broadened. The selection and appointment of the two-committee leadership team should draw from all echelons of society, including experts in poverty alleviation, demobilized soldiers, college students, village officials, and skilled migrant workers. At present, out of the cadres being sent into villages for assistance, 170,000 will be first secretaries of village committees. Fourth, the training of reserve personnel for two-committee leadership teams in poor villages must be intensified. Villages and towns must be taken as units to establish and improve the talent pool of reserve cadres at the village level. It is important to systematically select outstanding young farmers, demobilized soldiers, and exceptional village officials in poor villages to receive various vocational and professional training, allowing them participate in practical work to gain experience, and placing them in pivotal roles as quickly as possible.

b) Strengthening administration and supervision

First, the assessment mechanism must be improved, and standards must be set for assessment. Quantitative and qualitative assessment should be carried out for the performance of the two-committee leadership team, covering poverty alleviation policies, basic organizing, development and management of agricultural sidelines, social undertakings, safety, and maintaining stability. Assessment methods are supposed to be varied, and can also be carried out in the form of creative activities, such as "Star Party Organizations" (grading and classifying primary-level Party organizations from one star to five stars).

Second, training should be improved and training resources should be leveraged. It is important to offer theoretical and technical training in stages and batches to the members of two-committee leading groups, especially the village Party Secretary and village director, helping them update their ideas and enhance their ability to rise out of poverty and earn a living. It is necessary to select some typical two-committee leading groups of high quality and strong ability to play the roles of demonstration, radiation, education, and inspiration. Efforts should be made to encourage the two-committee leadership teams in poor villages to learn from the examples and successes of other places, and explore ideas.

Third, management must be improved and made comprehensive and gridded. It is necessary to establish and improve the system for inspection and democratic evaluation, as well as the communication between the superior Party committee and the two-committee leading group. The openness of village affairs and democratic management must be improved, focusing on a comprehensive audit of the financial revenue and expenditure of poor villages and the use of poverty alleviation funds once a year, for the sake of transparency.

c) Improving villages' collective economy

Developing and expanding the collective economy in poor villages is the material basis for intensifying the building of two-committee leadership teams. The cases discussed above have a common feature, that is, the village-level collective economy continues to grow in the process of development, establishing the foundations for the village to grow upon. For one thing, the two-committee leadership team should manage and make good use of the existing collective economy to maximize its economic benefits. Meanwhile, it is also necessary to develop a new collective economy according to local conditions, making full use of resources such as land, minerals, and ecology of poor villages, and exploring various modes to develop the collective economy in combination with national poverty alleviation as well as development policies and measures, turning resources into economic advantages. Superior Party committees and governments should intensify their leadership over the collective economy of poor villages, improve economic management and development planning, establish an incentive mechanism for the development of the collective economy, and provide good conditions for economic development in poor villages.

d) Improving the treatment of village cadres

In addition to giving appropriate consideration to political treatment, two-committee leadership teams in poor villages should be given a guarantee in terms of economic treatment, so as to inspire cadres' enthusiasm and initiative and stabilize the teams. The basic salary of cadres in poor villages should be increased year by year with the development of the county economy, and welfare should be adjusted in good time according to the collective economic conditions of poor villages. The remuneration of the cadres in the two-committee leadership teams in poor villages will continue to implement the overall planning and unified development system. Their salaries should also be included in the financial budget to ensure good treatment. At the same time, it is necessary to establish an incentive mechanism for cadres of the two-committee leadership team in poor villages, and commend and reward officials for outstanding performance. Appropriate subsidies should be given to retired village cadres according to the length of their term of office, so as to solve their financial worries and make current cadres feel confident and secure.

- **Case Study**

The "Training Project for Leaders of Entrepreneurship and Prosperity in Poor Villages"

In order to implement the objectives and requirements of targeted poverty alleviation, the Poverty Alleviation Office of the State Council created the "Training Project for Leaders of Entrepreneurship and Prosperity in Poor Villages" in 2014, aiming to lift poor people out of poverty and into wealth through the development of industries on a larger scale through systematic training, entrepreneurship guidance, and continuous services for the poverty alleviation personnel in poor villages.

Group photo taken at the Rongzhong training base in Fujian, including the leader of the "Training Project for Leaders of Entrepreneurship and Prosperity in Poor Villages" from the Poverty Alleviation Office of the State Council

This successful training practice has particular significance for intensifying the establishment of two-committee leadership teams in poor villages.

The first training base for this project was set up in the village of Rongzhong in Fujian Province. Since the scheme was officially launched in October 2014, under the direct leadership of Li Zhensheng (Secretary of the village branch and deputy to the National People's Congress), nearly 500 students from provinces and regions such as Gansu, Ningxia, Fujian, and Hubei have been trained. Many of them are now branch secretaries in poor villages, and the directors of village committees. More than a year's practice has proved that choosing members of village-level leadership teams as the recipients of training improves an individual's ability to rise out of poverty and earn a living, and also contributes to poverty alleviation across whole villages.

The Rongzhong training base uses the innovative "1 + 11" training mode. "11" refers to the deployment of poverty alleviation volunteers (assistant mentors) for 11 months of continuous assistance and supervision after the trainees return home. The core tasks in this stage are to train poverty alleviation volunteers, screen assistance projects, and realize the implementation of assistance projects in combination with the industrial reality of the villages where the trainees are located.

The core content of the "1 + 11" training mode at the Rongzhong training base can be summarized as the "1–2–3" project, that is, the creation of one model, two key points, and three teams.

One model refers to the industrial poverty alleviation model. It takes the assistance industry as its mainline and the "master and apprentice" model as its driving force. The cultivation points (trainees and poverty alleviation volunteers) are connected into a line (i.e. teachers and apprentices pair up), forming a film (multiple assistance industries are implemented). Finally, via poverty alleviation through industry, a development environment is created comprising one town, one industry, one village, and one product.

Two key points refers to training members of village-level leadership teams and poverty alleviation volunteers as private entrepreneurs.

The cultivation of the two key objects will lay a human and intellectual foundation for poverty alleviation through industry.

The three teams are a team of expert consultants, a team of trainees, and a team of poverty alleviation volunteers. The expert consultant team is composed of a well-known national brand, market, industry, capital, e-commerce experts, well-known entrepreneurs in the industry, breeding experts, and professors based on the trainees' regions. Its responsibility is to evaluate the feasibility of entrepreneurial projects and put forward opinions and suggestions. The participants are mainly members of the village-level leadership team. The teaching in the "1" stage inspires trainees' entrepreneurial passion, and encourages them to formulate plans. The poverty alleviation volunteer team is composed of private entrepreneurs and well-known figures, and functions to identify advantageous resources such as projects and markets for the systematic development in the "11" stage. In the "11" stage, the training base applies a method of promotion and elimination through the scientific design of assessment indicators according to the driving ability and radiation range of poverty alleviation volunteers, and commends exceptional performance according to the poverty alleviation situation that year.

References

Bao, Erwei. *Research on Poverty Alleviation in Old Revolutionary Areas: A Case Study of Yulin City.* Northwest Agriculture and Forest Science and Technology University, 2013.

Ding, Jianjun. "A Comparative Study of the Poverty Levels of 11 Concentrated Contiguous Areas of Hardship in China: A Perspective Based on the Calculation of the Comprehensive Development Index." *Geography Science*, 2014.

Huang, Guoyong, Min Zhang, and Bo Qin. "Social Development, Geographical Conditions and Rural Poverty in Frontier Areas." *Chinese Journal of Population Resources and Environment*, 2014.

Li, Xiaoyun, Xuemei Zhang, and Lixia Tang. "Current Poverty in Rural China." *Journal of China Agricultural University*, 2005.

Li, Zhongshen, and Ying Luo. "Research on Rural Anti-poverty in Ethnic Areas." *Management Observation*, 2015.

Liu, Yaping, and Yi He. "An Analysis of Basic Education in Poverty-stricken Areas in China." *Science and Technology Horizon*, 2014.

Tu, Weiliang, and Kanxiong Nie. "Development Trends of Family Farms in China – Problems and Options." *Journal of Anhui Agriculture and Science*, 2006.

Wang, Lin, and Cangping Wu. "Focusing on the Poverty of the Elderly in Rural China." *Socialist Studies*, 2006.

Xi, Jinping. *Up and Out of Poverty.* Fujian People's Publication House, 2006.

———. *Zhejiang, China: A New Vision for Development.* Zhejiang People's Publication House, 2001.

———. *Being a County Party Secretary in the Style of Jiao Yulu.* Central Party Literature Press, 2001.

———. "Working Together to Eradicate Poverty and Promote Common Development." Speech at the 2015 High-level Forum on Poverty Reduction and Development, 2015.

Yearbook of China's Poverty Alleviation and Development. Unity Press, 2015.

Zhang, Jianlin. "Between Community and Farmland: The Direction of Evolution of Villages in Central China, Based on 30 Villages." East China University of Science and Technology, 2015.

Zhang, Zhao. "Research into Changes in China's Consumer Culture Since Reform and Opening, Using the Case of Beijing." Beijing Jiaotong University, 2013.

Zhao, Huaming. "Reflection on the Economic Development in Impoverished Border Areas." *Journal of Kunming Metallurgy College*, 2002.

Zhou, Mengliang, and Yating Peng. "Research on the Creation of a Financial Poverty Alleviation System in Contiguous Poverty-stricken Areas." *Contemporary Economic Management Practice*, 2015.

Zuo, Changsheng. *Inclusive Development and Poverty Reduction*. Social Sciences Academic Press, 2013.

Postscript

The book *The Final Battle: Winning the War Against Poverty* is both an account of my personal experience and a summary of my participation in China's voluntary service for poverty alleviation in recent years. According to the decisions made at the Central Conference on Poverty Alleviation and Development at the end of last year, it is necessary to ensure that all poor people will be moderately prosperous by 2020. The real battle to alleviate poverty has begun. To win it, public participation is necessary, with enterprises, social organizations, and individuals playing important roles.

In 2012, I undertook the training of the Party branch secretaries of the top 100 villages selected by the CPC Central Committee as the advanced model of national grassroots Party-building. I also established the "Advanced Training Course for Village Officials" at Renmin University, for which I received high praise and affirmation from the then president, Mr. Chen Yulu. In the two years I spent with these student village officials, I was hugely inspired, educated, and moved. Most of them were leaders who were lifting villagers out of poverty and into prosperity, and each was a "living textbook" when it came to poverty alleviation. Many of their experiences and practices are worthy of reference in poor areas.

In 2014, the Poverty Alleviation Office of the State Council took the lead in piloting the "Training Project for Leaders of Entrepreneurship and Prosperity in Poor Villages" in Rongzhong Village, Nan'an City, Fujian Province. On the invitation of Li Zhensheng, an outstanding alumnus of the village official course and Secretary of Rongzhong Village, I participated in the preliminary planning and design of the pilot project, and have been a dedicated member of the poverty alleviation volunteer service ever since. Later, entrusted by the Poverty Alleviation Office of the State Council, I hosted its "Poverty Alleviation and Entrepreneurship Volunteer (Mentor) Training Course" and the 2015 High-level Forum on Poverty Reduction and Development, and Rural Development. Through participating in this work, I acquired a deeper understanding of the reality of China's fight against poverty and its determination and confidence to win this war. It has also given me some personal knowledge and experience of how to ensure that under existing standards, all poor people will be lifted out of poverty by 2020. I hope to speak and exchange ideas with people from all echelons of society who care about and support national poverty alleviation and development. This was my original intention when writing this book.

The publication of *The Final Battle: Winning the War Against Poverty* is inseparable from the care and support of enthusiastic national leaders, experts, and exceptional student village officials in the field of poverty alleviation and development. First of all, I would like to thank Mr. Liu Yongfu, Director of the Poverty Alleviation Office of the State Council. I have also benefited greatly from the top-level design of special poverty alleviation projects by Si Haibo, Director of the Development Guidance Division of the State Development Assistance Office, such as photovoltaic poverty alleviation and the "Training Project for Leaders of Entrepreneurship and Prosperity in Poor Villages." I would also like to thank Mr. Lou Xiangpeng (an expert on Chinese agricultural brands), Mr. Kang Hualan (Director of China's Family Culture Research Center), and Mr. Huang Zhihao (general planner of the Beijing Agricultural Festival) for their considerable support and assistance in the poverty alleviation volunteer service. I would also like to pay special tribute to some of the outstanding students from the village official course – Li Zhensheng, Ma Xianfu, Pan Jianzhang, Yan Jing, Zhang Wende, Tan Zeyong, and Yang Zailing. They have participated in national poverty alleviation in many different ways, hoping to set an example in their specific fields.

When I started writing this book, I established and headed a research group. The members were Liu Zhenqi (a professor, doctoral supervisor, and teaching supervision expert from the Military Academy of the Chinese People's Liberation Army), Tian Limin (Assistant Director of the Institute of Rural Development at China's Renmin University), Wang Xiaotian (a Masters student in risk management at Monash University in Australia, and CEO of Beijing Juchayuan Network Technology Co., Ltd), Zhang Yuanyuan (Deputy General Manager of Beijing Zhenqi Green Health Management Co.Ltd.), Qi Dandan (from the Institute of Rural Development at China's Renmin University), and Liu Deyu (a graduate student at China's Renmin University). Professor Liu Zhenqi and I were responsible for the overall planning, framework design, and compilation of the book, which I finalized; Tian Limin wrote, organized, and coordinated Chapters 3, 4, and 5; Wang Xiaotian and Liu Deyu wrote Chapter 5; Zhang Yuanyuan wrote the opening material; and Qi Dandan wrote Chapters 1 and 2. I would hereby like to express my heartfelt thanks to the members of the research group for their hard work and efforts. Colleagues such as Zhao Dongfang, Sun Yan, Zhang Lijun, Shen Qi, and Hu Zhigang did a lot of auxiliary work, for which I am thankful.

Mr. Hu Xiaowen (president of the social sciences branch of the Democratic and Legal Publishing House of the China Publishing Group) tracked the writing of this book from start to finish, offering many valuable opinions, and making significant contributions to its completion and publication.

Winning the battle against poverty and building a moderately prosperous society in all respects by 2020 was a major strategic decision made by General Secretary Xi Jinping and the Central Committee of the Communist Party of China. It has been a major task of the national 13th Five-Year Plan, and is a huge project with national and social dimensions. For this book, I have only performed superficial research from a certain angle, so it is inevitable that there will be errors and omissions.

Wang Jiahua